When Sammie arrived at Brad's, she retrieved a flashlight from the backseat and used it to light her way to the river side of the studio. The river had washed over the bank some, and she could see that the studio floor was wet. But Brad's paintings were either on easels or walls and, so far, were safe.

Please God, please God, send help soon. Right now, those paintings were her responsibility. She felt sick to her stomach. How long would it take someone to get here?

When she flashed her light into the kitchen, she could see that water covered the floor there, too. Futilely, she rattled the doorknob. Walk to the car, she told herself. Lock the doors and wait. She laid her head back on the car seat and tried not to dwell on the fact that she was alone on a deserted, wooded road in a flood late at night.

Brad was right. He should have stayed.

A PALISADES CONTEMPORARY ROMANCE

REMEMBERING THE

Roses

MARION DUCKWORTH

PALISADES®

REMEMBERING THE ROSES
published by Palisades
a division of Multnomah Publishers, Inc.

© 1998 by Marion Duckworth
International Standard Book Number: 1-57673-236-3

Cover illustration by C. Michael Dudash
Design by Brenda McGee

Scripture quotations are from:
The Holy Bible, New International Version © 1973, 1984 by International Bible Society, used by permission of Zondervan Publishing House

Printed in the United States of America

For information:
**MULTNOMAH PUBLISHERS, INC.•POST OFFICE BOX 1720
SISTERS, OREGON 97759**

Library of Congress Cataloging-in-Publication Data
Duckworth, Marion.
   Remembering the roses / by Marion Duckworth.
       p. cm.
   ISBN 1-57673-236-3   I. Title
   PS3554.U278R46 1998   98–11953
   813'.54—dc21   CIP

98 99 00 01 02 03 04 — 10 9 8 7 6 5 4 3 2 1

To Louis Hutchins,
who gentled me
to Jesus

Remain in me, and I will remain in you.

JOHN 15:4

ONE

Was this the town she'd been looking for?

After weeks of driving north from Los Angeles, stopping at one dot on the map after another, shaking her head and moving on, Sammie had wondered if she should give up. Maybe the place she was looking for didn't exist. Maybe Pop was right. She should turn around and head back to Los Angeles. Never mind trying to start over.

She clenched the steering wheel more tightly. Absolutely not. If Pineville Beach here on Washington's Olympic Peninsula wasn't the place, she'd keep searching until she found it.

Sammie drove across the Iseeyousee River Bridge and on to Main Street. In front of her, in the center of the street, was a village green. The large, oblong piece of grass was lush, nourished by April rain and sun.

The trace of a smile spread across her face as she slowly drove down the several blocks of Main Street. Pineville Beach was a picture from one of her childhood storybooks come to life. The town was pure greeting card Americana that the rational, grown-up part of her was certain existed only in the artist's imagination. Was this merely an illusion created by the town's merchants?

When she turned a corner at the end of the Main Street shopping area, she sucked in her breath, opened her eyes wide, and stared. Back off the road on her right was an English style cottage with a wooden sign across the front: *English Country Tearoom.*

In front was an English garden with tables and chairs where customers could nibble crumpets and sip pots of tea among yellow, pink, red, and purple spring flowers. The windows of the tearoom were hung with lace curtains and decorated with flower boxes. Probably a bell at the door tinkled when you opened it.

A year and a half ago, Sammie would have slammed on the brakes, jumped out of the car, and rushed down the path. When she got inside, she'd have gasped her excitement to whomever she met. "I can't believe it! Mom would just love this place! We'll have to come back here together."

Instead, she pulled her red Suburban slowly to the curb and sat quietly as she took it in, then choked back a sob. If Mom were here she'd walk through the garden slowly, inhaling each fragrance, examining each flower and shrub, naming this variety and that.

"Oh, my God." It was a groan. It was a prayer. A day didn't go by without reminders of the past.

Mom was dead, and all the moaning and crying in the world wouldn't change that. Sammie glanced in the rearview mirror and dabbed at her moist dark eyes with the back of her hand. She smoothed her closely cropped black curly hair and stepped out of the car. As she walked toward the tearoom, she tucked her T-shirt into her jeans, noting again how big the denims had become on her. These last months, she'd gone from a size eight to a size six without trying. That was one of the things Pop kept harping about. It didn't matter that she was twenty-seven years old. Pop would always speak his piece to his only child.

But what could she expect with a father who owned a restaurant and was a first-class chef? He simply couldn't stand seeing her disinterest in food. "A five-foot-nothing half-pint like you will become a quarter-pint if you don't look out."

A bell did indeed tinkle as Sammie walked through the tea-room door. Instead of following the waitress to a table, Sammie wanted to turn and make a run for it. The English Country Tearoom was Mom's dream inside as well as out. It consisted of one small room filled with round lace-covered tables with a vase of flowers in the center of each and a brick fireplace at the far end of the room. Both sides of the shop were lined with shelves of teapots, cups and saucers, tins of tea, and dainties.

Sammie sank down in a chair by the nearest table and stared at the wallpaper, splashed with pink roses. The final blow. That's where Mom spent so much of her life the last years. In her rose garden. That's where they found her that day, lying between the rows, the pruning shears at her side.

"Will you have tea, ma'am?" The waitress, wearing a black uniform with white apron and cap, spoke softly as if she did not want to intrude on Sammie's thoughts.

"Yes. Tea." Sammie studied the menu a few moments. "And crumpets, please." Pop would be pleased. She was eating breakfast.

When the tea came, the pot wore a hand-knit cozy, and a dish of raspberry jam accompanied the warm crumpets. "What a beautiful day after all that rain." The waitress's English accent was a sprinkling of sugar on the moment. "Are you vacationing?"

Sammie hesitated. "Not exactly. It's more of a business trip." For more than six months, she'd been rationing her words. They seemed safer staying in her head than coming out of her mouth.

"I hope you'll have time to enjoy Pineville Beach. There's a minus tide in about an hour. If you're into beach-combing, you might find some treasures. Just follow Main Street to the sign that says Beach Access."

Another reason this was the right town. She'd always been able to think more clearly walking the shore.

The waitress got a tide chart from the counter and handed it to Sammie. "In case you decide to stay a few days. There's plenty to see and do here. My name is Abby. I've owned this shop going on ten years, so I can probably tell you whatever you'd like to know about the area."

"I'm Sammie Sternberg." Even though she felt reluctant to do so, she knew that giving her own name was the polite thing to do. Now that she had, part of her wanted to push aside the rules and ask the questions she'd been clutching tightly since she left home: *Can I start over here? Open a shop? Make acquaintances but stay safely detached?*

What she did ask was, "Do you happen to know of a Victorian-style house I might be able to rent? One that could be used as a shop? I'd like to call it the Treasure House and fill it with previously owned items, lovely things like pie safes and candlesticks, things that were an important part of someone's life."

The only other patron, seated at a far table next to the fireplace, looked up from her tea and the book she'd been reading. "How about the old Nelson place?" The handsome woman, with shoulder-length chestnut hair that looked like a model's in a shampoo commercial, smiled over at Sammie. V.J. would have said she had style, with her long denim dress and silver loop earrings.

"Good location," the woman continued. "Ideal for what you want. Besides, we'd get to know one another because it's right across the street from my book shop."

At the offer of friendship, Sammie wanted to pull inside herself like an anemone poked with a stick. Before she could respond, Abby introduced the other customer as Claudine and gave Sammie's name.

"It's short for Samantha," she explained hastily, thinking that there might not be many women named Sammie this far from Los Angeles.

"Mrs. Nelson has been waiting for just the right person to come along and rent the place," Abby said. She looked over at Sammie. "Maybe you're the one she's been looking for."

Sammie tried not to appear too eager. "I'd like to see it."

"After you finish your tea, I'll give you directions."

When she turned off Main onto Orchard, Sammie spotted the bakery on the north corner, as Abby had indicated. The front window was shaded by a green-and-white striped awning and decorated with white starched curtains. On display were trays of pastries fit for the Regency in Los Angeles. No question, the bakery belonged in the picture book.

Across the street was Claudine's book shop. *The Reader's Guide: Rare and Previously Owned Volumes,* the lettering on the door read.

People in books were safer friends than ones with flesh, Sammie had learned. They didn't pry. If she settled here, she could run across the street and choose new ones at will.

Careful, her cautious side warned. *Don't set yourself up for disappointment. This might not be the town after all.*

Next to the bakery, she saw the Nelson place. She pulled slowly to the curb, turned off the motor, and stared in wonder. *If I designed a place for the Treasure House myself, it couldn't be more perfect.*

The Nelson place was a stunning Victorian Gothic, a turn-of-the-century beauty who drew all eyes to her. The house was painted blue-gray with lacy white trim and decorated elegantly with curved and circled gingerbread. Deep down, Sammie knew that this Victorian dollhouse-come-to-life *was* the place for the Treasure House. Did she dare to think that God had brought her here?

She hopped out of the car, and, instead of yelping with

delight the way she wanted, Sammie forced herself to slowly examine the details. But her heart raced as though she were meeting a dignitary and was too overwhelmed to say how do you do.

The house had a front porch, the way she'd dreamed it would. Not a token porch. This porch swept across most of the front of the house and had the same lacy white gingerbread trim. On it she could arrange white wicker furniture and pots with marigolds and lobelia spilling color.

When she shifted her gaze to the left of the porch, she grew light-headed. *Another of my dreams for the house*—a white-trimmed bay window and shutters! If that wasn't enough, on the second floor over the porch were two steep, gingerbread-trimmed gables with a third one over the part of the house with the bay window. The windows, with their straight sides and arched tops, were embellished with tracery. She knew that fragrance from the wisteria climbing up one side of the house would fill the air.

Her gaze swept to the far side of the house where a red brick chimney rose as high as the highest peak. To Sammie, it seemed to be a protective elder brother promising safety and warmth during chilling times.

This *was* the Treasure House. The walnut chairs and Tiffany lamps, the yellowed samplers, chintz pillows, hand-sewn quilts, and lace table covers, the crystal and silver all belonged in these rooms. She knew without seeing.

She wanted to run up onto the porch and touch the stained-glass pane in the front window and dash around the side of the house to inspect the backyard. Was there a back porch? A place for a porch swing where she could sit and sip tea after the Treasure House was closed for the day?

It was time to grab herself by the collar. Neighbors might be watching and think she was a trespasser, and she certainly didn't want to get off to a bad start. So instead of running and peering, she read the sign in the front window: *For rent. Inquire at the bakery next door.*

A bell tinkled when she opened the bakery's front door. No customers were in the shop and no one was behind the counter.

Her first impression was of cleanliness. The walls, the curtains, the cluster of tables and chairs in one corner were all white. Here and there the white was splashed with red: a log cabin quilt on one wall, crocks of geraniums on the floor, gingham cloth squares at the center of each table.

Gleaming cases held breads of every variety as well as pastries, cookies, muffins, cakes, and pies. She wanted to store the fresh-baked aroma in her memory to recall at later times. But was it possible that she could live next door and be able to smell it every day?

A slender, attractive blonde, perhaps a few years younger than Sammie and wearing a white uniform, came from the modern kitchen carrying a tray of freshly baked donuts and slid them into the case. "How may I help you?"

"I'm inquiring about the house for rent next door."

The young woman looked uncertain for a moment, her eyes darting. Then with a slight nod, she said that she'd get her husband.

She returned from the kitchen accompanied by a tall, dark blond-haired man about the same age as the woman, whose strong good looks were guaranteed to make women's eyes linger. He wore a white baker's uniform, and the short sleeves revealed muscular arms like those of the bakers she knew from Pop's restaurant.

"You're interested in the Nelson place?" His tone was flat.

Sammie nodded.

"Why do you want to rent it?"

Sammie felt as though her answer was crucial to her future. *Speak confidently,* she told herself. *Convince him that you're the one he's been waiting for.*

After she'd introduced herself and described the Treasure House, explaining that it would be a year-round business and that she wanted to make Pineville Beach her home, his expression softened slightly. "I'm Mike Le Duc. This is my wife, Autumn."

They shook hands all around. "Get the key," Mike directed Autumn. "I'll show her the place."

The entryway steps were solid under her feet; not a board creaked as she crossed the porch. She remembered what Pastor Jim had said when she told him that she was going to take this trip. "Keep talking to God at every fork in the road even though you don't think he's saying anything back to you."

Did God understand that she couldn't have real conversations with him right now? Taking one more chance that he did, she breathed his name the way she had outside the tearoom, only this time with hope.

Mike swung the door open and stood aside so she could enter. How she wished Mom and Pop were by her side, stepping through the looking glass with her! Place had always been important to Sammie. The beach. The noisy kitchen of Pop's restaurant. Mom's garden. The newsroom at radio station KTWI. She'd become part of the environment and the environment part of her.

Mike Le Duc stood and watched silently as she slowly walked the length of the parlor which looked out onto the porch. *What a background for my treasures!* The wallpaper was the same blue-gray as the house and patterned with white fleurs-de-lis. At one end was a stone fireplace. Her eyes swept the room.

Sammie gasped another one-word prayer at her next discovery—a pump organ! It stood alone on the shorter wall opposite the fireplace.

"The only things Mrs. Nelson left in the house are this old organ that the captain gave her and the kitchen stove," Mike commented. "She says they belong here. I turn on the heat when it gets cold for the sake of the house and the organ. My wife keeps the place dusted and clean."

Was Mr. Nelson a real captain? Sammie stored the question to ask at a later date. Instead, she sat on the organ bench and ran one finger lovingly over the ivory keys and stops.

"Mrs. Nelson doesn't want just anyone to rent this house." Mike hesitated. "She…she has other ideas."

Sammie panicked. Surely the owner wouldn't want customers walking through the rooms. *How could I have been so foolish as to let myself think that God would let this dream come true?* Still, Mike knew her plans for the house and showed the place to her anyway. Why would he bother if there was no use?

They moved on to the dining room, and when she saw the bay window, hope burst in her like time-lapse photography of a budding blossom. *I'll drape a quilt here on the seat, a bank of pillows and a family of stuffed cats there.*

Mike interrupted her thoughts. "You married?"

She shook her head. *Well, it's true, Sammie. You never were married. You only thought you were.* That ceremony in Mom and Pop's garden with Pastor Jim officiating notwithstanding, there hadn't even been time enough with V.J. Magellan for the skin under Sammie's wedding band to turn white.

They moved into the old-fashioned kitchen with highly polished wooden cabinets and glossy wood flooring that matched the floors in the rest of the house. Mike was watching her carefully. "Where are you from?"

"Southern California."

"Family there?"

"Just my father. My mother died about a year and a half ago." *And that's all the family history you're going to get.*

"How do you feel about living in a place like Pineville Beach after southern California? We don't have that kind of excitement, you know." He paused. "Well, in the summertime it can get pretty crazy."

She turned her head toward him to look into his face. When her neck crunched and ached, she realized how stiff and sore she'd become from months of tension and inner pain. "Pineville Beach is exactly what I've been looking for."

Why couldn't this man be quiet and let her enjoy this once-in-a-lifetime experience of seeing the house? But he was probably using the walk-through as an information-gathering expedition. To control the interrogation, she'd settle for a quick look at the rest of the house, much as she hated the idea.

But not before she savored her first look at the stove. It was a Home Comfort graniteware wood burner with warming ovens on top. It was an ample, well-turned-out grandmother that outclassed modern metal boxes and was a perfect place to display copper kettles and kitchen linens. "Another gift from the captain to his wife," Mike explained as he opened the back door so she could look outside.

There it was—the back porch she'd hoped for and not just an entryway unworthy of the name.

Rhododendron bushes had been planted along the fence, interspersed with flower beds. At the back of the yard sat a cottage painted the same blue-gray with white trim.

"That's the guest house. The Nelsons had lots of people coming and going. It's still furnished."

They stepped back inside, and she took a quick look at the dining room, master bedroom, and bath and then climbed the stairs with Mike leading the way. On the second level were five rooms and two baths. "Here's the room most people want to see."

He escorted her into the turret room. Five-sided, with windows from floor to ceiling, the morning sun turned the room golden. From the window bench at the front, she could see a stretch of blue sea spreading to the horizon. If Mr. Nelson had been a sea captain, had his wife sat up here and watched for his ship?

As they made their way back downstairs, Mike spoke over his shoulder. "Well? Do you want it?"

"It's exactly what I've been looking for. Do I talk with you about the arrangements?"

"Not to me. Mrs. Nelson may be ninety, but she's perfectly capable of talking for herself. Matter of fact, she wouldn't have it any other way."

"When can I see her?"

"After I finish a couple of hours' work left at the bakery, I'll take you to the nursing home across town where she lives."

Sammie breathed a sigh of relief. At least Mike thought she was a possible renter. "I'd appreciate that. Meanwhile, maybe I can bike around town. Any particular direction I should go?"

"One place folks people generally like to see is Fort Barker." They walked out on the front porch, and he locked the door behind them. She'd get a look at the rest of the town and relay the description to Pop. It might help convince him that she wasn't crazy to open a business in such an out-of-the-way place. The fort, along with the beach, must bring a fair number of tourists, and Mike had said the town was wild in the summertime.

After she removed her bike from its car rack, Sammie pedaled at an easy speed in the direction Mike indicated, through a residential section of Pineville Beach with two- and three-bedroom homes, most with well-kept lawns and a couple of renegades with ankle-deep grass. Children squealed on a playground at the grade school and flew into cluster around a teacher when she blew her whistle.

Across the railroad tracks on Center Street was what looked like the bread and butter district. The Economart—a scaled-down version of a supermarket—had handmade signs in the window that offered canned chicken soup, hamburger, and cabbage on sale; Bob's Meat Market; Coxell's Drug Store; Greenbaum's Hardware Store; Crane's Department Store with mannequins in distorted positions modeling polyester pantsuits and toddlers' Sunday dresses in the window. These stores looked like they'd been part of town life for decades and probably nothing much about them had changed in all those years.

The back side of Pineville Beach felt comfortable and provided a connection to its past.

A sign directed her around the corner to the beachfront road and Fort Barker. She passed a miniature white church with a cross on its steeple and a tiny cemetery beside it. Definitely another page in the picture book.

The sprinkling of homes on the bank overlooking the water was reminiscent of places where she'd spent summer vacations with Mom and Pop when she was a child. Around another curve was the entrance to the fort and a historical sign. She hopped off her bike to read it. Forts and wars never had been an interest of hers, but Sammie felt a strong desire to learn about this one.

Fort Barker was built in 1811 and was named for General Amos Barker. She hopped on her bike again and pedaled around another curve. What had the forts in history books looked like anyway? Old war movies came to mind with John Wayne types shouting orders behind stone walls over the deafening sound of cannon fire.

Suddenly, it was there in front of her—a protective wall, perhaps two hundred feet long, that followed the contour of the cliff on which it was built, with openings for weapons. Adjoining structures had probably been used to store ammunition and supplies and house troops.

Except for the sound of the surf below, the place was deadly silent. It was a cemetery without lawn or flowers or a sense of loved ones at rest. Only emptiness.

Laying her bike on the ground, Sammie walked slowly toward the wall. In back of her, forested mountains rose majestically. Ahead was this desolate curiosity and the sea. All the fort was good for now was to be stared at by sightseers on their way to somewhere else.

It's a picture of my life.

Was she fooling herself to think God would help her heal and start over?

Her only answer was the pounding of the surf below.

TWO

Mike stood waiting for her on the sidewalk in front of the bakery looking like a stone lion she'd once seen. Although she wasn't late, she felt reprimanded.

Quickly, she applied fresh lipstick and brushed her hair. He'd changed to navy slacks and a white knit shirt. His crisp look made her wish she had time to switch from her jeans and T-shirt to the loose-fitting pink cotton dress in her suitcase. Maybe then Mrs. Nelson would picture her in a white wicker chair on the porch of the house sipping iced tea.

Mike was silent as he drove his black panel truck with *The Bakery* lettered on the side to a road that ran along the Iseeyousee River. When Sammie spoke, she sounded like a child trying to get back in her parent's good graces, the way she had when V.J. had become wooden with disapproval.

"I appreciate you taking me to see Mrs. Nelson. Have you two been friends long?"

For several seconds he stared ahead as though he hadn't heard her. Then, without shifting his gaze, he spoke in the same unleavened tone. "Yeah." His response didn't allow any probing.

A sprinkling of fishermen cast lines from the bank of the Iseeyousee River. A few stood hip deep, casting and reeling in the bright April sun. Another page in the picture book.

"Ahead, just past the little park," Mike offered.

The River Rest Retirement Center was a sprawling, modern brick building with a carefully manicured and landscaped lawn. The interior was just as slick. To the left of the entry was a sitting room with windows overlooking the river. As Sammie rode with Mike in the elevator to the second floor, she tried to imagine the matriarch of that Victorian house living in this modern architectural setting.

On their way down the corridor, Sammie noted the decorations on each person's door: a bouquet of flowers, a poster picturing a cat desperately holding onto a ledge by its claws and the words "Hang in there," a wreath of sunflowers with "Welcome" in the center. Like a college dorm.

Mike stopped in front of number 26 and knocked. On Mrs. Nelson's door was a poster, too. Hers was of a huge rock on the edge of the seashore and the words "The Lord is my refuge and my fortress, my God, in whom I trust." A statement of faith by the woman on the other side?

The door flew open. "Hallelujah! You're a shrimp like me! Someone I can look right in the eye."

Sammie knew she was staring. The tiny, wrinkled woman who looked like Grandma Moses at her artistic prime wore a Dallas Cowboys sweatshirt, jeans, and a green eyeshade. Instead of greeting the woman or introducing Sammie, Mike said simply, "Like I told you on the phone, she wants to rent the house."

Mrs. Nelson's tiny apartment looked as though it had been scaled down to fit her. They entered a playhouse-sized kitchenette and living room. Through an open door Sammie could see the bedroom. Mrs. Nelson motioned for them to sit on the sofa. Lowering herself into a chair, she directed her words to Sammie, "Who are you?"

"I'm Sammie Sternberg."

"Mike told me your name on the phone. But who are you?"

Fear prickled Sammie's insides. What kind of question was that?

"I'm afraid I don't understand."

21

Mrs. Nelson smiled slightly. "When you're ninety, you get to ask whatever you please. Never mind. Just tell me why you want to rent my house."

When Sammie began to talk about the Treasure House, her words rushed out like kids at the three o'clock school bell. She tried to line them up in an orderly fashion but some refused to cooperate. When she got to the part about selling previously owned treasures, things that had history and meaning because they were part of people's lives, Mrs. Nelson interrupted.

"Whoa, little girl. Slow down. Now you're getting to the good part." Her voice was firm at the center but frayed on the edges.

Obediently, Sammie took a deep breath and issued another order for her words to line up nicely. "I have pieces from estate sales in California. As often as I could, I got history about the families so I'd know a little about the story behind what I bought. In one home I found a cradle made by the father of eight children and a bedspread his wife had crocheted. I even saw a photograph of the whole family when the kids were little. The Treasure House will give me an opportunity to offer these pieces for adoption to someone who cares about them. Often I'll be able to tell at least some of the item's history."

Mrs. Nelson raised a hand for silence. "Do you want to settle down in Pineville Beach? Make it your home? Or do you want it for a summer place, going back to California in the wintertime?"

"Oh no!" Fly back and forth like some kind of migrating bird? Absolutely not. Sammie wanted a place to *be*.

The other woman rose carefully from her chair and adjusted her eyeshade. "Not fashionable, but it helps me see." Even in her Dallas Cowboys sweatshirt she looked like the queen of a Lilliputian kingdom. Sammie wondered at the fact that she could stand so straight at ninety.

"You may have the house."

Have the house? Surely Mrs. Nelson wasn't giving her consent. Not just like that. She hadn't asked for references. Hadn't even talked about a price. Was this woman mentally alert enough to know what she was saying? She certainly appeared to be.

Mike, who'd been sitting quietly, jumped to his feet. "Are you sure?"

Mrs. Nelson gave him that same slight smile. "Mike, you know me better than that. Of course I am." She turned to Sammie. "God assured me he'd let me know when the right person came along. You are that person."

Sammie shook her head in disbelief. It couldn't be this easy.

The woman continued, "Little girl, the house isn't mine. It belongs to God, you know. He's the landlord, not me."

No, I didn't know, Sammie responded silently. *The poster on the door wasn't enough to tell me that.* Should she tell the woman that she was a Christian? But how could she, when she hardly felt worthy of the name?

A minute ago, words were pushing one another to be heard. Now her brain was frozen and her words trapped inside. *Say something,* she told herself frantically. "Thank you, Mrs. Nelson," she managed. She felt like curtseying.

The next voice she heard in her head was Pop's. *Think about what you're doing here. This is business. Remember?*

"We do need to talk about business arrangements," Sammie stammered. "For one thing, I want to be sure I can afford the rent."

Mrs. Nelson stiffly made her way to the tiny kitchenette. "I'll put on the coffeepot and we'll talk." Instead of adding one measure of coffee per cup, she added two. "Captain had to have his coffee thick enough so the spoon could stand alone. He said it was because he was a Swede and a fisherman."

So he *was* that kind of captain. Mrs. Nelson also put on a kettle of hot water. "I got used to having my coffee strong, and Mike likes it that way. I tell others they can add hot water so it won't have quite so much wallop."

They sat around the tiny table in the tiny kitchenette drinking coffee from mugs. Sammie's read "Bloom where you are planted" and pictured an ample matron watering flowers through a shuttered window. Mike's was decorated with white whales swimming in a blue sea. Mrs. Nelson's said "I love my Grandma" in childlike letters.

Mike spoke abruptly. "We need to talk about money." Sammie could see the muscles working in his face.

Mrs. Nelson looked into Sammie's eyes. "Are you rich?"

"Rich?" She couldn't help but laugh at the incredible directness of the question. But if this woman could ask something like that, what other interrogation might Sammie face? "No, I am definitely not rich. I recently sold my house in California so I have that money to get me started here."

Thanks to Pop, she added silently. Right after her marriage, he'd handed her the key to a house he owned that she and V.J. loved. "I want to give you this," he said. "Be happy." He hadn't approved of the marriage, but he'd done everything he could for her.

Mrs. Nelson responded quickly. "Then we'll set the rent low at first. Say one hundred dollars a month. After you get the business going, we can raise it." She pushed up the sleeves of her sweatshirt. "In a year, pay fifty more a month. Maybe fifty more a month after two years."

Mike objected. "You can't do that! It's worth a whole lot more. I've told you what other places in town rent for."

"This isn't other places. This is my place. More important, it's God's place."

Mike shook his head and took a deep breath. Would he see

Sammie as taking unfair advantage of an old woman?

Sammie spoke up. "Mike's right. That's not enough rent."

Mrs. Nelson shook her head. "It's settled." She set down her coffee cup and extended her thin, veined hand. After hesitating, Sammie shook it. "It's a deal, little girl. You can move in anytime. Today if you like."

Sammie could only stare at the wrinkled face, the faded blue eyes. "I appreciate your faith in me," she said softly.

"It's not in you, Sammie. It's in God, and I sense his okay."

"Mrs. Nelson…" she began, and hesitated. *Just say it,* she urged herself. "My heritage is Jewish, but I'm a Christian. I believe Jesus is the Messiah. I saw your poster on the door, and I wanted you to know." Mike stared down at his coffee cup, examined his fingernails, and then stared at a blank spot on the wall.

"Sammie Sternberg is a *Christian!* Imagine!" Mrs. Nelson slapped the table, then leaned back in her chair. "I want to hear more about that next time. That's part of the deal, you know. For you to visit me and tell me about the Treasure House, about your life here in Pineville Beach. Maybe you'll even tell me who you are."

Not a chance, Sammie shot back silently. "When the shop is open, maybe I can take you there for a visit. You can tell me what you think." Mrs. Nelson smiled and nodded slightly in response as Sammie took out her checkbook to pay the first month's rent.

Sitting beside Mike on the ride back to the bakery, all Sammie could think about was that she had to get to a phone and call Pop. Instead of asking to call from Le Duc's, she'd use a booth. That way she'd have privacy.

Pop answered on the second ring. She didn't have to force

herself to sound cheery. "Hi. How's the restaurant business?"

"What I want to know is how's your business."

"You won't believe what happened. I found the Treasure House."

"What do you mean, you found the Treasure House?"

"I mean I found the perfect location. A beautiful Victorian house in Pineville Beach, Washington."

"And would you mind telling me where Pineville Beach is?"

"It's on the Olympic Peninsula. Gorgeous mountains, the ocean. Everything I wanted."

"So how long have you been there? A day? Two days? And already you know this is the place? Some things never change."

Sammie took a deep breath, reminding herself to inhale patience and exhale anger. "You'd have to see it. Besides, everything is falling into place."

"Yeah, right."

Her father stirred up her uncertainty. Had she gotten carried away? What made her think she knew what she was doing, anyway? Would she find herself splattered on the sidewalk one more time?

All she could do now was keep her heels dug in. "Pop, you said you'd bring up my inventory for the Treasure House and my personal things when I found a place. I need you to do that as soon as you can. I've already rented the house."

"Excuse me if I don't jump up and down."

Sammie waited, and he continued. "I know I promised to bring the stuff to you, and I'll do it. But it's against my better judgment."

She gave Pop directions to Pineville Beach and asked when he thought he could get there. "Two days to get ready on this end, maybe three to make the trip. I'll call along the way to let you know for sure." He hesitated for a couple of seconds. "Listen, kid. I just want things to be right for you."

Sammie's voice softened. "I know you do. I miss you. Get lots of help loading the truck. Don't push yourself to get here. A day or so won't make that much difference. Just get here in one piece."

"You sound like your mother."

"Good."

"Are you eating right?"

"Hey, I had a crumpet for breakfast, and I'll get some lunch after I hang up. There's no phone in the house yet, so I'll call you tomorrow evening."

He paused. "You're on the Olympic Peninsula in Washington? That's practically out of the United States."

"I love you, Pop."

"Eat lunch *and* dinner. You hear?"

"I hear." She closed her eyes and ran her hand across her forehead. "Any word about V.J. from the police?"

"Nothing. What we need is to get the story on one of those crime-stopper shows."

"No way. I'm not having my stupidity televised for Mr. and Mrs. America's after-dinner entertainment."

Pop backed off. "How about I fix salmon while I'm there?"

Your answer to everything, dear old Dad. Food. "I'd like that. See you soon."

Sammie cradled the phone and ran her finger along the mouthpiece before hanging up, thinking words she couldn't say to him. *Pop, we're all we have now. Please, let's make it easier between us.*

She had to get on with it. First on the list was to get the phone hooked up. But before that, she'd walk through the Treasure House all by herself. Right after lunch, though, because she did have to keep her word to her father.

Where to eat? The English Country Tearoom, she decided. That would give her an opportunity to thank Abby for the tip about the house and let her know she'd be moving in!

Abby greeted her at the door. "Sammie! Did you see the house?"

"Not only did I see it. Mrs. Nelson rented it to me."

Abby slid the menu she was carrying under one arm and took both of Sammie's hands in her own and squeezed them. Her words were a bouquet. "Congratulations and welcome to Pineville Beach. Lunch is on the house."

Sammie allowed herself to bathe in the delight of the moment as she sipped her tea and savored a cucumber and cream cheese sandwich. Right now, she'd choose to believe that renting the house was right. She'd choose to bask in Abby's enthusiasm and imagine that this was a party in her honor and that the others in the tearoom were guests who'd come to wish her well.

For the moment, she'd dismiss her father's words of criticism and remember his love. For the space of a cucumber sandwich, she'd let the rose wallpaper and the teacups on the shelves make the memory of Mom so vivid that she'd be at the celebration too. Sipping her tea slowly, Sammie studied the portraits of the British royal family on the wall. *Hey, Mom, look! The king and queen have come to our party.*

Hating to see the interlude end, she took tiny bites of her sandwich. It was when she was chasing the crumbs around the plate with her finger that she realized what came next. The walk through the the Treasure House by herself!

Her hand trembled as she fitted one of the keys Mike had given her into the lock of the front door. When she closed the door behind her, she stood in the center of the living room and felt the layers of the house around her.

She was really here!

Guilt suddenly overwhelmed her. She didn't deserve this. She deserved to fail. She walked through the rooms, listening to her own hollow footsteps echo in the emptiness like the sound of her soul. Like the fort, desolate and empty.

Should I pray? Have a private dedication ceremony? Pastor Jim had advised her to keep talking to God. But what would she say? How could she ask God to help her succeed when she didn't deserve it?

Listen, stupid. You have to succeed. Have to go on with your life. And how do you expect to do that without God?

Planting herself in the middle of the kitchen, she prayed, "God, I'd like to believe you led me here. But why should you do that for me? Even so, I do want you to be involved in the Treasure House." She paused and thought hard. "That's all I know to say. I'm sorry. Amen."

Even though the prayer didn't sound like much to her, she felt better because she'd gotten beyond "dear God." Her words had been honest. She hoped that counted for something.

As she walked through the rest of the downstairs, she began to sense a shaft of hope like the first ray of early morning sun. She could put a Georgetown circle quilt on this wall and star of Bethlehem quilt on that one. A breakfront with china and crystal in that corner. The oak dining table in the center of this room.

She climbed the stairs and walked through the bedrooms. In one, she envisioned the four-poster heaped with pillows and hand-embroidered linens hanging from racks. In a smaller room she'd use as a nursery, she'd display children's furniture, toys, and animals.

The turret room? She wasn't sure. But she sensed that it had to be planned with special care. The turret room had to be just right.

A glance at her watch made her realize she'd better hurry.

First, though, a stop at the guest house.

The sun was playing hide-and-seek behind the clouds, and the grayness pressed at Sammie as she crossed the backyard. But the sight of herb beds, like ruffles around the front of the cottage, made her feel as though she'd turned the page in *Country Living* from an advertisement for plumbing fixtures to a photo layout of a country garden.

Thyme, oregano, sage, lavender, mint. Gracious living. She would have pot au feu simmering on the back burner seasoned with sprigs picked fresh that morning. A cup of fresh mint tea on the front step as the sun set.

Like Goldilocks discovering the three bears' house! she thought as she walked through the door into the living room. Not because it contained three of everything, but because it was bursting with cheerfulness and seemed to smile a welcome.

The rooms were small but not cramped. The living room and kitchenette were painted white and splashed with yellow. Next to the yellow print sofa was an oak rocker with a carved back and a matching print cushion on the seat. Like Goldilocks, she had to try it. It was just right.

There were dishes in the cabinets to serve four, pots and pans, glassware, silver—all she'd need to keep house and plenty of utensils to please even a cook like Pop.

The bathroom had a shower for hurry-up mornings and a tub for leisurely evening soakings with candles to set the mood.

She shook her head in disbelief. A Tudor rose quilt covered the bed in the only bedroom (decorated pink and white—her favorite colors) with a teddy bear waiting on the pillow. At the foot of the bed sat a chest, empty and ready for her belongings. The dresser and the closet were also empty and waiting for her to fill them. It was silly, she knew, but she did feel as though the whole house had been waiting for her.

Move on, Sammie, she prodded. *Go to the phone company, pick up groceries, come back and unpack the car.* On her way out, she noticed a guest book on a tilt-top desk. The last entry was "Bob and Marlee Kohler, Kenya, Africa," dated June of last year. They'd written, "Thank you, thank you, thank you." The album was thick with names and addresses and comments written by guests from around the world over many years.

At Olympic Bell, Sammie arranged for phone service. From there she drove to Economart and filled her cart with tea, coffee, cereal, milk, cans of soup, cheese, crackers, butter, jam, eggs, apples, and oranges.

Before going home, she stopped at the bakery for a loaf of bread and a coffee cake. Autumn bagged a loaf of crusty sourdough bread and an apple cinnamon ring. Her words were soft. "I'm glad we'll be neighbors."

Sammie responded sincerely. "I'm glad, too, Autumn." *Why do I feel as though I want to pat her hand? Say something to her like, "Hey, I'm the new kid next door. Do you want to come over and play?"*

Questions about Autumn would have to be shelved for later. Right now there were suitcases and bags to carry into the guest house. For the next hour, she put the first pieces of herself into drawers and chest and closet—hair brush and toothbrush and changes of clothes. *My bare bones,* she thought. But the house wouldn't be truly hers until Pop brought the rest of her personal stuff.

She began a mental "to do" list. Apply for the store's license at city hall. Order a sign for the Treasure House. Order stationery and business cards and the promotional folder she'd already designed. See about insurance and a bank. List supplies. Decide ways to advertise.

The next evening she called Pop at home to check on his progress. "I borrowed a truck from Ben who owns the appliance store," he told her. "We'll load it tomorrow. That's Friday.

Early Saturday, I'll be on the road." Sammie still had no phone, so she arranged for Pop to leave a message with the Le Ducs.

Each evening, Sammie sat at the table to eat a bowl of soup with cheese and crackers or an omelet and toast and wondered how she wound up in Pineville Beach, Washington, the almost-proprietor of the Treasure House. Afterward, she'd brew a pot of tea with mint leaves she picked fresh and sit on the front step of the cottage listening to the silence.

Shades of green, the scent of lavender on her fingers, the chirping of birds, the country stillness normally would have combined to create a sense of place, a place where Sammie could *be*. But strangely, it wasn't happening this time. Each evening she hoped it would be different. When it wasn't, she'd jump to her feet, toss the remainder of her tea, and hurry back in the cottage and into bed. Buried under the Tudor rose quilt, clad in her red nightshirt, she tried to think of words to say to God as a good night. Before she slept, she'd promise herself that tomorrow she wouldn't sit on the step in the evening. But she always did.

On the third day, the phone was installed, and Autumn gave Pop Sammie's number when he called. Before he left Los Angeles the next morning, he phoned. "I'm on my way."

She was watching for him from the front porch of the Treasure House and wishing the sign she'd ordered was finished and hung, when he rounded the corner and pulled up. He hopped out of his vehicle, grabbed her by the shoulders and kissed her squarely on the lips, then held her at arm's length.

"You look so little! A good wind would blow you away!" He pulled her to him, and she buried her face in his broad chest, feeling the soft flannel of his shirt against her cheek. He stepped back, his arm still around her shoulders, and stared at the house, then shook his head. Sammie winced until he declared, "Your mom would go crazy over it." She began to feel relieved until he ran his hair through his thick gray hair and frowned. "But, Sammie, it's in the middle of nowhere. You need customers to have a business."

"We have tourists. Lots of them. And in the winter time, I'll make my jewelry to take to shows."

He dismissed her words with a wave of his hand. "And by the way—what kind of name is Iseeyousee for a river?"

"A funny name. There must be some story that goes with it. I just haven't had time to find out about it yet."

The two men Mike had located to help unload the truck drove up. For two hours, the four of them hefted china cabinets and tables and chairs and washstands and chests of drawers and boxes and more boxes into the Treasure House. Boxes that were labeled "personal" went in the guest house. When the moving was over, Sammie felt like a child who couldn't decide which toy to play with first. Should she open the box marked "linens"? the one marked "quilts"? "Franciscan ware"?

Her practical side intervened. She'd unpack her personal items in the cottage so the place wouldn't be chaotic and so Pop could see how homey it was.

Back in the cottage, she made coffee. "I'll drink sitting on the front steps by the herbs," she decided. "Then I'll walk through the house and take a better look." Pop went back to pay the movers, and Sammie sorted through boxes until she came to the one marked "personal and private" and lifted it on the table. No skipping off to do the fun stuff. Hard work first, fun for dessert.

She removed the metal box inside, set it gently on the table, and opened the lid. The first item was a thirty-year-old framed photograph of her parents on their wedding day. Pop, solid, strong, and sober; Mom, tiny, fragile, and looking as though she were planning some mischief. Sammie gently lifted the photograph out of the box and ran her finger across her parents' faces.

Next in the box was a memento from another wedding day—her own. She removed the small white book titled *The Marriage Service*. She stared at it as if from a faraway place. *Funny*, she thought, *it was designed to be a keepsake, with its gold lettering and tassel*. Taking a deep breath, she turned to the inside cover. The words "Declaration of Intention" were printed in the kind of red letters found in family Bibles. Next was written: "We do engage ourselves, so far as in us lies, to make our utmost effort to establish this relationship and seek God's help thereto."

Yeah. Right.

She stared at the signatures that followed as though the book was one she'd come upon at an estate sale and the signers were strangers. *Vincent James Magellan.* Careful, precise, as though traced over a penmanship model. Had he practiced his signature the way he'd practiced playing his role? *Samantha Sternberg.* Swirls and curlicues. Excited. Believing the fairy tale.

She sank into a chair. She wouldn't cry. She'd despise Vincent James Magellan, but she wouldn't cry over him.

Of course she did cry. That's how Pop found her, crumpled in the chair, tears running down her cheeks. Lifting her gently upright, he cradled her head against him the way he'd done after she'd seen her dog run over by a car when she was six.

Sammie's words came out in chunks and then in shuddering sobs. "I'll hate him until the day I die. All the time he was smiling at me and squeezing my hand, Mr. Happily-Ever-After was planning how he'd con me." Her father looked mournfully into her tear-streaked face. "I was just someone ripe for the picking. Another wife to fleece. And not even a wife at that."

Her father gently stroked her head.

"Pop, I'm such a fool."

THREE

For precious seconds when Sammie awakened the next morning, it could have been any day.

Then her mind, a thin-lipped, narrow-eyed person-in-charge spoke sharply before she could slam the door shut: *Remember last night? The Marriage Service? Your anger at V.J.? At yourself? The way you broke down and Pop comforted you?* Yesterday's pain, undigested, was a hard lump in her chest.

Come on, Sammie. Think about something else. Think about this place. Why you're here. What's happening today.

Today, she thought dully. What was today?

She jumped wide awake, for today was the day she and Pop would begin to shape the Nelson family home into her dream. Yesterday may have tasted bitter, but today held the promise of tasting sweet. She prodded herself to get moving. But first she needed to digest last night, and now, with today ahead, she felt strong enough to walk slowly through it.

She recalled Pop's soft shirt growing soggy with her tears. The feel of his arms enfolding her. The words she choked out through sobs. Now that her mind had stopped playing tennis inside her head, she became aware of Pop humming "The Yellow Rose of Texas" in the kitchen. She took a deep breath and swung her legs over the side of the bed.

For years, people commented on Pop's humming. "You're so lucky to have a father who's that happy about life." Loyalty kept her from setting them straight. Sammie knew that humming "The Yellow Rose of Texas" meant that Pop's mind was full of *shoulds* and *oughts*. It was because he couldn't speak them that he had to make some kind of noise. A hum was acceptable. At least he wasn't singing the words now the way he sometimes did, getting them all wrong because he was occupied inside his head with some stream of rhetoric.

She got up, put on her robe, and opened the door, ready for a "Pop" explosion.

"There's nothing to eat in this house." He stood in the kitchen with two oranges in his hands. "No potatoes. I need to go shopping."

"I went shopping right after I got here."

"You call these groceries?" He opened the cabinet and gestured at the boxes of crackers and tea, the lone cans of soup and coffee.

She giggled. "They do look pretty pathetic."

He shook his head and groaned. "What a *meshuga* daughter!"

"Aw, Pop, there you go, calling me pet names again."

He waved her away in mock disgust. "I know you. Work like a truck driver on a diet of butterfly eyelashes."

From the place of used-to-be, she felt a wave of well-being. Bantering with Pop in the kitchen in the morning. His half-smiling reprimands that she was working too hard, eating too little. Pop's way of caring for people was to feed them. And the more he cared, the bigger the meals.

Inhaling the fragrance of the coffee he'd made and gesturing at the pot, she spoke in a little girl voice. "Please, Daddy dear, can I have a cup? With a piece of coffee cake? And an orange cut in wedges?" She knew he enjoyed the game as much as she did.

"Yeah, yeah. Coming right up." At home, he always cut her morning orange in wedges.

She sat at the table, suddenly aware of its emptiness except for a blue Wedgwood bowl of pine cones. "*The Marriage Service* was here on the table last night. Did you do something with it?"

He worked with his back to her at the kitchen counter, pretending not to hear.

"Pop?"

In a voice soft and washed of banter, he answered, "It was in the way so I put it in the drawer."

Silence settled between them. Then she rose, walked to the desk, took the white book out, and placed it on top of the desk. She wasn't sure why, but the book had to be out right now.

Pop sighed and shook his head. "Sammie, why do you have to torture yourself?"

"Today we're going to launch my new life. Maybe it's important to acknowledge who I am and why I'm here."

Suddenly, the idea of the book being in plain view made her panic. What if someone came to the door unannounced?

Calm down, she told herself. *You could slip it back in the drawer before you let them in.*

But as she moved to the table and sat down, Sammie could feel the book like a pair of eyes, staring relentlessly at her as though V.J. himself were in the room watching her.

Nevertheless, she thought. *Nevertheless. It stays.*

Pop brought two cups of coffee to the table and followed up with coffee cake and plates of prepared oranges. With each step back and forth he hummed "The Yellow Rose of Texas" again, only this time he'd picked up the tempo. She knew that meant his interior monologue was fist-pounding.

Between bites of Mike's cinnamon apple ring, which Pop verbally applauded, Sammie asked, "How did you sleep last night?" He'd insisted on bedding down on the sofa bed in the living room despite her urgings that he take the bedroom.

"Let me put it this way. That sofa should be advertised as a guarantee that guests don't stay very long. It's not your fault. I'll look for a motel to spend the nights."

She knew there was no use arguing. It wasn't in him to take the bedroom away from her, and he'd never be happy in the living room. The sofa bed could have been made especially for the White House, and it wouldn't make any difference because the real problem was that her father needed a private place, not a couch next to the front door surrounded by communal furnishings. She should have known. He'd probably felt as though he were sleeping on the freeway. Place mattered to both of them.

"I'm sorry. Later I'll ask Mike about a motel." Looking at her watch, she gasped. "It's nearly 8:00! We need to get started." In every town she'd driven through she'd imagined this day, but in each version of her fantasy she was hard at work already!

He cleared the table while she dressed in jeans and a black turtleneck. They headed through the yard to the back door of the Victorian house. "Another sunny day," she said triumphantly, as though it were her own doing. "Now you won't be able to put down Pineville Beach when you get home as the place where Noah should have built the ark."

Instead of answering, he sniffed the air and made a face. "What's that smell?"

"That, Father dear, is fresh air. You remember. That's what outside used to smell like when you were a boy."

They walked up the back steps, Sammie unlocked the door, and they stepped into the kitchen. The natural wood, fresh as a tree, welcomed her warmly. A generic house fresh from a carpenter's tool box had not been what she'd wanted. This one had lived long enough to have individuality and a history. Again, she savored the sense that people had lived and loved and struggled here.

Trying to behave, Pop asked for directions. "Should we unpack the boxes in the kitchen? Rearrange the furniture?"

"We'll begin with what the customer will see first. We'll imagine the sweep of her eyes as she walks in the front door and arrange furniture in that area first. Then we'll follow her steps through the house and move furniture to make it look the most pleasing. After that, I'll unpack boxes and begin to arrange small items."

Pop followed her silently into the living room.

No arguing to do it a different way? No objection that she could make it look like a dollhouse, but the place was still in the north woods?

Before long, though, his frustrations found a voice. "All this work for what? To prove something you don't have to prove!" Sammie turned away, took several deep breaths. Then they went silently about their work.

All morning, they hefted and shoved and pushed and grunted. Though her father was past middle age and only five feet ten, he was square-cut and solid. He made sure he took the heavy end as he followed her orders. "The dresser over there. The hutch in the corner. The chest in front of the love seat."

The anticipation she'd felt the moment she realized what day it was kept her feeling carbonated inside. Bubbling with anticipation, she wanted to jump here to do a job, then over there. It wasn't winning the prize, but striving toward it that exhilarated her. She smiled to herself as she stepped back and surveyed a bedroom, remembering how hard she worked to win the sixth grade essay contest and to be elected president of the eighth grade. She'd won both times.

Motivated to push on, she requested a shelf here, some pegs there, a bracket for a lamp on that wall. Mumbling and grumbling, Pop obliged.

By lunch time, they'd arranged most of the furniture. Pop had taken measurements for the lumber he'd need and made a list. Putting it in his shirt pocket, he made an executive decision. "Time to eat!" Pop was unequivocal when it came to food. "Time to eat" had always meant "Put down your toys and wash your hands. Now!"

He raised one eyebrow. "Of course we'll go to a restaurant. All you have in your cupboard is bird food."

She grinned at him. "Last one to get washed up is a stale bagel."

After a mock race to the sink, they walked to Mike and Autumn's bakery. Pop headed straight for Mike. Hastily, Sammie introduced them.

"Now *that's* coffee cake," Pop said, "Moist but not doughy, the right kind of apples. Believe me, I know my coffee cake."

Sammie explained that Pop's restaurant was widely known for its cakes and pies. Her father jumped in on the end of her sentence. "Right now, we need you to recommend a restaurant for hungry furniture-movers."

The taciturn baker couldn't hold out against her father's compliments. "The Farmer's Wife. That's the place if you have an appetite." He even turned to Autumn for confirmation. "Don't you think?" She nodded shyly.

Before they left, Sammie also asked the Le Ducs to recommend a motel. "Amy's Bed-and-Breakfast is better than a motel, and it's only two blocks away." Mike turned to Pop. "When Amy says breakfast, she means *breakfast.*"

The Farmer's Wife was a big white farmhouse up a hill just outside the residential district. A white and black matching barn stood behind the house.

"This must have been a working farm," Sammie commented as they walked up the sidewalk. She noted that the front yard was landscaped Pineville Beach style with gleaming milk cans of pink and purple petunias and tiny white fences enclosing bursts of color.

An ample woman about her father's age met them with a broad smile and led them to a polished wooden table in one of the many rooms in the house. "Today's special is pot roast with vegetables, potatoes and gravy, biscuits and coleslaw."

"Are you the farmer's wife?" asked Pop with a grin. Sammie shook her head imperceptibly. *That's my pop!* she thought.

"Sure am. My husband has been gone nearly ten years, though. I decided to turn the place into a restaurant. Figured I might as well earn a living doing what I've done most of my life. Today I'm the hostess. Other days I'm cook, baker, waitress, or pot scrubber."

When the farmer's wife brought today's special, even Pop gasped. The plate was heaped with mounds of fluffy potatoes covered with dark gravy, thick slabs of meat, tiny carrots and onions. She arranged in front of them a basket of biscuits as high as popovers, a crock of real butter, a glass dish of homemade strawberry jam, and side dishes of creamy coleslaw.

Throughout the meal, her father groaned with pleasure to others eating near them. Afterward, he lavished praise on the farmer's wife, whose name he found out was Pearl. "I'm Sam and this is my daughter Sammie. She's opening a business in Pineville Beach." He nudged Sammie. "Tell her about it."

Pop, you should have been head of public relations for General Motors, she thought as she described the Treasure House.

Pearl seemed genuinely enthusiastic. "I'll stop in and take a look after you open. I'm always in the market for things to decorate my place."

As they walked to the car, Sammie was stabbed with regret. With Pop here, she felt safe. It was so much easier to count on him to make acquaintances, knowing he'd somehow set boundaries so nobody would pry into her past.

Throughout the next two days, her father sawed and hammered and nailed and painted and objected and complained that all this was a waste of time. Sammie ran to this establishment and that, made phone calls, and tried to be patient with Pop who checked and rechecked to make sure she went here to do this and there to do that. She pored over catalogs, placed orders, worked on setting up an accounting system.

About four o'clock each day, her father put down his hammer and went shopping for dinner. "I found a fish market on a side street near Economart with salmon so fresh it hasn't stopped wiggling its tail," he bragged as he unpacked his groceries. "But it's a good thing we don't keep kosher. The only kosher foods you can buy are dill pickles and hot dogs."

At 5:30 he was cooking. The first night he served grilled salmon steaks seasoned with dill accompanied by tiny potatoes and peas in cream. His chicken breasts and asparagus accompanied by noodles and fresh tomatoes and basil on the second night would have won a gold medal in any competition.

When they started yawning, he went to a king-sized bed at Amy's Bed-and-Breakfast. Despite the woman's insistence, he refused the lavish morning meals of eggs, country-fried potatoes, thick bacon, cinnamon rolls, and fruit that she prepared. Instead, he came early to the guest house to cook for Sammie and himself.

And then it was over. Time for her father to go home.

The last evening, they sat on the steps of the guest house listening to night sounds, reluctant to look separation square in the eye. When Sammie reached over and took her father's hand, he enveloped it in his own. "Thanks for all you've done," she told him softly.

He studied her hand in his. "I wish I could stay." He stroked her fingers, a ritual he'd always told her would make them grow longer. "But I have to get back to the restaurant."

"I know." They savored the moment in silence.

"Sammie, you know I'm not a religious Jew. But I was brought up orthodox. One thing I remember is when I opened my first restaurant, that little hole-in-the-wall delicatessen, my poppa gave me his blessing. Of course, being orthodox, he said it was the best thing he knew how to give.

"I don't want you to live here away from me and your home. But I can't stop you." He stood, took several steps into the yard and held out his hand to her. "I know that blessing by heart and like my poppa did for me, I want to say it over you now, my Sammie."

She rose and joined him. They stood facing each other. He placed his hand on Sammie's bowed head and looked up to the lavender blue sky. "The Lord bless thee and keep thee; Lord make his face shine upon thee and be gracious to thee; the Lord lift up his countenance upon thee and give thee peace."

They held one another silently.

The next morning she bought a fresh cinnamon apple ring from Autumn for Pop's trip home and filled his thermos with hot coffee. She waved brightly as he drove down the road. As the distance between them grew, she wanted to run down the street after him, yelling for him to come back. When he was out of sight, she walked slowly into the Treasure House.

Separation, she thought angrily as she threw herself into the job of unpacking boxes. *Separation from Mom. From my dream of a "happily-ever-after" marriage. From Pop. From everything I used to be.* She paused, *worst of all—separation from closeness to God.*

Pineville Beachers began stopping in throughout the day, as if they knew she needed voices to break the Treasure House stillness. Mike suspiciously checked on what she'd been doing to the house, Claudine from the bookstore scrutinized and approved the position of this china closet and that chest and the lace tablecloth draped over the Windsor chair. Ben from Printer's Inc., where she ordered business cards and stationery, stopped in "on my way to the bank and had to see what's going on."

She continued to fill every moment of the day with work to crowd out the heaviness of separation, and fell into an exhausted sleep that night. Hours later, she found herself trapped in a dream place and, sobbing frantically, pulled herself awake.

"Oh, God." It was the same dream that had plagued her for months; in it she was searching for Mom. She sat up, still sobbing, and remembered.

In the dream, Mom had disappeared, and Sammie was running through deserted night streets, searching desperately for her. In the next flash of interior images, Sammie was pushing up the side of a mountain, only to find that Mom wasn't at the top. Just as suddenly, Sammie was in a hospital ward, going from bed to bed, hopefully scrutinizing each face. In the last bed, her mother lay motionless beneath the sheet, staring straight ahead, refusing to look at Sammie or to say a word. When she awakened, Sammie was pleading. "Momma! Momma! I'm sorry. Forgive me, Momma!"

She sat up straight. *Get out of bed,* she told herself. *Get busy unpacking and arranging items. So what if it's three thirty in the morning? Put on yesterday's work clothes and get going.*

Not knowing why, on her way to the front door, she stopped to take the *Marriage Service* from the drawer where she'd placed it. Once inside the Treasure House, she knew she couldn't work. Instead, she climbed the stairs to the turret room and slumped to the floor in the dark in front of the windows with the *Marriage Service* in front of her, and stared out into the blackness.

Keep talking to God about everything that happens.

She'd try. "This dream, oh God. Are you telling me that I'm a terrible daughter? That I failed Mom completely? God, what are you trying to tell me?"

A single word came to her mind. *Remember.*

Remember what? She waited. Her eyes fell on the white

book, glistening in the dark.

She remembered a certain Tuesday about ten in the morning. She was seated at a table in the restaurant next door to radio station KTWI where she'd been a reporter.

"Pretty crowded today." She looked up and saw a tall, slender, dark-haired man in a navy three-piece suit and red-print tie. The man looked to be in his midthirties. In one hand he balanced a cup of coffee and in the other a cinnamon roll. "Aren't you Sammie Sternberg, the reporter on KTWI?"

She nodded, only slightly surprised. Publicity photos and public appearances for the station made her recognizable to true KTWI fans. He looked around at the full tables. "May I join you?"

She gestured for him to sit down. He said he was in the neighborhood on business and had a sudden urge for one of the restaurant's famous cinnamon rolls. V.J. was his name, he said.

When she rose to return to work, he said he came there frequently and would look for her. He said it casually, as though this was a chance encounter and not a carefully contrived scheme.

And I played right into his greedy hands, she thought. *It's not that I didn't know enough to be careful, considering my experiences as a reporter and the cases I've covered.*

As the darkness pressed in at her, the word came to mind again. *Remember.*

Snippets that came to mind were from their courtship. Browsing through art galleries. Licking ice cream cones as she and V.J. window-shopped. Candlelight dinners at their favorite restaurant on the twenty-fourth floor overlooking the night city.

All the time, V.J. had been weaving his web. "You like the Impressionists? They're my favorites." "Pistachio nut ice cream?

My first choice, always. We're made for each other." Doing what he called "diving deep into her eyes" as they sipped their coffee.

Remember.

Their wedding day. May 12. Sunny and nicely warm. Mom's rose garden. The fragrance of the flowers scenting the air. Sammie, in an old-fashioned white satin dress with a tiered skirt, a band of pink rosebuds in her hair, a spray of pink roses in her arms. Maid of honor and bridesmaids in pink carrying sprays of white roses. The men in the wedding party in black tuxedos.

Walking in the garden between the rows with Pop who gave her away. Sorrow at seeing Aunt Tessie sitting in Mom's place in the front row. V.J. stepping up beside her. Standing before Pastor Jim in the white gazebo. The vows. Their tender kiss and the celebratory walk back between the rows.

She wanted to rip those pages out of history. But it had really happened. She had to face it. She had willingly given her love to V.J., not knowing he was Satan in a three-piece suit.

She remembered how delighted she was with his playful, verbal swats, his purr of contentment when he was with her. All the time he was planning to take well-to-do restaurateur Sam Sternberg's daughter for all he could get.

She needed to write her thoughts down, to express her feelings in words on paper. Just for herself. She had to lay out all the pieces of the puzzle, turn them face up, and see how they fit.

She turned on a lamp and ran to fetch a notebook and pen. Back in the turret room in front of the window, she began to write.

Two hours later, the sun was rising, casting an orange glow on the water. She'd written and written. She looked down at the *Marriage Service*. She'd go to the cottage and put it back in the drawer and put the kettle on to boil.

About midmorning, fighting off bone weariness, she was arranging a collection of prisms so they'd catch the light, when the phone rang. "My name is Alexa Alexandria. I own Alexa's Interiors. The Merchants Association is having their monthly potluck this Friday at the community center, and we'd like you to come and get acquainted. You'll be the guest of honor, Sammie. Please say you'll be there."

Sammie knew she didn't have a choice.

"Being guest of honor means that you don't have to bring any food," Alexa went on, "and you get to wear a corsage. How can you beat a deal like that?"

Sammie frowned as she hung up the phone. Alexa Alexandria? The name sounded like a member of the jet set.

The night of the potluck, Sammie dressed in a long, loose-fitting pink and lavender flowered print, hoping it would be appropriate. When she walked into the large meeting room in the community hall, she realized that almost anything would have been appropriate. Mike and Autumn in jeans and T-shirts arranged dishes at a long table. Claudine, in an animated conversation with a knot of people at the back of the room, had on shorts as did several others. Some, like Sammie, wore dresses, others wore shirts with ties.

Alexa Alexandria, a plump, middle-aged redhead with very fair skin, in silky, wide-legged yellow pants and flowing top, swept forward and greeted her expansively. "Welcome, my dear." Deftly, she pinned a white carnation corsage on her shoulder.

"Let me introduce you." Taking Sammie's hand, she led her to a microphone. After presenting her to the forty or so Pineville Beach merchants and their spouses, Alexa turned to Sammie with a broad, dimpled smile. "Please do tell everyone about yourself and your shop."

The room was silent; every eye was fixed on her. *Pop! I need you.* She rallied, careful to talk only about her plans for the shop. After applause, she mingled.

As she greeted people, her eyes fell on Mike and Autumn alone in a far corner. Mike's face looked like a storm brewing, and Autumn looked as though she heard thunder and expected a bolt of lightning. He stopped spitting words when a guest approached and engaged him in conversation. The fleeting incident unsettled Sammie.

After about half an hour, Alexa rescued her. "Being guest of honor means you're first in the food line," Alexa insisted, taking her hand. After Sammie spooned homemade baked beans, spinach dip and chips, fruit salad, and meat loaf on her plate, she settled at an empty table and surveyed the room.

"Sammie Sternberg. You're from California, right?" Everything about the middle-aged man who sat down next to her was big—from his height to his girth to the helpings of food on his plate to the decibel level of his voice.

"Yes. My father owns a restaurant in the Los Angeles area."

"Sternberg. Jewish, right?"

Sammie nodded cautiously.

"What made you decide to settle here? We don't have much of a Jewish community, you know."

"That's not important to me." She side-glanced at him as she dipped a chip. "I fell in love with the town. Ethnicity doesn't matter to me."

"Really? Well, you need to know that we don't conduct business here the way the Jews in Los Angeles do."

"And how is that, Harry?" The voice came from a fortyish man who slid into the chair across from Sammie.

"Come on, Art. You know what I mean. Kikes can't be trusted to play by the rules."

"You're a piece of work, you know that, Harry?" He turned

to Sammie. "Forgive us our trespasses. Please?"

Sammie sat stunned. How could this conversation be taking place here in Pineville Beach, where merchants hung baskets of flowers and kept the town square litter-free?

When Harry headed for the serving table to refill his plate, Sammie sighed heavily. *No matter how many times it happens, it still hurts,* she thought. *Especially now. I'm already squashed flat.*

"Please believe that Harry doesn't represent Pineville Beach." The man extended his hand. "Art Humble, and with a name like that I've had to develop a sense of humor. I own Petland."

She grinned in spite of herself as she shook his hand and studied him more closely. He was compact, had salt-and-pepper hair and blue-gray eyes that spoke as much as his words. In khaki Bermuda shorts and black shirt, he looked like he probably jogged on the beach each morning, played tennis each evening, and ordered from the low-fat menu. Art Humble had no hard edges. Even his voice was gentle.

As soon as she could manage, Sammie escaped for home, anxious to put away the day. The next morning as the sun was rising, she filled her backpack with fruit, a thermos of coffee, her journal, and a pen and biked the route to the river. Around a turn was a stretch of undeveloped land with forest on one side and the river on the other, now exposed, now hidden by trees.

At a bend in the road, she had a clear view. The river was wide, alive, rushing over rocks with a sound she'd like to fall asleep by. The air was so fresh it would have made Pop wrinkle his nose and exclaim in mock horror.

She parked her bike, shouldered her backpack, and climbed down the bank, heading for a grove of evergreens just ahead. They were clustered together like family, their branches bowed protectively to the ground. She crawled underneath and sat on a bed of dry needles.

For a long time she sat very still, allowing herself to breathe in the feel of the place. It reminded her of "Sammie's House," a hideaway she'd created with blankets over a card table when she was a little girl. She felt again the same delight she had felt when she crawled inside "Sammie's House" and snuggled down with her stuffed animals and tea set.

Sipping her steaming cup of coffee, she watched the water flowing downstream and listened to its persistent, rushing sound.

Setting down her cup, she pulled out her journal and pen and began to write.

Last night at the Merchants Association potluck, I met Harry. He hates Jews. If this were the old West and I were a man, he would have challenged me to a gunfight at sundown. Harry doesn't want me in Pineville Beach. Especially in business. After all, Jews can't be trusted. I'm so glad Pop wasn't there to hear him.

This morning at the river, I found my secret place. That's what I'm going to call it. She leaned against the thick trunk of a tree and studied its protective, needled arms.

For isolated moments, she savored this sense of place here under the protection of the evergreen branches and watched the river, surrounded by hulking mountains.

"Dear God," she said aloud. "Will life always be bitter-sweet?"

FOUR

As Sammie sipped her coffee on the front step of the cottage the next morning, she realized with surprise that it was beginning to feel comfortably familiar. *This is my house,* she thought with resolve.

She smiled to herself as she thought of her father. A pint-sized house for a pint-sized person, he'd say.

This pint-sized house was beginning to feel like home.

That's when she saw the bird. It was probably the female because it wasn't very colorful. The bird flew to a corner of the eaves, ruffled its feathers, and settled down.

Ordering herself to stay still, Sammie strained her neck to see if there was a nest. She wanted to jump and yell when she caught sight of the bird's home carefully crafted, beakful by beakful. And Mama sitting, protective and immobile, probably incubating eggs.

Oh, sure. Mama stays put hour after hour, day after day. No food. No flitting and soaring. Where's the man when she needs him?

As if to defend himself against her unfair accusation, the spiffy male swooped into sight and lit on the phone wire. Immediately, the female flew from the nest, and the male took her place. A few minutes later, the female returned, and the male flew away. Mama bird settled on the eggs. For as long as it took Sammie to drain her cup, she watched the pair repeat the process. Mama was the primary brooder; daddy relief parent. *Maybe all guys don't fly away irresponsibly, squawking that they put one over on a dumb female.*

Had God purposely caused these birds to build their nest here, so she could observe them?

Come on, Sammie. Why would God Almighty do that for you? More questions without answers.

Part of her wished the birds would pack up their nest and eggs and move somewhere else. She didn't want to share her house with a family-to-be. Not even a bird family.

But there was no more time for bird-watching this morning. For today was *the* day.

Today she'd open the doors of the Treasure House.

At ten, she'd turn the sign in the curtained front door from Closed to Open. And hope and pray that, before the day ended, someone would make the bell she'd hung over the door tinkle.

She bit her lip. Maybe no one would come. She'd sit and pace and put out stock and arrange and rearrange and the bell wouldn't tinkle once. Maybe Pop was right. The north woods, he'd called Pineville Beach. Why had she thought it was a good place for her shop? Had she been led by her heart and not her head one more time?

As she packed a sandwich to eat for lunch, she defended herself against the accuser in her head. Hadn't she done her best to be business-like? Besides, Pop, who knew business the way Mom had known roses, had come to make sure she didn't miss anything.

Maybe there was more she should do to attract customers. But what? She'd advertised in the *Pineville Herald* and would be running a grand opening ad. Brochures, expertly done at Printer's Inc., were in racks where tourists could take them.

She'd done what she knew how to do.

On her way through the yard to the shop, she paused at the spot where Pop had spoken the blessing over her. Were the words a promise that God would bless her? Or merely a moving family tradition?

Inexplicably, she thought of Mrs. Nelson. What would the

ninety-year-old in the Dallas Cowboys sweatshirt who'd spent her life in this house think of the changes?

Focus, she told herself. *Take care of business.*

It wasn't long after she turned the sign in the front door from Closed to Open that the bell tinkled. Her first customers were a squat, gray-haired couple who looked as though they'd grown to match one another.

"From Grants Pass, Oregon," the husband told her. They bought a tin top for twenty dollars.

"For Ed, here," his wife explained. "He collects old toys." She poked him playfully. "It's just an excuse for him to act like a kid."

As soon as they closed the door behind them, Sammie wanted to celebrate. Call Pop. Run up and down the street and wave the twenty-dollar bill like a banner. Instead, she breathed a deep, emotional "thanks" and tucked the bill away to frame.

All day, people came. In campers and trailers and suburbans and sedans. In pairs on bikes loaded with gear. Twenty-some-things warning their kids "don't touch!" Thirty-somethings wearing shorts and message shirts and sun glasses tucked in their hair. Forty-somethings looking for gifts to take home. Retirees in matching jackets. Homemakers from the neighborhood who had to get back to the vacuuming or gardening but just wanted to wish her well.

Not only did they come, but they bought: a tea pot, a butter churn, an embroidered linen tablecloth, a rocker with a rush seat, Depression glass—all before noon.

The rest of the day was just as good. One couple bent their heads close and whispered to one another as though they thought a family lived in the house and they mustn't wake the baby. A vacationer smiled reminiscently over a bone china tea pot. "Grandma had one like it."

"You been here long?" bored husbands would ask while

their wives sauntered through the rooms.

Every day that week, the bell tinkled frequently. Sammie smiled and greeted people and offered help. She answered questions. "This silver candelabra belonged to a couple in Beverly Hills. They used it for formal dinners." She was courteous and helpful but kept a professional distance.

Early Saturday morning, she hung the grand opening banner across the front porch. Just after ten o'clock, the Bloomin' Place made a delivery. "Two for you," the red-haired, freckle-faced boy announced as he set down a potted azalea and a bouquet of yellow roses.

Turning quickly away from the roses, she opened the card with the plant. *Congratulations! Come have tea and crumpets to celebrate. It's on the house!* It was signed, "Dear Abby." It must be a local joke. People must call her "Dear Abby" and ask what in the world they should do about their boyfriend or mother-in-law.

For a moment, she allowed herself to sit still and feel warmed by the tea-shop owner's kindness. But the truth was, she was avoiding the roses.

She told herself to get on with it, so she opened the other card and read the message aloud. *Our love, no matter what. Mom and Pop.* Mom's name on the card made her feel weak. *I can't cry,* she thought. *There are customers in other rooms of the shop.*

But sorrow paid no attention to mental resolve. Quickly, she blew her nose hard and wiped her eyes and took several deep breaths and hoped she only looked allergic.

A couple entered the room. "Those cobalt blue bottles in the kitchen are beautiful. I'm trying to convince Chris here that we need them for our bay window." Convinced or not, Chris paid for the bottles and the couple left. A few minutes later, Autumn walked in the front door carrying a huge cake decorated with pink roses and held it out for Sammie to take. The pink lettering across the top read *Congratulations*.

"For your grand opening," she explained. When Sammie squealed with delight, Autumn said softly, "It was my idea. Kind of like a party."

"That's so nice of you," Sammie said. Of course the cake would be decorated with roses.

All day, congratulatory gifts came. Balloon bouquets. More flowers and plants from the Bloomin' Place. Cards from two of the bouquets she read quickly and tucked into the pocket of her red patchwork skirt. *Praying for you. Pastor Jim,* the first said. The other was signed *Go for it. Love, Dave.* She experienced pangs of homesickness for the pastor and her burly detective friend.

The delivery that left her laughing and shaking her head, though, was a bouquet of chocolate roses from Claudine. First a delivery of hothouse roses, then icing roses, and now chocolate roses. Was she being deprogrammed? What kind would be next? Paper roses? Fabric roses?

At the end of the day, when she checked the place after closing, every room in the Treasure House was festive with bouquets. How she wished Pop were here to see it.

Changing into sky blue slacks and matching top, she hopped on her bike and rode past the English Country Tearoom through downtown to the village green and parked her bike. Several couples sat on benches, a few young people lay on the grass. She remembered thinking the day she first drove across the Iseeyousee River Bridge into town that Pineville Beach looked like greeting card Americana.

What did she think after a few weeks? Pineville Beach and its citizens had taken on dimension. Some of the people had names and faces and personalities. But familiarity hadn't changed her impression. Mrs. Nelson and Alexa Alexandria, for example, could have posed for a poster with an American flag waving in the background.

Sammie stopped at a sandwich shop for a turkey on wheat with sprouts and ate it on the front step of her house. A cool breeze played gently with the rhododendron leaves. She looked at the bird sitting on its nest in the eaves. *Tuck your feathers around those eggs. It's going to be cool tonight, Mama.*

A wave of loneliness swept over her. What an ingrate she was. Her week had been gloriously successful, the shop was full of plants and bouquets, the bank deposit had been sizable. But she had no one of her own at her side to share her victory with.

Pop. She'd call Pop now. Take him on a tour of the shop over the phone. They'd celebrate long distance.

As she sat at her desk in the Treasure House kitchen and dialed the phone, she felt as though she'd won a battle. Taking charge, instead of allowing the deep well of sorrow to rise and break through the surface like a flood, made her feel strong.

"Hey, Pop, it's your long-lost daughter here in the north woods."

"Sammie! *Mazeltov* on your grand opening. I'm afraid to ask how it went."

"Guess."

"It was like a funeral. You gave a party and nobody came."

"Wrong. You get the gong. It was fabulous. A steady stream of customers from the first hour. Lookers, but buyers, too." Her voice softened. "I think maybe it's going to work for me here in Pineville Beach.

"Yeah." He sounded as thought he was swallowing what he really wanted to say. "Did you eat today?"

"Just finished a turkey on wheat so thick I thought maybe you taught them how to make it. Listen, Pop, I want to take you on a tour of the shop. Now. Here on the phone. Okay?"

"How did you know? I was just sitting here saying to myself, 'I wish Sammie would take me on a tour of her store.'"

"What a coincidence. Okay, then, we'll begin in the parlor." She kept talking as she walked with the phone. "On the table next to the door are the roses you sent. Beside it is a picture of you and Mom. Not for sale, of course."

Her voice became tender. "Thanks for sending the flowers." He meant well, she knew, by sending roses and including Mom. The last thing she'd do would be to tell him how much it had hurt to look at them all day.

He entered into the game. "They smell wonderful." Sammie knew Pop wouldn't spoil her celebration even though what he really wanted was to take her by the nape of the neck like a stray kitten and move her to the safety of his house in California.

"Look over here at the azalea plant from Abby who owns the tearoom. And the bouquet on the organ. It's from Pearl. You like the way I arranged the miniature houses over the fireplace? the Tiffany lamp and the wooden boxes?"

"I'm speechless, believe me."

"I gave the dining room a formal look. After these things sell, I'll probably change it. See the bouquet of pink baby carnations on the table between the pink candles? It's from Printers Inc. The whole house smells like Mom's garden."

"I have the real thing right outside my window." Pop didn't know how to be subtle.

"I love the kitchen," she went on. "On the stove, I've displayed copper kettles and stacked linens. The shelves you built are perfect for folded quilts and crocks. And you'll never guess what's on the dry sink next to the back door."

"Who could guess?"

"It's a bouquet of chocolate roses from Claudine across the street. I'll tell you what: I'll mail you one. Eat it and think of me."

"I was right. You are *meshuga.*"

"It runs in the family."

In the master bedroom, she described the teddy bear collection, the pressed flower pictures, and a bouquet from the Merchants Association. When she went on to describe the candles and crystal and dresser sets in the pink upstairs bedroom, the spinning wheel, baskets of hand-spun yarn and handwoven fabrics in the mauve bedroom, her father groaned that it all sounded too feminine for him.

His response to the collection of cuckoo clocks in the yellow bedroom was an "*oy vey*" so loud she had to hold the receiver away from her ear. "All those birds sticking their heads out every hour would drive me cuckoo." But he did ask questions about every congratulatory bouquet and plant in every room so he could get an accurate picture in his mind.

"Here's the children's bedroom. This is the one for you. Don't you love the balloon bouquet on the dresser from the people who made my sign? and the toys? the trucks and steam shovel, rag dolls, tiny tea sets? I'll let you play with them next time you come."

"Just what I've always wanted."

Keep it light, Sammie, she prodded herself, pushing out of her mind V.J. and the talks they had as they lay in bed at night about the nursery they'd decorate with Pooh Bear and Eeyore and Piglet.

She walked down the hallway. "Last but not least is the turret room. Remember we put the glass-fronted bookcases in here? I've filled them with old books. Tea cups are on the tables next to the love seat and rocker we arranged so people can sit in them and look out the windows at the sea. In one corner, I have a children's table and chairs with picture books."

"So are there plants or flowers in this room?"

"Sure are. A gloxinia from Pastor Jim and a mixed bouquet

from Dave." Pastor Jim and Dave were two of the few people from Los Angeles who knew where she was, except the police working on her case.

"What do you think?" she prodded.

"I think you're a Sternberg through and through. Set your mind and get the job done." Silence stretched between them. He turned the question back to her. "What do *you* think?"

She took a deep breath. "I think…I think…I have a lot of different feelings. I guess I want to prove to V.J. that I can be successful in spite of him. Of course, he doesn't even know about all this. Not that I want him to. Nothing short of prison will make any difference to him, anyway."

"If I could get my hands on that rotten bum…"

"That would only make things worse." Pop never blamed her. What he could have said was, "I told you from the first day that I didn't trust him." But he didn't.

"It should be like the old days when the family went out and took vengeance."

She sighed. "That was when they didn't have police and jails."

"If you had to quit your job, why did you have to go so far away?"

She'd answered these questions so many times before. "You know there are too many people there who ask too many questions, Pop. Too much notoriety. Too many memories." Of Sunday afternoon drives to the beach. Bike rides in the park where they stopped to feed the squirrels. Times they stepped inside their private world.

"Pop, thanks for the blessing. I think about it a lot. I think about you a lot."

"Bubbela, you know what I said on the card with the roses? I mean it."

"I know. I love you. Goodnight."

"Stay well, you hear?"

"I hear."

As she walked downstairs, she wished she felt exhausted so she could go home and fall in bed. Why did she have to feel agitated?

She had to move. Accomplish something. Another achievement. Another triumph. Unpack and polish the stunning silver tea set she'd purchased in Beverly Hills at the estate sale of an investment broker and his wife who were retiring and moving closer to their children and grandchildren. Put it in the dining room. Make the pieces shine so customers gasp when they walk in the room.

Far into the night she worked, riveting her mind to the task. She could sleep in tomorrow because it was Sunday. Like most storekeepers in Pineville Beach, she wouldn't open until 1:00 P.M.

Conscience pricked her. *What about church?*

She felt guilty. Go to church and listen to a sermon about trusting God? About how all things work together for good? *No, thank you very much.*

The second week went as well as the first, but by Saturday night Sammie found herself panting like a puppy after a run. Before too long, she'd have to find someone to work a few hours a week so she could at least run errands.

On May 12, her wedding anniversary, she felt as though someone had pierced her heart with a knife. She flashed cries of help to God and kept her day filled with toe-to-heel activity.

Gradually, life settled into a routine. Sip coffee on the steps, watch Mama and Papa Bird, and listen to the morning. Eat breakfast to please Pop, make a sandwich for lunch, and turn the sign around in the front door of the shop at ten. Make polite conversation with customers, talk about the background of this item or that, make transactions, restock, do book work, phone in orders, dust, and polish.

On Memorial Day, businesses closed, one of Pineville Beach's traditions. Claudine stopped by. "You *are* planning to go to the Memorial Day commemoration." Claudine didn't ask questions; she made statements.

When Sammie hesitated, Claudine pressed. "As one of the merchants, you need to be there. Besides, this is a chance to experience grass roots patriotism. Pineville Beach actually remembers the war dead just like our parents and grandparents used to."

The next morning, Sammie took time to wash and condition her hair so it fell in a cap of soft curls. She looked at herself with disgust in the mirror. Even the hair on her head brought back bad memories. V.J. had caressed it, then pulled a curl straight, and laughed when he let go and it sprang back.

She slammed down the hairbrush to sever the reverie. It was Memorial Day, and she was going to a Pineville Beach commemoration. What should she wear?

Patriotic colors. After surveying her wardrobe, she selected navy slacks, a crisp, button-down white shirt, a navy-and-red vest, and red blazer. Almost defiantly, she fastened a red bow in her hair. When she looked in the mirror, she could hear Pop call her "sample size" and insist she drink a milkshake.

By the time Claudine came, throngs of people were walking past the shop toward the largest cemetery in town. "It's traditional. A sign of solidarity."

They were met at the cemetery gate by the high school band playing "America the Beautiful" and a color guard from a local veterans organization wearing uniforms and carrying flags. Together, townspeople slowly moved inside and circled around a section of graves. The band faced them playing

"America," flag bearers on either side.

When the song ended, from the front row, a tall, fortyish man with kind eyes behind steel-rimmed glasses, stepped forward.

"Jack Bishop," Claudine whispered. "Pastor of the community church."

His words were gentle as an evening breeze. "We're here to remember and pay tribute to those who fought for us. Freedom has a price. Today, the price for us is to stand for our convictions. The men and women we honor put their lives on the line. They were wounded. Some died. They may have been your loved ones."

Precisely at eleven o'clock, Pastor Bishop called for a minute of silence. Sammie bowed her head. She tried to think of young men hitting the beach at Normandy all those decades ago. What came front and center instead was the night in the turret room when she'd heard that word. *Remember.*

You're disgusting, Sammie Sternberg. Here you are standing by the graves of those who fought for your country, and what are you doing? Feeling sorry for yourself. Remembering your own battles, feeling your own pain.

Pastor Bishop spoke again. "We look forward to a day when there will be no more war. The dwelling of God will be with men. He will live with them. He will wipe every tear from their eyes. There will be no more death or mourning or crying or pain, for the old order of things will have passed away."

The band began to play "The Battle Hymn of the Republic," and elementary-school children moved through the cemetery, placing a single carnation on the graves of those who fought in wars. Tears streamed down Sammie's face, and awkwardly Claudine reached over and took her hand. Sammie wanted to wrench her hand away, ashamed that her tears were for herself and not for others. She wept out of the desperate need she felt to have God wipe the tears from *her* eyes; for the old order of things to pass away in *her* life.

A gray-haired, proudly erect black man from the color guard marched to the center front of the band carrying the flag. He stood, chin up, eyes straight ahead, as the band played the national anthem. With hands over hearts, townspeople sang lustily, Sammie with them. Young trumpeters pushed themselves to hit the right notes. Children who'd placed the flowers on graves, stood transfixed. With the sun warming her back, the sound of the national anthem filling her head, and the scene filling her eyes, for a blessed few moments, Sammie forgot herself.

When the anthem ended, the flag bearers led the way out of the cemetery followed by the band, playing a march. Together, they all walked from the cemetery to the town square.

Claudine fell in alongside her. "There'll be barbecued hot dogs and booths with games. It's the town's annual scholarship fund-raiser. The principle is that if we help send kids with potential to college, in the long run we're helping the country and ourselves."

Along the way, the townsfolk's mood gradually changed from somber to celebratory. "The committee works for months getting this organized," said Claudine. The green was lined with booths and tents. In the gazebo, a group of men with instruments, wearing straw hats and red-white-and-blue jackets, were getting ready to play.

"Other years, I've worked a booth. That's good for business. But I took this year off," Claudine explained. "Let's buy some tickets and have fun."

Sammie joined in halfheartedly as they tried to knock down milk bottles, make four baskets in a row, and toss rings over spindles. Children squealed, teenagers yelled across the green to one another, men and women who manned booths called customers to play their games, and the band played one old tune after another. But Sammie wanted to run through the village green until she found the volume control so she could turn it down.

When she made a face, Claudine noticed. "All the noise getting to you? Too much fun and games?"

Sammie shrugged. It wasn't only that. She'd seen couples all morning, and she was sick of them. They held hands tearfully at the cemetery and now were wiping ice cream from each others chins and cheering when their partner knocked down the milk bottles or won a prize. Dutifully, she ate a hot dog when Claudine was hungry and then followed her to a booth. "There's someone I want you to meet."

Face painting, the sign said. "He's our resident celebrity." Claudine pointed to a man seated at a table, his head turned away, and she whispered in Sammie's ear. "Brad is a well-known, professional watercolorist. Don't expect much when I introduce you because he keeps to himself pretty much." She side-glanced at Sammie. "He makes my heart beat faster, I can tell you."

They walked to the table where the artist was concentrating intently on a small, blond girl whose face he was about to paint. Claudine placed her hand on his shoulder, and he turned to look at her.

He sounded as though he'd been brought back from a foreign country. "Claudine. Hello."

Claudine pushed Sammie forward. "Brad MacKenzie, this is Sammie Sternberg. She's the owner of the Treasure House, a new business in town. It's right across from my bookstore."

Brad's long stare made Sammie feel as though he could see beneath her eyes, her skin. "Hello, Sammie Sternberg."

It was hard to stand unflinchingly under his gaze. "Glad to meet you," he added. He was tall, with soft, dark hair that looked freshly blow-dried and chocolate brown eyes like her own. He was dressed simply, in blue jeans and a denim shirt.

He looked to her as though he'd ripped the brand names from his life. He was in good physical shape but had no bulging muscles that would call people's attention to him, no witty repartee that said "Look at me, I'm clever." Still, he hadn't been able to scrub himself of magnetism. Involuntarily, she took a step backward.

He turned back to the little girl and began painting Noah's ark on her cheek. Claudine looked with curiousity at Sammie as they walked away. "What do you think?"

"I'll bet no one calls him 'Mac.'"

Claudine nodded as she guided Sammie to a booth across the green. "There's one more thing we have to do before we leave." They turned at a sign that read *Ye Old Photo Gallery.*

A photographer, with red garters on his white shirt sleeves and a straw hat over straw-colored hair, was shooting pictures of townspeople standing behind a life-sized tintype of an old-fashioned bride and groom with openings for people's faces.

Selecting a black beard, handlebar mustache and wig, jacket and top hat, and standing before a mirror, Claudine applied her disguise while Sammie stared dumbly. "I played boys' parts in the all-girl school I attended," she explained as she grinned at her reflection. "And believe me, this is the only kind of bride I ever want to be again."

A wedding picture? Sammie looked around for an escape and realized there was none.

Tough it. She put on a white lace headpiece and bridal gown, then stepped beside Claudine and posed. At least she didn't have to smile. Brides and grooms in tintype photographs rarely did. She thought of her own wedding pictures as the photographer focused and snapped the shutter. If she'd known what was ahead, she wouldn't have smiled then, either.

On the walk home she was silent. "You didn't want fun and games today. Don't think I didn't notice. Let's just say you're tired from opening a new business." Even though Claudine hadn't asked a question, she waited for an answer.

"Yes, I guess I am tired," she answered reluctantly and hoped what she said would be enough. *Not tired the way you think, though. I'm tired inside my bones.*

At home, she set the tintype bride and groom photograph on the dining room table. In the bedroom, she removed a wide, plain gold band from the tin box in the dresser drawer. Squeezing it in the palm of her hand, she thought of the day V.J. had slipped it on her finger and repeated after Pastor Jim, "With this ring I thee wed and with all my worldly goods I thee endow."

She wanted to throw the ring through the window. Bury it beneath egg shells and coffee grounds in the garbage can. Instead, she carried it back to the table and picked up her journal on the way. Seated, she placed the ring next to the photograph and began writing.

This morning, I cried for myself at the Memorial Day service, instead of for the veterans. I hated every laughing couple I saw. Then Claudine insisted we have a tintype wedding photograph taken at the celebration.

She fingered the wedding ring. *That day in the rose garden I thought V.J. and I were being united before God. I thought on our wedding night, as I stood feeling shy in my white satin nightgown and V.J. took me in his arms, that our union was about to be consummated in purity. That it was right.*

Pressing so hard she almost tore the paper, Sammie printed in huge block letters across the page: *I WAS A VIRGIN.*

FIVE

That night, Sammie lay in bed listening to music playing softly on an FM station. A cool, gentle breeze brushed her face, and she was trying to calm her ragged emotions when suddenly from next door, Mike's voice knifed the air.

"I thought I told you…" He grew louder. "Read my lips, Autumn!"

Next she heard a clatter of what sounded like pans or baking tins. The screen door to the patio slammed.

Sammie sat up in bed, straining to hear, but the only sound was the barking of a dog in the distance.

Oh, Lord. Marital misery in picture-book Pineville Beach? Right next door?

She chided herself. *What do you think? That small town marriages are as serene as the scenery?*

Maybe it was only an isolated argument. She turned over in bed, and hugged Mrs. Nelson's stuffed bear, trying to turn away from the unpleasantness.

The next morning, Sammie was stepping out of the shower when the phone rang. Wrapping herself in a towel and trying not to drip, she answered with a reluctant hello.

"Samantha Sternberg?"

"This is she."

"My name is Mattie Mead. I'm editor of the *Pineville Herald*, the town's weekly newspaper. Sorry this is last minute, but I wondered if you could meet me for breakfast. I'd like to do a story on the Treasure House."

Sammie wished her brain didn't feel as though it had gone into hibernation. "A newspaper article?" she asked, as though they didn't have such things where she came from.

"Can you meet me at Hotcake Heaven in forty-five minutes?"

"Hotcake Heaven?" She was annoyed with herself for repeating whatever her caller said. "I thought I'd found all the restaurants in town, but I missed that one."

"It's in the old section, the place locals go. Breakfast all day. Platter-sized pancakes." Mattie Mead gave her directions.

Sammie responded with a brightness she did not feel, "I'll be there in forty-five minutes."

She willed herself into action. The *Pineville Herald* was the only newspaper in the area and did a pretty fair job of reporting local news. The townspeople read it religiously and tourists scanned it to find out what was going on. So this article was important publicity.

As she brushed her hair, Sammie scolded herself. *Quit worrying because you're afraid the past will come out. You wanted to open a business. Having a business means publicity. You don't have to say anything you don't want to. Besides, that was a risk you decided to take, remember?*

She chose a black skirt, black blazer, and a fuchsia silk blouse with an embroidered collar that made her look more like an efficient business owner than she felt. In her mind, she created an image of herself speaking crisply yet politely, her personal life safely tucked away.

As she slid behind the wheel of the car, she shook her head. *You're not the crisp type.* "I can't psyche myself up, God," she prayed aloud with her heart in every word. "Help me get through this interview."

The blue sign over Hotcake Heaven's door showed pancakes with wings floating on a cloud. As she walked into the long, narrow, no frills eatery, on the left she saw a series of open grills with cooks in white aprons arranging bacon, pouring a line of hotcakes, browning home fries, and breaking large eggs with bright yellow yolks. Her brain told her that the food looked wonderful but her stomach was shouting "no, thank you." Last night she'd wept until she was exhausted, and now she had an emotional hangover. Her eyes burned, her head pounded.

She spotted a sturdy woman in her forties with bobbed gray hair sitting at one of the scrubbed pine tables in the back and facing the door. The woman broke into a smile when she saw Sammie.

That must be Mattie Mead, she guessed. When they shook hands, the older woman's large one enveloped Sammie's own.

"On the way over I realized I didn't know what you looked like, and I forgot to ask on the phone what you were wearing so I'd know you."

Mattie Mead looked down at her blouse and skirt. "It's usually denim. Jeans, skirt, dress. But I've been past the Treasure House and saw you inside, so I knew what you looked like. Sorry I missed the potluck they had welcoming you."

Sammie acknowledged her apology with a smile and slight nod. "I've heard people around town refer to you as 'Miss M.'"

The older woman's chuckle was so deep that Sammie had to keep from looking startled. "Miss M. is what people call me. And sometimes lots worse."

"People call me Sammie, Miss M."

Miss M. chuckled again. "Our parents must have had monograms in mind when they named us. MM and SS."

Sammie faltered because her initials were supposed to be SM and not SS. But the name "Magellan" was as phony as he was.

They each ordered coffee and a single hotcake that resembled the one on the sign: light, thick, and platter-sized. After buttering hers and pouring blackberry syrup on top, Sammie took a bite and groaned dutifully with pleasure even though her stomach was holding up red flags.

Miss M. efficiently cut her hotcake into squares with a knife and fork and ate quickly while Sammie managed a few more bites. They made safe small talk about the heaping plates waitresses hefted by.

When the newspaper woman finished eating, she pushed her plate aside, took a pad and pen from her purse, leaned forward, and looked directly at Sammie. "What's special about the Treasure House?"

Breathing a tiny sigh of relief and chiding herself for thinking Miss M. would grill her like a detective with a suspect, she answered. "Every item has a history. I try to find out as much as I can about a piece so I can pass the information on to the purchaser." She told Miss M. a few stories about items in the shop.

The editor looked down only rarely to make notes. Most of the time, she kept her eyes focused on Sammie's face.

Maintain eye contact. Come across as though you have nothing to hide.

When she learned that Sammie had been a radio news reporter in Los Angeles, her eyes widened. "Ha! In the news business, eh? Don't we have a lot in common!"

Then her voice turned a corner. "But you've made quite a leap, haven't you? From covering the city scene to selling Waterford crystal? Why such a drastic change?"

Don't panic. It's a reasonable question.

"Opening the shop has been a dream. I finally decided to go for it."

A faint smile curved Miss M.'s lips. "People from California settle here to get away from something and maybe to find something. They want to get away from the smog, the traffic, the congestion, and maybe to find peace." She cocked her head. "You say that with you it's different?"

Sammie's head began to pound harder, and her stomach threatened to reject the bites of hotcake. "Actually, I enjoyed my life in the big city." She hesitated because she didn't want to lie, but neither could she tell the whole truth. "This just seemed to be the right time to open the Treasure House, and Pineville Beach looked like just the right place."

Miss M. leaned back in her chair. "Interesting. I went from a big-city newspaper to the *Pineville Herald*." She sat forward again and looked piercingly at Sammie. "But this is your story, not mine." She glanced at Sammie's ring finger. "You're not married?"

For a moment, Sammie held her breath, trying to keep the pain from making its way to her face. "Not married."

"What business plans do you have for the winter, when tourist business slacks off?"

Her stomach relaxed slightly. "I make lapel pins. One-of-a-kind, called 'Originally Yours.'" This woman had honed concentration to a fine art. Customers came and went, waitresses brushed by, groups at other tables laughed raucously, but she was never distracted.

"Wouldn't sales in the shop be better if you were in the city and not way out here?"

Just as Sammie scrambled for a safe reply, she heard a male voice at her elbow. "Miss M. and Sammie Sternberg." Not a greeting, simply a statement. When she looked up, Sammie saw it was Harry, the unwelcoming committee of one at the Pineville Beach Merchants Association potluck. Harry, the Jew hater.

Miss M. looked up and nodded curtly, and Sammie did the same. Harry raised an eyebrow, nodded back, and walked silently to a table in the corner at the very back of the restaurant.

"I heard about what he said to you at the potluck. I'm

sorry." Miss M. watched him; her eyes narrowed. Her voice grew hard. "He won't try that around me."

When she looked again at Sammie, her face softened. "Let's finish the interview at the shop, okay? I'd like to do a walk-through for the article, anyway."

It was more than okay. Maybe now they'd be talking about her merchandise and not her.

But the first thing Miss M. asked about in the shop was the photograph of Mom and Pop. "What do they think about your new venture?"

"Mom died nearly two years ago. Pop thinks any place with rural mail delivery is nice to visit but he wouldn't want to live there. The day of the grand opening, I took him on a tour of the shop by phone. How about if I take you on the same tour in person?"

The editor gave a decisive nod. In each room she made notes and asked questions. How had Sammie come by an exquisite star of Bethlehem quilt? antique map? set of thimbles?

In the kitchen, Miss M. stood silent. "This is a fancied-up version of the farm where I grew up. My grandmother should be standing at the stove stirring apple butter and my mother at the counter kneading dough." For a moment, she was not Miss M. but Mattie Mead, warmed by memories. She turned to Sammie. "You have a feel for this, all right."

Upstairs she paused by the spinning wheel and baskets of yarn. "Sometimes I wish we had to spin yarn in order to have a new dress. That would slow us down, wouldn't it?"

Instead of Pop's "oy vey" when she saw the cuckoo clocks, Miss M. gave her deep chuckle. "I'll send a photographer over to take pictures to go with the story. Be sure he gets a shot of these."

In the turret room, she scrutinized the book titles. "I'd like more time to look these over." At the window, she sighed, then turned and made eye contact with Sammie. "This room was special to the Nelsons, you know. You knew that when you fixed it up, didn't you?"

"Not exactly. I just sensed it."

The editor put her hand on Sammie's shoulder. "As my father would have said: 'You done good, kid.'"

On the way downstairs, Miss M. asked, "Are there any of your personal items for sale in the house? Ones that were yours or belonged to your family?"

Fear prickled Sammie's insides and made her weak. "Err, yes." *Things V.J., the bigamist, and I collected,* she thought. "A few pieces here and there."

"When I have more time, you'll have to tell me the stories behind them." Miss M. turned to her and smiled. "When I come back for a visit, not to write about you for the paper."

Sammie simply smiled back and said she'd welcome another visit and thanked her for the interview. After the editor left, Sammie stood staring out at the street. The woman was suspicious. Would she come back to pry?

More tourists filled the streets of Pineville Beach that June week now that school was out. They passed one another going in and out of the shop, so Sammie had little time to worry about Miss M. These days she couldn't lock up long enough to run errands. Restocking and book work had to wait until after hours. Even though she wasn't sure she could afford it, the time had definitely come to hire a part-time employee.

Maybe Mike and Autumn would know someone. She hesitated to go over and talk to them after overhearing Mike's outburst. Setting him off was the last thing she needed, but Mike wasn't someone she could avoid. Anyway, she didn't want to avoid Autumn.

After closing on Friday, she walked around to the Le Ducs' patio. Mike was sitting at a table by the back door drinking iced tea and talking to Autumn through the screen door to the kitchen.

He motioned to a chair across the table. "You want iced tea?" If he suspected she'd overheard him that night, he didn't let on.

Since this was the most hospitality he'd offered since she met him, Sammie accepted. Through the screen door, she could see Autumn fixing the tea with rabbitlike movements.

Mike gestured toward his shop. "Business has picked up over last spring. It doesn't hurt having you next door. Your place is popular with women, and they stop here on their way past."

So that's why he's more friendly! Keeping the conversation on a business level, she agreed that sales had been good and asked if he knew someone reliable who could work in the shop a few hours a day.

Autumn handed her the tea and mentioned her sister Jennifer to Mike.

He nodded.

"Jen is seventeen and very responsible," Autumn told Sammie. "She lives with our folks out in the country. Hoffman—that was my maiden name."

Mike drew a map locating their house on a pad Autumn gave him and handed it to Sammie who said she'd contact Jennifer the first chance she could.

That night, Sammie stocked the nursery with toys, including her personal favorites: a doll with a china head, a kaleidoscope, a toy scooter, and a worn set of wooden alphabet blocks. When she finished and sat back, she felt hungry. Not for food, but for history—the history of the house; for the sounds this house heard when it was young. She wanted to know who the house was.

With its porches and fireplace and bay window and turret, it had personality. But what had it sounded like during the years when a youthful, feisty Mrs. Nelson scurried through the rooms? Had the house been noisy with family and guests around the table?

Mrs. Nelson. She remembered her promise to visit her unpredictable landlady. Would the woman be willing to tell her about what life was like during the early years when she and Captain lived there? She grimaced. *Why should I expect Mrs. Nelson to tell personal history when I'm not willing to do that myself?* Nevertheless, she'd promised to visit. *Besides, I really do want to see her again.*

Before opening the shop the next morning, Sammie prodded herself to take photographs of the rooms from several angles and drop the film off to be developed. Munching a muffin she'd picked up at the bakery on the way back, she telephoned Mrs. Nelson.

"I'd like to come over next Wednesday after I close the shop and show you photographs of the place." A phone tour, a walk-through tour, and now a photographic tour!

"I don't happen to have a date that evening. I'll fix us a little supper."

"Don't go to the trouble, please. I'll settle for a cup of your industrial-strength coffee."

"My generation considers it rude to turn down hospitality. It'll be a simple meal. One course and no finger bowls. Anyway, as busy as you've been lately, I don't suppose nourishment is something you get a lot of."

Her father had an accomplice. If she didn't know better, she'd have thought he'd been talking to Mrs. Nelson.

There was a new poster on her landlady's door picturing a black cat curled up beside a white dog, with the caption: "Let's be friends."

Mrs. Nelson's grin was unchanged, but this time she wore a red baseball cap and a navy sweatshirt with a picture of another cat and the words, "I don't do mousework."

Sitting across from her landlady at the kitchen table, eating homemade pea soup seasoned with chunks of ham, accompanied by toast and watered-down coffee, Sammie felt at ease.

Why should she feel safe in this miniature apartment with this tiny old lady? It wasn't because the woman was too fuzzy-minded to ask pointed questions.

Sammie commented on how delicious the soup was. Then she asked about two plates hanging on the kitchen wall. One pictured stick people dancing in midair and the other a blue house with smoke curling from the chimney. "Were they made by your grandchildren? Or maybe your great-grandchildren?"

"Not exactly." She crooked her neck to look up at them. "Not blood relatives, anyway. But as sure as I'm sitting here, they're my kids."

She arose, picked up her cup, and headed for the living room. "Come. We'll sit on the sofa and I'll show you." She set her cup down on the coffee table and removed an album from the bookcase. It was so heavy she had to grasp it to her chest with both hands. Sammie knew better than to offer to help.

They settled on the sofa. Mrs. Nelson squinted under the bill of her cap. "It tickles me that I don't have to get a stiff neck looking up at you." Running her hand over the album's embossed cover, she spoke as though she was about to open a door to some private room in her life. "This is my family album. The family God gave me, that is.

"Right after we were married—I was eighteen and Captain was twenty-one—we came across the Sound by boat. There were no roads into this part of the country. And he wasn't Captain, then, either. Just Peter. Because he hadn't captained anything.

76

"But he was a fisherman. My folks warned me not to marry him. My father was a doctor, and he said he wanted a better life for me." She gave Sammie a sly look. "Does it surprise you that I was headstrong? Anyway, Peter and I built a one-room cabin and called it home.

"We spent everything we could scrape together on a boat, and he started fishing. I was alone in the wilderness when he was gone, which was a lot, and that gave me plenty of time to worry about him. I knew the sea could turn treacherous at any moment.

"He felt bad about me being alone. There were bears and coyotes and moose and elk in the woods around our cabin, but you did what had to be done in those times.

"An older couple on a place about a half mile away checked on me and helped me when I needed it. Matter of fact, they kind of adopted me. And Peter taught me to shoot a gun for protection."

Sammie tried to imagine this wrinkled woman at eighteen in the wilderness with a rifle at her side. "Didn't you wonder if you'd made a huge mistake?" she said.

"You bet I did. Every night when I went to sleep alone with the coyotes howling. But I loved Peter, and besides, I was too proud to run home to my folks.

"Peter fished and hunted and I gardened and canned and sewed. We kept cattle and saved every penny to buy land. That's where the future was, Captain said. He was right."

She brought the coffeepot from the kitchen and refilled her cup. Sammie declined more and wondered how the woman had made it to ninety drinking that brew.

Mrs. Nelson took a sip. "We wanted children, so we began work on the new house. Our aim was to fill it with kids." She paused. "But that wasn't to be. God didn't give us children, and as the years passed, I became more and more resentful. Captain

77

kept telling me that God had something else in mind for us, but I wouldn't hear it."

She breathed deeply as she opened the album cover to fading photographs of two small children—the younger, a sober-faced boy on her lap, and the older, a girl with long curls, standing at her side.

She leaned back. "It was right after we moved into the new house. A family named Brownell had a cabin several miles upriver. It caught fire one night, and Maude Brownell was burned to death. Joel, her husband, saved the babies but he was pretty badly burned.

"They didn't have many close relatives, and the ones they had were back east. Someone had to take the children. Captain and I prayed together and knew that's what God wanted us to do."

Her eyes caressed the photographs. "I didn't know anything about raising children, being the youngest at home, but I learned fast. And little Billy, here, was a good teacher.

"He was two, with a mind of his own and a one-word vocabulary—'No!'" She tasted the memory as though it were one of Mike's pastries. "Ellen, here, was four and a quiet little lady. She followed me everywhere.

"After about a year, their father was well enough to take them back. He married a girl from Seattle, and she made a good stepmother to them. I missed them something awful. But Captain was right. God had plans. I kept insisting that he show me what they were up front, like a blueprint for our lives. Of course, he didn't do that."

She shifted so she could look directly at Sammie. "What he showed me was that he wanted me to trust him. I didn't have to know all about what was going to happen. I only needed to know what he wanted me to do now."

She closed the album. "Enough of that, little girl. You

brought pictures of your shop, and I want to see them."

Sammie protested. "Please go on. I want to see the rest of the pages, hear about what happened after that."

Mrs. Nelson laid the album on the coffee table. "When it's time, I'll show you more."

Sammie pointed to the plates on the kitchen wall. "Who made them? Grandchildren of the kids in the album? Great-grandchildren?"

"It's a long story because I've had a long life. Now, you show me your pictures, little girl," Mrs. Nelson prodded.

Mrs. Nelson erupted with "hallelujah!" as she scrutinized the photographs through a magnifying glass. She looked satisfied when she finished and handed them back to Sammie with a request for a set of her own. "They belong in the album. At the end."

Sammie pressed them back in Mrs. Nelson's hands. "Keep these. I'll get another set for myself."

They both rose, and the old woman expressed her appreciation as she set the photos on top of the album. Then, she took Sammie's hands in her own. "Remember, I had to learn, little girl. To trust God for this page of my life and then to trust him for the next page."

They said goodbye at the open door to the hallway. "Come back. I make a mean pot of clam chowder. Captain's favorite."

This time Sammie didn't object that it would be an inconvenience. She looked forward to sitting at Mrs. Nelson's table again. "And I do want to take you for that visit to the Treasure House so you can see it in person."

"Now *there's* a plan!"

Sammie waved and walked down the hall, turning to see the tiny, deceptively frail-looking woman standing outside her door watching her go.

~ ~ ~ ~ ~

Thursday evening, Sammie answered the phone and heard Detective Dave Vivano's unmistakable greeting. "Hey! Sammie, my man!" He'd been calling her that ever since she'd known him.

"I'm in Seattle to attend a law enforcement conference. It runs all day Friday and Saturday. I thought I'd skip the last workshop on Saturday and drive over there to the north woods, as your father calls it, for a quick visit. I'd have to leave by noon Sunday. Would that be okay?"

"No, it wouldn't be okay. It would be absolutely wonderful!" Time with big, burly Dave? What could be better!

It still amazed her that such a long, deep friendship had resulted from a chance meeting between her mom and his mom at a flower show. After that, it was lasagna at Mama Vivano's and knishes at Sternbergs. When Dave was assigned to V.J.'s case, she was relieved.

After she hung up, questions ran head-to-tail through her mind. Should she call the bed-and-breakfast immediately and reserve a room for Friday night? Cook dinner or take him out? Where would he like to go sightseeing? What would he think of her new life? Did he have any news about the case?

Finally, she'd have someone safe to talk to. With Pop she had to be careful because he became so emotional about the V.J. mess and overwhelmed her with his paternalism.

She was waiting on the porch of the Treasure House when Dave drove up. As they hugged on the sidewalk, she giggled to herself. Was Claudine watching? Did she suppose this was her out-of-town boy friend? Who knew what kind of stories might be around this small town in twenty-four hours!

Dave was hungry and breakfast for dinner sounded good to him, so they headed for Hotcake Heaven. Crisp, brown home-fries filled half his platter and a cheese omelet filled the other half. Fat, locally-made link sausages and toast were served on the side. She settled for a hotcake and gave Dave a taste.

It felt good just to look at him. Powerful at forty-five, he was barrel-chested and broad-shouldered with rugged good looks. It came as no surprise when people found out that he had almost become a pro football player, but then opted for police work instead. Blocking on the field for his college team had earned him write-ups in sports columns. When life turned sour for her, he'd tried to block interference and lessen the blows.

His widowed mother and married sisters and brothers gathered around him when his wife divorced him because she couldn't handle being married to a cop. As the eldest son, he'd stepped into the role of patriarch, the relative everyone came to when they needed advice. His nieces and nephews loved him and argued over who got to sit next to him at family dinners or play one-on-one with him on the school playground.

Sammie had so many questions. "How's the family?"

A grin warmed his craggy face. "They're having babies, being confirmed, getting in trouble, and listening to me tell them to shape up or else," he said fondly. Then he added, "At least I hope they're listening."

"What about Mama Vivano?"

He looked pensive. "Mama's okay. She works too hard and worries too much. We have trouble when she tries to gather her chicks under her wings. They keep escaping."

"Sounds like Pop. Except that he's only got one chick."

She knew he wouldn't bring up the subject of V.J. in a public place. As soon as they'd settled in the living room of her house, she brought the subject up herself.

"Are there any leads in the case?" He'd know that for her there was only one case.

"We've had leads, but V.J. still manages to stay ahead of us. A man answering his description fleeced a woman in El Cajon out of her savings and disappeared. He didn't marry her, though.

"The wife he married before you hired a private detective. You met her, so you know that woman is determined to get revenge." He slapped his thigh. "Why he picked an attorney to victimize, I'll never know. It could have been pure ego." He frowned slightly and scrutinized Sammie's face.

She remembered meeting V.J.'s first wife at police headquarters. Blond, attractive, sharp, but obviously not sharp enough. That's probably what made the woman even more furious.

"How are you feeling now about what happened?"

"I seem to have a different feeling for every day in the week. Monday anger, Tuesday sorrow, Wednesday guilt..." Sammie said with emotion.

"*Guilt!*" His voice sounded like the blast of a boat horn. "Anger and sorrow I understand. But why in the world would you feel guilty?"

She felt a need to wrap her arms around herself so she wouldn't fall apart.

Before she could think of what to say, Dave sighed deeply and shook his head. "I'm sorry, Sammie. I didn't meant to yell at you. It's just that I'm angry about what happened to you. And right now, you're the one who's paying the price."

Now *she* wanted to comfort *him*. "You'll get him, Dave." Even though she wasn't sure she meant the words, she hoped they were a reassuring pat on the shoulder.

"But, guilt, Sammie?"

She studied her fingernails. "I should have known better. I covered stories about con men, and I wound up being conned myself."

"Hey, he's as slick as they come. His first wife is an attorney, remember?"

"But I walked right into it. I might as well have said, 'Here I am. Make a fool of me.'"

Dave chose his words carefully. "I was going to try to talk you into coming back. But now I think you may need to be here. For a while, anyway." He paused. "It's quiet here. You need that." Leaning forward, he drove home every word. "What happened is *not your fault.*"

She tried to absorb what he said and hoped he sensed her gratitude because she had no words to give him.

After he left for the bed-and-breakfast, Sammie curled up on the yellow-print sofa. Her thoughts lingered over the unsinkable Mrs. Nelson in her red baseball cap and "I don't do mousework" sweatshirt as an eighteen-year-old alone with a rifle by her side. What other stories about the Treasure House lay between the pages of her album?

As she drifted off to sleep, Dave floated into her thoughts. *Big papa bear...*

It was nearly midnight when she awoke, stiffened from her crunched up position, and dragged herself to bed.

The next morning she was sitting on the front step sipping fresh peppermint tea and eating toast when Dave showed up. "Sammie, my man! I had breakfast for dinner last night and breakfast for breakfast this morning." He looked at her tea and toast. "I had a real meal. Can that woman cook!"

"I can't wait until Pop eats there."

He sat down beside her on the step. She reached over and picked a sprig of lavender and stuck it under his nose. He backed off and looked at her quizzically. "Perfume straight from the vine," she laughed. Sammie pointed to bushes of white and crimson rhododendron blossoms, pink azaleas, and clusters of bright yellow daylilies. "What would Mama Vivano think about those?"

"She'd go wild. Mama loves the city and wouldn't think of

moving away from the family, but I know she'd go on about each plant as if it was one of her grandbabies." He hesitated. "I'm glad I came. I feel better about your being here now. Except that you're alone."

"When you see Pop, tell him it's okay that I'm here, will you? He needs convincing," she said dryly. She brushed toast crumbs from her mulberry sweater. "And it's okay that I'm alone, Dave."

Sammie named off the places she could show him in the brief time he had left. When he chose Fort Barker, she feigned enthusiasm.

At the fort, he climbed out of the car and surveyed the scene. "Man!" He ran a hand through his hair. "Originally built in 1811 under General Amos Barker?" He hadn't needed to read the sign. He walked toward the wall and called over his shoulder. "Makes me want to go home and find out more about it."

When he returned from his slow tour, they stood quietly, side by side. Sammie hesitated and then told him that she saw the ruins as a picture of her life.

"You didn't really want to bring me here, did you?" Dave said.

She hesitated.

"It's okay," he told her. "I appreciate that you did it for me."

She recognized his Papa Vivano tone, the one she'd heard him use with his kid sisters and brothers and nieces and nephews. It was the one he'd used with her when V.J. took off.

She followed the sweep of his arm as he spoke. "You see ruins, but I see a monument. I see victory. We fought and we won, Sammie my man. And so will you."

SIX

Her birthday, June 17, was sweet-smelling and accompanied by bird song.

It was just what she'd have ordered for her birthday a couple of years ago. But today the contrast between how things looked outside and how she felt inside only made her feel worse. Oregon rain would have fit her mood better today.

The last week or so, she'd been engaged in an internal tug-of-war about turning twenty-eight without Mom. And without a happily-ever-after marriage and family. Since she'd opened her eyes about an hour ago, she'd been fighting the black feeling that threatened to suck her into a pit of hopelessness.

Stop the pity party. Put on a dress that makes you feel pretty. The grayed-pink A-line with darker pink sprays of flowers looked right. She fastened a star-shaped, gold-on-gold pin she'd crafted onto the shoulder. As she fussed with the pin, she continued the internal lecture. *Walk around the pit, climb over it, but don't get pulled down into it.*

She took a deep breath and exhaled with a sigh. It was just that determination took so much energy.

Sammie walked into the yard and picked herself a present. Now she stood admiring the delicate, pink rhododendron blossom floating in a glass bowl on the table. *Yes, Mom, a flower.*

Birthday cards had come in the mail from Aunt Tessie, Dave and Mama Vivano, and Mina, her mother's spiritual mentor and her own as well. And there was a package from Pop. No one else back home who knew it was her birthday had been told where she was.

All her growing-up years, birthdays meant parties. Balloons and a clown on the lawn when she was six. A dress-up dinner when she was sixteen. Every year before, after, and in-between, Mom was the official party-giver: organizing and shopping and designating herself Captain in Charge of Secrecy in the years when the parties were a surprise. Pop griped and moaned and prepared the meal and loved every minute of it.

No party this year, not that she wanted one. Pop would call this evening, of course, and she'd save his package to open then. That was one more reason to detest V.J. Because of him, she was separated from family.

Birthday or no birthday, it was Thursday and she had to open the shop. Midmorning, right after a couple had browsed and then purchased a soup tureen, she felt the sick, sinking feeling threatening to take over. Today she dreaded going home after work to a silent house. Initially, she'd craved solitude. But when Dave visited, she realized how good it felt to talk freely with someone.

She was pressing a lace tablecloth to put on display in the kitchen of the Treasure House and searching for pleasant thoughts to block misery's way. Her mind drifted to the first birthday she'd celebrated away from home.

She'd just completed her sophomore year and was working in a resort for the summer. Peggy, her college roommate, was working there too. When Peggy's family, who lived about an hour away, heard it was Sammie's birthday, they invited the girls for dinner.

While Peggy's dad barbecued steaks in the backyard and her mom got the rest of the food ready, her roommate gave her the grand tour. The moment she met Casey, the Zimmerman's parrot, the tour was over as far as Sammie was concerned. Without prompting, Casey greeted her. "Casey good boy."

"Hello, Casey," she'd answered, wondering what to say to a parrot. She needn't have worried. Casey could hold a one-sided conversation just fine. Fascinated, she barraged Peggy with questions about the conversant bird with a rich gray body and a bright red tail and was told it was an African Gray and that they were good talkers. Ever since Casey, she'd been fascinated with birds that could talk and thought about what fun it would be to own one.

Now, she stood the hot iron up on end and carried the tablecloth to the dining room. *A parrot! I'll buy myself a parrot for my birthday. A present from me to me.* It would be a way to get back at V.J. She would choose to do something crazy and fun. To celebrate twenty-eight, no matter what. Then V.J. wouldn't win. Not today he wouldn't. Besides, a parrot would be someone to talk to. And he wouldn't be able to broadcast secrets because Sammie wouldn't tell him any.

Take it easy, Sammie, she told herself. *A pet is a responsibility. Don't get one on a whim. It may sound great now. But you'll still have this bird six months from now. Years from now. Parrots live a long time.* She'd have to think it through rationally. Should she pray about it? Did God even care if she got a parrot?

Suppose she just looked around to see if one was for sale in Pineville Beach. That's when she remembered Art Humble, owner of Petland and her savior from Harry the Jew Hater at the Merchants Association potluck.

During a lull between customers, she called, explaining that she'd heard African Grays were good talkers and asking if he had one.

"No, but I know where I can get one," Art told her. "I'll bring him to the store. Come after closing, and I'll wait for you so you can see him."

"You'd do that?"

"Sure. Be glad to."

She drove up and spotted Art waiting outside the front door in faded jeans and a yellow knit shirt and smiled to herself because she'd changed to the same thing. The Pineville Beach uniform, she thought, jeans and knit shirts in a rainbow of shirt colors.

In stalls, a beagle pup was lying with his fat, pink belly up; a dachshund was curled nose-to-tail on a soft blanket; a cockapoo was crouched and yapping under a fringe of white fur.

In a cage in the front corner of the store was the parrot she'd come to see. He eyed her suspiciously.

"He's gorgeous," Sammie breathed in wonder. It had the same delicate gray body and vivid red tail feathers as Casey. She noted that the feathers on its head and at the nape of its neck were darker gray with lighter edges that looked scalloped. At her close inspection, the bird squawked and made her jump back.

Art laughed. "Let me introduce you. Sammie Sternberg, this is Beauty." He started to add that the bird's name wasn't really Beauty, when the Gray suddenly spoke. "You're a beauty." Sammie giggled.

"As you know, African Grays usually learn to talk more easily than most breeds. The more they learn to say, the less likely they are to squawk. And they're gentle. Of course, they have to be handled and trained."

Sammie stepped closer to the bird and examined the golden eye with a black pupil that stared relentlessly at her. It was surrounded by a pale gray oblong, like some painted, tribal decoration. She couldn't help thinking how much artistry God put into creating this parrot. No question about it, it was a beauty.

"Do you know much about parrots?"

She shook her head. "We've had only a passing acquaintance. I've been interested in them since college, though."

"This bird is only about six months old. That means it'll be easier to train. See how erectly it holds its head? How it looks you in the eye? What full plumage it has? Those are all signs of good health."

He motioned with his head to a terrier puppy who'd awakened from his nap and was woofing at them from his cage. "You wouldn't want a dog, too, would you?"

"I'm wondering if I can give a bird the time and care he needs, never mind a dog." Uncertainty nibbled at her composure. Parrots took a lot of time to train. Was this a bad idea?

"I tell you what," Art walked to a literature rack and picked out a book on the care and training of parrots while the bird ruffled his feathers and squawked some more.

Art handed her the book. "Take this home, read it, and see what's involved. If you still think it's for you, I'll deliver Beauty personally, cage and all. And I'll come by and help you get started training him."

"Bad salesmanship. You're supposed to convince me it'd be a cinch and push me to buy now." She considered telling Art that it was her birthday, but said only, "I'm impressed."

He looked pleased at her compliment. "This isn't really a pet store. It's a pet adoption agency. We match parrots and people, puppies and people, you know. Besides, I want you to like it here in Pineville Beach. Think of me as your Welcome Wagon representative."

As she reached out and took the book from him, the animal sounds suddenly ceased. In the silence, she felt awkward and realized that she hadn't been ill at ease with this man in the store after hours.

"It's a deal."

"If you decide to take the bird, I'll bring pizza when I deliver him." He made the offer sound casual. Just the way V.J. had, she thought.

Nonsense. Can't a man be friendly without an ulterior motive? Besides, he must be Dave's age, at least. He wore no wedding ring, though.

Art waited patiently for her to answer. "I'm just being practical. I'll be hungry, and you'll be hungry. I don't know about you, but a growling stomach would keep me from concentrating on training a parrot even more than his squawking would."

"You're right. In case you were going to ask, I like pepperoni."

"How about olives and mushrooms, too?"

"Perfect. I'll call you."

Just as she curled up on the sofa with the book about parrots, the phone rang. Instead of a hello, she heard a rendition of "Happy Birthday" so unmelodious it could only be Pop. Mom was the one in the family who could carry a tune. But Sammie had to give Pop credit. Tone deaf though he was, he persisted in upholding family tradition.

"Thanks. This is the next best thing to a hug."

"So how did you celebrate?"

"I'll tell you in a minute. First though, I'm going to open the package you sent. I saved it because I knew you'd call."

"While you're opening it, tell me what you want for your birthday dinner. I'll cook it next time I come up. Or when you come home," he added pointedly.

I'm not coming home. Not to stay, anyway.

She carefully untied the white satin ribbon and unfastened each taped end of the silver paper that covered the small, square box. "Guess what I want for dinner."

"How can you do this to me? You have a father who's a Jewish chef and what do you want? Spaghetti and meatballs! I can't believe it!"

"Did I ask for spaghetti and meatballs?"

"You've been asking for it since the third grade." Most years, he'd make it as a side dish and prepare something exotic for the main entree.

She rattled the paper into the mouthpiece. "I have the box unwrapped." Engraved in gold on the black velvet lid was the name Goldstein Jewelers. How like Pop to keep up with old friends like Mo Goldstein, whom he'd known when he first started in business. She was pleased, especially since Mom's death, that they still had coffee once a week or so.

"I'm opening the lid."

As soon as she snapped it open, Sammie gasped into the phone. Nestled against the white satin was a gold charm bracelet. "Oh, Pop…" Her voice was soaked with emotion, not only because of the loveliness of the gift, but because the first charm her eyes fell on was a rose.

She took some deep breaths and swallowed hard. Her father took over. "The rose is a happy birthday from Mom. Make up a fancy Latin name for the variety. *Rosicus Momicus*, maybe."

"That's terrible," she was able to laugh in response. "Thanks for making Mom part of my birthday."

Was she really grateful? Sammie wasn't sure. The important thing now was to assure Pop that she was okay or he'd be on the next plane ready to pack her up and ship her back. Twenty-eight years of age made no difference to him.

After more deep breaths and swallows, she examined each charm. "There's a tiara…"

"Because you're my princess."

"A microphone."

"Because you used to broadcast the news at the top of the hour."

"A shell."

"Because you love the beach."

"A heart that says 'I love you.'"

"That's from me."

"And a…bagel? Pop, a bagel?"

"Why not? I wanted one with cream cheese and lox but Mo said that was impossible."

"Pop…thanks. You couldn't have given me a more perfect present."

"I hope it makes you good and homesick. Wear it in good health."

He was ready to switch to some father-daughter sparring. "So how did you celebrate your birthday up there in the north woods where the buffalo roam?"

"Sorry. No buffalo roaming here. We have deer, a herd of elk, and a bear now and then." Immediately she regretted mentioning the bear that came down to the river to catch fish occasionally. Before her father could explode, she changed quickly to another subject, one she knew would bring fireworks as well, but one she wanted to get over with.

"I went shopping for a parrot."

Sammie held the receiver away from her ear because every word of his response was like a ball slammed into the outfield. "You…went…shopping…for…a…what?"

"A parrot, Pop," she responded calmly. "The one I found is an African Gray. I'm not sure yet if I'll buy it or not."

"Not, Sammie. The answer is *not* to buy it. A cat maybe. But a parrot? They squawk and make a mess. Parrots don't even make a decent pot of soup."

She ignored him. "It's beautiful and smart and I could actually teach it to talk."

"So now my daughter the pioneer wants to be a bird woman! 'The Bird Woman of the North Woods!'"

As usual, her father's call was therapeutic and not just because of the bracelet. He'd managed to make her forget how miserable she felt; she was too busy defending herself for wanting a parrot.

"How could my kid be such a *schlemiel?*" He groaned. "Bird, schmird. I could talk all night, and you'd do what you please."

"A chip off the old block, right?"

"No comment." His groan meant that she was hopeless. "Sammie, do you have a candle?"

"Right here on the table."

"Good. Light it. It'll stand for the twenty-eight we'll light on your birthday cake when I come up. Or when you come down."

Obediently, she got a match and lit the fat, cinnamon-scented candle. "Now make a wish and blow it out. You want me to tell you what to wish?"

"No, I absolutely do not." She stared at the flame. "I'm thinking, Pop." What should she wish for? Since wishes on birthday candles weren't prayers, it didn't seem right to choose something serious. But everything that came to mind was serious.

What was the matter with her? She knew the answer: she didn't believe in wishing any more. She'd lived by wishes and dreams and fairy tales. But they didn't come true.

Instead of telling Pop that she had no wish, she said simply, "I'm ready" and blew hard, extinguishing the flame. Wishes and dreams and fairy tales were over, like good-night tuck-ins and kisses on banged knees and elbows.

She and Pop exchanged "I love you's" and as she hung up, Sammie shook her head. *We would have made a good vaudeville team; Sternberg and Sternberg.*

The next day, after closing the store, Sammie got out the map Mike drew directing her to the Hoffman place so she could find Autumn's sister Jennifer and talk to her about coming to work.

The Hoffman place, she thought, amused, as she drove out of town. I talk like a Pineville Beacher. People don't have "homes," they have "places." The Hoffman place. The Nelson place.

The directions led her along the river through a wooded area interspersed with an occasional "place." Mostly, they were small ranches with frame houses, beds of flowers in the front yard, gardens, cattle and occasionally sheep grazing in the pasture, barns, outbuildings. Sammie mused about how much the "places" revealed about their owners. These were generally people ingrained with the work ethic. They weeded and hoed and mowed regularly. They cared.

She looked for house numbers on the rural mailboxes, many painted with what Pop would call "north woods" scenes. Soon she decided that 622 Old Country Road, where the Hoffmans lived, had to be just past the line of pine trees up ahead.

No one had painted mountains and evergreens on 622's mailbox. It was plain, and dented where someone had apparently backed into it.

"Unadorned" described the entire Hoffman place. No flowers in the front yard, only a few overgrown bushes. A saltbox house with its white paint chipped and peeling and the window shades pulled down. A nondescript, medium-sized, skinny brown dog was chained to a sagging dog house. If she walked over to it, she knew it'd yap, then slink, head down, tail between its legs.

To the right of the house was a huge garden plot, one of the largest she'd seen on Old Country Road. A logging truck was parked in the driveway, and in the backyard machinery sat idle looking like nondescript squatters.

After several moments, the door to the house opened slightly. The man who stood staring silently at her was cut from the same cloth as Paul Bunyan. Not tree-sized, but huge nevertheless. Massive shoulders and chest, a square face partly hidden by a thick, black beard made him look like a poster boy for the Pacific Northwest.

If she'd chosen his clothes herself, they couldn't have been more appropriate. Red and black flannel shirt, black twill pants with suspenders, and a hard hat. Probably he was wearing logging boots, but his stony stare kept her from looking down.

Autumn and Jennifer's father? "Mr. Hoffman?"

He grunted.

"I'm Sammie Sternberg." She didn't bother offering her hand.

His face remained expressionless, his eyes piercing.

"I own the Treasure House. Your daughter Autumn and I thought maybe Jennifer would be interested in working for me part-time."

When she got to the part about a job for Jennifer, he opened the door. Taking that as an invitation, she entered the darkened living room. The furnishings—a worn sofa and chair, a couple of tables and lamp—reminded her of pieces she'd seen sitting curbside in middle-class neighborhoods with a sign: Free.

Mr. Hoffman bellowed. "Jen! Get out here!"

A slender blond girl in jeans, a teenage version of Autumn, appeared in the kitchen doorway and stared at the floor. "This lady came about a job." Without another word, he turned and walked through the kitchen and out the back door.

Sammie extended her hand, introduced herself, and explained her mission. "I'd need you part-time. When I get more established and if it works out, I'd want you to work longer."

Jennifer's grin was spontaneous. "I'd do a good job, Miss Sternberg. Honest. I'm a hard worker. You can call other places where I've worked and ask them about me."

Her eagerness struck Sammie as more than that of a teenager who wanted to earn some money.

The two of them sat on the sofa while Sammie wrote down names of former employers. She tried to shift without being noticed because a spring was poking her. "It's okay with your mother if you come to work for me?"

"Mama? Oh, sure." Jennifer looked startled by the question. "I'd introduce you to her, but she's sick today." As though wanting to change the subject, Jennifer rose. "Are we done?"

"I think so. If the references check out, I'll call and arrange a starting date."

On their way to her car, Sammie motioned to the truck in the driveway. "Is your father a logger?"

"Yes. He's a gyppo."

Sammie laughed. "I'm a city girl, Jennifer. What in the world is a 'gyppo?'"

"That means he's an independent logger. He works for himself." Sammie couldn't help wondering if that was because he couldn't work for or with anyone else.

When she called the owners of the Burger Barn and the C & J Market later, they assured her that Jennifer had been an outstanding employee, so Sammie called and told the seventeen-year-old that she was hired.

As arranged, Jennifer arrived promptly at the Treasure House at one o'clock the following Saturday. "I parked my bike behind the shop. I hope that's all right."

"Sure, but it's quite a ride into town. It's about five miles, isn't it?"

"That's okay. I'm used to it. I ride my bike everywhere." She hesitated, as though expecting to be cut off. "On days like this one," she looked out at the clear blue sky and warm sun, "it feels good."

From a pocket of her brown slacks, Jennifer took a small notebook and pen and wrote down Sammie's instructions. "Gradually, you'll learn about the various items for sale and their history so that you can tell it to customers."

"Miss Sternberg, I love the things in your shop." Jennifer gestured toward a display of goblets. "I just hope I don't break anything."

Sammie smiled. "You'll do just fine. And please call me Sammie."

Jennifer's only problem appeared to be lack of confidence.

On her second day of work when she spilled a heavy jar of glass marbles on the floor, she recoiled in horror. "I'm sorry. I'm sorry." She fell to her knees grabbing them frantically.

"Jen, it's okay. No harm done. Accidents happen." The girl looked up in disbelief. When she stood and replaced the jar, her hands were shaking. Sammie thought of her sister Autumn, next door, who always seemed to be seeking permission.

On Jen's third day in the shop, Sammie felt confident that she could leave her alone long enough to run to Claudine's bookstore. "Phone me over there if you need to, and I'll come back. But I know you'll do fine."

On her way, Sammie resisted an urge to sprawl on the front lawn and sniff the grass. When she walked through the door of the book shop, Claudine was behind the counter talking with a man whose back was toward Sammie.

Claudine looked up. "Sammie. Finally able to get out? Come over here. I want to show you something."

Sammie walked to the counter somewhat apprehensively. As she did, the male customer turned around and looked at her. It was Brad MacKenzie, the artist she'd met at the Memorial Day celebration.

When she walked closer, she saw a large watercolor painting, with the signature "Brad MacKenzie," on the counter in front of them. It was hard not to stare at Brad. Everything about him was compelling. He wore a soft, beige, suede shirt that she wanted to run her hand across, and coffee-colored slacks.

When she shifted her gaze back to the painting and took a closer look, she stared open-mouthed. Collecting her thoughts, she asked, "This is your work?"

An amused smile curved the corners of his mouth as he nodded.

Claudine broke in. "You mean, what is someone who paints like that doing in Pineville Beach? Sammie, he's our hidden treasure! But think of it. What better place for a painter? We've got the scenery and the solitude. Matter of fact, from time to time we've had something of an artist's colony here."

Sammie wished Claudine would stop talking for Brad. Though he seemed content to let her do it.

"I bought the painting from Brad for my new house and he's delivering it to me here." Claudine looked lovingly at it. Sammie knew Claudine was divorced and that her settlement had been more than ample. Proof of that was the house townspeople described as lavish that she'd recently had built on beachfront property.

A customer entered the store and asked to see books on gardening, and Claudine led her down an aisle. Brad stood silently watching Sammie as she stared at the painting. She slowly shook her head, as if it were too much to absorb all at once.

In the left foreground was a tiny village that included a church spire, a city hall, a school. In the center of Main Street was a funeral parlor. Bunched like friends in a strange place were clusters of houses.

But her eyes were drawn to a lone English-style cottage on a hilltop at the right that glowed from the rays of the sun setting behind it. In the doorway stood a child. To the left of the cottage, a garden burst with color. The road leading to the cottage was bare and winding,

"Did something inspire you to paint this?"

Brad stared off through the window to the street. "I can't say." His voice drifted off. He looked at her challengingly. "It needs a title. What would you call it?"

She knew he was asking why the painting had such a profound impact on her. Now it was her turn to fumble for something to say. "I...I'd have to think about it."

There was something more than just the gentle blending of colors and dreamlike images, the hazy landscape, the glowing house at the end of the winding path. Something illusive.

Brad was silent, so she asked, "Do you show your paintings here in Pineville Beach?"

"No. I show in a gallery in Seattle."

"Maybe it's presumptuous, but I'd love to hang a couple of your paintings in my shop. I'm sure they'd sell quickly."

He looked thoughtful. "Selling locally isn't something I've done so far."

Claudine returned with the customer and rang up her purchase. "Do it, Brad. How fitting to have your paintings in the Treasure House." When the customer left the store, she looked at Sammie and then at Brad. "Besides, I think you two could work well together."

Sammie felt her face flush and turned away, pretending sudden interest in a volume of photos of the Northwest. As she did so, she noticed Brad shake his head slightly as though Claudine were a child who'd been badly trained.

Grateful for an excuse to make a graceful exit, Sammie peered across the street and explained that Jennifer was new and she'd better get back. Quickly, she found a new mystery by Lillian Jackson Braun and paid for it. "I'll wait to hear from you," she told Brad in what she hoped was a business-like tone.

His face remained impassive. "I'll stop and see your shop and give you my decision." For the first time, she heard teasing in his voice as he called after her. "And Sammie! Maybe you'll have a title for this painting by then."

As she crossed the street in the midmorning sun, she shivered. This artist, who'd created a painting that stroked her soul in a way that she could only feel but not describe, had called her by name. *Sammie.*

She thumped each foot firmly on the wooden steps of the Treasure House. *Keep your mind on business.* And it would be good business to be the only place in town that showed Brad MacKenzie's paintings. Even Pop couldn't argue with that decision.

After she closed the store that day, Sammie had a powerful urge to get out into the day, still warm and clear. Hopping on her bike, she rode through town and across the Iseeyousee River Bridge, stopping to peer at the river. Then turning, she rode back across the bridge to the candy store in the center of town that sold homemade ice cream. She rested on the bench licking a waffle cone of pistachio nut. Eating green ice cream made her feel like a kid.

Instead of feeling pleasantly tired after she parked her bike and went in the house, she was unable to sit still. Still hungry, she steamed a fish fillet, spooned on a mustard sauce she'd learned to make from Pop, tossed a salad to go with it, and warmed a roll from the bakery.

The meal didn't relax her. Tea on the steps watching the birds in the nest under the eaves feeding their open-mouthed babies also failed. Maybe she'd find something to watch on TV. But flipping through the channels proved fruitless.

Should she work on the shop's books? The idea didn't appeal to her.

She picked dead leaves off a prayer plant in the kitchen window, rearranged canisters and bric-a-brac, wiped the kitchen counter. Should she telephone someone? But who in Pineville Beach would she call to have a friendly chat? There was no one. And wasn't that her own fault?

Why did she feel so unsettled?

Brad MacKenzie's image flashed into her mind. Had such a brief meeting affected her so strongly?

Was it because she couldn't read him? That must be it. Most

people she could read. Brad made her feel insecure. He was a closed volume. She suspected that the only way he revealed himself was through his paintings. When she queried him about the one he sold Claudine, she sensed a raw vulnerability that caused him to retreat into the shadows where he could hide. He made her feel unsettled. And she felt unsettled enough already.

It was more than that and she knew it. *Admit it, Sammie. You find him attractive. And that's the last thing you need right now.*

She paced the length of the cottage, paused, and picked up the book she'd bought from Claudine. *A mystery,* she thought, staring at its cover. *How appropriate.* But reading was out of the question, and she dropped the book on the sofa.

Think about something else.

Her dilemma over buying the parrot came to mind. Should she go ahead? What if she made a mistake? She frowned at herself. Did she expect God to write the answer on the living-room wall?

She'd do it. Tomorrow morning, she'd call Art and arrange to buy the parrot.

She was undressing for bed when Mike's voice cut through the night air. "I told you to do this today," he bellowed. "You're a screw-up, you know that, Autumn? Do I have to do everything myself?"

Peering out the bedroom window, she saw Mike jump in the bakery van and spit gravel as he sped out of the driveway. Was Autumn all right? Stupid question. How could she be all right after the way Mike chewed her out? But was she hurt physically?

In the stillness, she heard Autumn sobbing. Should she go over there? Maybe Autumn wouldn't want her. Mike certainly wouldn't want her to interfere. *And, face it, Sammie, you don't want to get involved.*

But the image of that butterfly of a girl motivated Sammie to throw on her robe and make her way through the bushes to the Le Ducs'. Crouched on the grass in the backyard, her head between her knees, sobbing, was Autumn. Sammie knelt beside her, putting her arm around the girl's heaving shoulders. "I heard. Did he hurt you?"

Autumn choked out her answer. "N-n-no. He doesn't hit me. Anyway, it's my fault. I forgot to do something important he asked me to do. If I weren't so stupid…"

A fire ignited in Sammie's insides. "I've watched you work, Autumn. You're conscientious. Stop blaming yourself. Mike is the one with the temper." As soon as the words were out of her mouth, she realized she was echoing what Dave had told her: "Not your fault. Not guilty."

Autumn wiped her tears with the back of her hand and stood up quickly. "Please go. Now!" She emphasized the last word frantically. "If Mike should come and find you here…"

When Sammie hesitated, Autumn grabbed her arm. "Please!" Autumn turned and ran toward the kitchen door.

Just as Sammie made her way back through the bushes, she heard Mike's van pull into the driveway.

SEVEN

T he next morning, Sammie squelched an urgent impulse to run next door and check on Autumn. *Not a good idea. Even if I didn't mention last night, Mike might get suspicious. Not hard for him, because he's suspicious anyway.*

Instead, she called Art Humble to tell him she wanted to buy the parrot.

"Great! I'll draw up adoption papers!" He arranged to bring bird, cage, food, and other necessities the following evening. "And a large pepperoni with olives and mushrooms."

But where in the tiny cottage would she put the oversized bird cage? Why hadn't she thought of that before? Had she rushed into this without thinking it through? Deceived herself into thinking she was doing the right thing?

Whatever happened, she wondered, to the Sammie Sternberg who was confident and not so easily pushed off balance?

She ordered herself to focus on the task at hand. First, something to wear. Since the morning's light rain was supposed to stop and the day turn sunny, she chose a pumpkin shell and a natural, drawstring skirt.

Second, a necklace to wear. From among the lockets and pendants in the black velvet box on her dresser, she withdrew a silver star of David with a cross overlaid on it. *I haven't worn this since I came to town.*

Then it hit her. *A lot of people here don't even know I'm a Jew who believes in Jesus. They must assume that being Jewish is not only my nationality but my religion as well!*

The silver star and cross glinted as a shaft of morning sunlight hit it. Years ago, when she first saw it in a jewelry shop window, the symbol had moved her just as it was doing now. "That's me," she'd thought instantly. With a sense that it was meant to be, she'd walked inside the store and purchased it.

Now she fastened it around her neck and smiled at her reflection in the mirror. She wasn't boasting about how great a Christian she was. Only stating her belief that Jesus was the Messiah that God promised to send to mankind.

But would people in Pineville Beach, where there were few Jews, know what the Jewish star and Christian cross stood for? If not, would they ask questions?

She'd find out. See which people only stared at it and which ones made some kind of comment. The idea made her feel mischievous, a welcome change from the bleakness she'd been experiencing.

Now maybe she could figure out a place to put the bird cage. On the way out the front door, she turned and surveyed the room. If she moved the dining table more toward the front door and the rocker to the other side of the room, there would be an empty spot next to the bedroom door. Yes, that would work.

She smiled more readily than usual because of the necklace when customers entered the shop. Some tourists were forthright.

"You must be a Jew who believes in Jesus. Am I right?"

Others were curious and asked questions. "I've never seen an emblem like that. What does it stand for?" To explain made her feel stronger and more confident.

"So," Claudine began when she saw it. "You're a Jew who believes in Jesus!" Sammie stared after her, amazed that she knew about such things.

A number of customers were like Autumn who, when

Sammie ran next door for a loaf of bread, glanced at her necklace and looked quickly away. Autumn, however, acted as if she expected a reprimand for being impolite.

Abby stopped in the Treasure House. "You're a Christian?" When Sammie nodded, the tearoom owner squeezed her hand. "Me, too!"

As customers came and went, she wondered if Brad would be among them. Did he mean it when he said he'd stop by and look the shop over in order to decide about hanging his paintings there? He didn't seem like the kind of person who made statements to satisfy people. But then, she'd proven herself a terrible judge of character.

Miss M. came through the front door midafternoon. Sammie struggled with a strong desire to slip off the necklace and hide it in her pocket. Like Claudine, Miss M. was direct, but she was more subtle and could easily guide the conversation out of the safety zone and into a mined area before Sammie realized it.

The editor gave no indication that she'd seen the necklace. "I want to buy something from your kitchen for my kitchen," she said as she headed to that room. "You may not know it, but I have a place on the river."

Sammie suppressed a smile at Miss M.'s designation of her home as a "place."

"Two-and-a-half acres and an old house that I'm fixing up. Slowly."

The front door bells jangled again. "Go ahead and wait on them. I've got to decide what I want."

When the customers left, Miss M. brought a copper tea kettle to the register. "I'll take this. And by the way, I'd still like to know if there are any items for sale that were yours or belonged to your family and have a personal history."

I was stupid to think she'd forgotten her promise to ask questions.

Sammie glanced around the room. "That tea towel belonged to my grandmother," she said, pointing to one appliquéd with red geraniums. "It hung in her kitchen when I was growing up. And this set of china has been in the family." What she didn't add was that it had been a wedding present to her and V.J., and it couldn't sell quickly enough.

Without waiting for a reply, Sammie changed the subject as she walked to the cash register. "I wanted to thank you for the newspaper article. It's brought quite a few people into the store."

Sammie had worried that a tourist from Los Angeles might see a copy and recognize her name, but nothing had come of it. Of course, they could see her name on the front door and recognize it from published reports anyway.

"You'll have to come and see my place one of these days," Miss M. said behind her. "Fifteen years ago, no one could have convinced me I'd be running a newspaper in a small town, remodeling an old house, pruning trees, and planting a garden. One of God's great surprises."

Sammie wished Miss M. would tell her more about her earlier life, but she decided not to ask questions she wouldn't want to answer herself.

Eventually Miss M. gestured toward Sammie's necklace. "That emblem you're wearing is one I saw when I worked on the paper in Chicago, but never around here. You must be a Jew who believes in Jesus."

Sammie nodded, thinking that Miss M. was as sharp as she had originally thought.

"Have you found a church yet?" Direct. Right between the eyes.

"Errr...No." She didn't add that she hadn't found one because she hadn't looked.

"I attend the community church on the outskirts of town." She nodded. "It suits me because it's practical Christianity. Will you come to church with me on Sunday? The service is at ten o'clock. Gives you plenty of time to get back and open the store."

A plain, direct question from a plain, direct woman. No chance here of hedging.

Sammie couldn't think of a legitimate reason to decline. She nodded. "Sure. Thanks for asking me."

After Miss M. left, Sammie wished she could take her words back. Of all the places in Pineville Beach that she knew of, church felt the most unsafe. Even when she'd been emotionally healthy, she often wept during worship services and during choruses about the majesty of God. In her present state, she probably couldn't get away with a few stray tears. More likely, she'd break down and bawl and humiliate herself.

What if the minister was a pulpit pounder who hammered about sin? Didn't she feel guilty enough already? Didn't the gap between God and her seem irreconcilable already?

But she'd given Miss M. her word.

After closing the Treasure House, Sammie decided to drive to the Farmer's Wife where she and Pop had had such a fabulous dinner. Disengaging her mind, she allowed waves of sensory impressions to sweep over her as she drove through the countryside. Vivid blue sky, green foliage, smoky peaks. The sound of the Iseeyousee River rushing past. The sweet, pungent odor of crops she couldn't identify. She surrendered herself to become part of the edenic environment, and, for the moment, peace without became peace within.

Pearl spotted her as she entered and escorted her to a table. "So when's that father of yours coming back for a visit?"

You made an impression, Pop. Sammie answered that she wished she knew and secretly hoped that he'd wait long enough for her to get settled with her parrot. The idea of dealing with Pop and a tropical bird at the same time made her shudder.

107

Diners were scattered around the large, gleaming room. Later, the restaurant would bounce with camaraderie. Now, it seemed to Sammie, people had come to purchase a private space in which to eat and drink and think their private thoughts in safety.

Pearl brought the chicken pot pie and fresh asparagus Sammie ordered. "Taste it. I want to know how you'll describe it to your father."

Sammie broke the flaky crust with her fork, cooled a chunk of white meat, then put it in her mouth. "I'll tell him it tastes like his chicken soup gone to college."

"Can I quote you next time one of those city restaurant critics comes by?" Pearl brushed imaginary crumbs from the table. As she walked back toward the kitchen, she called over her shoulder. "Tell your father I was asking for him."

For the rest of the meal, Sammie pulled privacy around her like her grandmother's afghan. Ordinarily, she would have read a book when she ate out alone to keep from feeling self-conscious about being solitary. Here, now, she didn't have to. She didn't even want to. Good food. A place where she and Pop had dined together. Friendly Pearl. A rural atmosphere.

Sammie savored the memory during lulls the next day. But when she got ready to close the store, she challenged herself to get ready to be a mother to a parrot.

She was bent over in the backyard pulling stray weeds from a flower bed when Art arrived in his panel truck with "Petland" on the side. Together, they unloaded bird and cage and boxes of supplies, a large empty cardboard box, and a pizza.

Art noted that she ate her piece backwards, from back crust to tip. "Probably psychologically revealing," he said soberly. That moment she was trying to capture a long thread of mozzarella so she waved him away, wishing she could eat pizza more delicately.

He grinned. "Enough about pizza and psychology. Let's talk about parrots."

The bird cage was covered and the bird silent. Art went over the supplies he'd brought. Parrot seed mixture, grit, a mineral block, toys, vitamins, bowls for food and water, thick gloves to wear while handling the bird, a couple of sticks. The paraphernalia looked overwhelming to Sammie.

"First, you want to let him get used to you." He placed the empty box on the floor with the open side facing them and removed the cover from the cage. The bird squawked indignantly. Sammie made a face. "How can anything so beautiful sound so raucous?"

Art grinned. "Dogs bark, cats meow, and parrots squawk. Just keep remembering that, more and more, he'll start talking to you instead."

Reaching in, he coaxed the bird to perch on his hand and transferred him to the box. "Put some seeds in the carton. Then talk softly to him while he gets used to being in there."

The bird stood in the box, cocking his head and studying Sammie with one golden eye. Satisfied he was safe, he began to pick up seeds from the box with his black bill and eat them.

"That's a good sign. He feels comfortable. But don't stop talking."

Sammie still didn't know what to say to a parrot. "Pretty bird. Nice bird. Pretty bird. You're a beauty. Sammie likes you." That was one of the words she wanted her bird to learn first, she realized. *Sammie.*

Art handed her the gloves, and after she put them on, he placed one of the sticks in her hand. "Hold it close to him and keep talking so he'll relax and step on the stick." Sammie did as she was told, and after some squawking, the bird finally obliged.

"Hey! Good start! Now, pick up the second stick and try to get him to transfer back and forth from one to the other."

Nervous but determined, Sammie held out the stick. After mulling the idea over, the parrot hopped from stick to stick as though he actually liked doing it.

"You're doing fine," Art said softly. "Keep talking to him."

"Good boy. Smart bird. You're a beauty. You're Sammie's good bird." She still felt foolish talking to a bird in language that sounded as though it came from a Dick and Jane reader.

"Now carry him on the stick into the cage and let him transfer to the perch."

The idea sounded pretty ambitious, but she did as she was told, with the bird jabbering gibberish all the way and Sammie encouraging him. "Good boy. It's okay. Stay with Sammie."

The parrot stayed. He hopped from the stick to the perch, cocked his head and studied Sammie with one eye, continuing to chatter indecipherably. "Here." Art cut off a piece of apple with his penknife. "Give him this."

The bird took it, flew to the highest perch in the cage, and began munching. Sammie studied his lighter gray underbelly and legs and anticipated the thought of being able to run her finger over those feathers.

Art pointed to the high perch. "That's where he goes to eat special treats." He reached out and shook Sammie's hand. "Congratulations. Good start. He's taken to you already."

I did it, Lord! A small victory, but it felt important. "Where do I go from here?" she asked Art.

Art ran through the feeding instructions. "The book tells you everything else you need to know. Take plenty of time with him. He's got to learn to know and trust you, and you've got to learn to know and trust him. Think of ways you'd build trust with another person. It's not so different with parrots."

Trust. The word made her want to shy away like a nervous mare. Would she ever get to the place where the bird would trust her? Would he say her name when she walked through the door?

Art assured her the Gray would begin to learn new words soon. "Take him out of the cage every day. Play with him. Let him get used to perching on your shoulder, your hand. He'll get excited when he hears your voice and start jabbering back. Start teaching him new words." He smiled at Sammie. "By the way, what are you going to call him?"

Sammie thought hard. She studied the parrot's soft, shaded gray feathers, his blood red tail, his awareness of her. "There's a word my mother used to use that means 'pleasure.' It's *mechiah*. I think he'll be a pleasure, so that's what I'll call him."

He chuckled. "Does that make him a Jewish parrot? I hope you get to introduce him to Harry some day." He carried their dishes to the sink.

Over her objection, Art washed and stacked them on the drain board. "Mechiah was born in captivity and was well taken care of," he told her as he rinsed out the sink. "So at least he won't have bad experiences to influence how he reacts to you. Birds who've been abused are very hard to train. And don't forget, each has his own personality."

With the pizza eaten and the bird training completed for now, Art headed for the door. "I'd better be getting on."

She shook his hand. "Thanks for everything. Let me make out a check for the bird and supplies."

"Not yet. He comes with a ten-day, money-back guarantee. If you're happy together, stop by the store with the check, and let me know how it's going between you."

Art Humble was too good to be true. If she were going to invent a pet store owner for a children's book about Pineville Beach, it would be Art. Kind, generous. All the animals loved him.

Was there more to Art than she'd seen yet? Suspicion didn't become her, but she couldn't discard it like an unflattering dress.

"Where are you off to now? More animals to deliver?" What

her female curiosity was pressing her to find out was if he was married and going home to his family.

"My next appointment right now is to run on the beach. That's one of the things I love about living here. Since I don't have a family, I can pretty much keep any kind of schedule I want."

She hoped she hadn't sounded as though she were on a fishing trip for information. As he opened the front door to leave, Mechiah called out his first intelligible words. "You're a beauty."

Art grinned at the bird. "You're a beauty, Mechiah." To Sammie, he said, "Have fun together. Any questions or problems, call me."

It seemed important to commemorate this moment, since getting Mechiah was an important part of her new life, her birthday present. Since there was no one she wanted to call, she'd write about it in her journal. Gathering book and pen, she sat on the sofa. Mechiah was eating.

Art Humble brought the parrot, whom I named Mechiah. He says we have to bond. Will trust come easy to him because he hasn't had bad experiences with humans?

She paused.

I have to go slowly—get to the place where I trust him too, though. With that beak, he could do damage.

Trust. It's all a matter of trust. Was there more behind her urge to get a parrot than she suspected?

Sammie slammed the journal closed. *You've been alone too long. Contemplating your navel too often.* People who spiritualized every aspect of their lives, saying that God led them to go to a particular restaurant or gave them a parking place, annoyed her.

She got up early the next morning to work with Mechiah before opening the shop. Scared to take him out of the cage by herself, she spent the time talking with the gray, repeating "Sammie's good bird" over and over. The bird just eyed her suspiciously and ruffled his feathers.

It was Saturday, and her first customer was Pearl from the Farmer's Wife. "Thought I'd stop on my way to get supplies." She walked around and touched a silver candlestick and blue willow dishes. "I should have left my credit cards behind."

In a ten-minute sweep of the store, she collected an antique apple corer, a sampler, several baskets, and a pewter pitcher. "I told you this was a dangerous place for me."

Customers came steadily. Among them was a couple in their early thirties who examined a small chest. The man was towering, swarthy and booming. The woman was as tiny as Sammie, blond, with a sliver of a voice that sounded at first as though it must be an affectation but then seemed to be genuine.

"Joe wants me to pick out an anniversary present on our trip," she said in tones that came from the *la, ti, do* end of the scale. "We just celebrated ten years."

Joe flushed behind his ample black beard and generous mustache, and spoke using the bass notes on the scale. "Get whatever you want, Tina, honey."

Sammie summoned enthusiastic anniversary greetings she didn't feel. She was showing the couple features of a small, carved chest when Brad MacKenzie walked in the front door. As she greeted Brad with a cheerful "hi" and a smile, she wished she'd asked Jennifer to come in earlier so she could get away and take him through the store.

When he saw the shop's interior, he looked as though his day had been sweetened. Slowly, he swept his eyes around the room and nodded at her approvingly. The Treasure House had captured his interest, Sammie decided as Brad wandered into another room. And not merely as a place he might hang his paintings.

Within a few minutes, Tina decided on the chest. As Sammie carried the purchase to the counter, she explained that the owner's grandfather had built it as a trunk for doll clothes when the owner's mother was a girl. Tina's face showed her appreciation.

Traffic in the shop thinned to a couple of browsers, so Sammie decided to go looking for Brad. She had to admit she hoped for compliments from him. Anything positive he had to say would mean a great deal. Because of his artistic eye, of course, she told herself.

Brad had gone upstairs. The old boards creaked beneath her feet as she walked down the hallway searching for him. She found him in the children's room. His back was to her, and he was bent on one knee in front of the wooden blocks on the floor. When he shifted, she could see him tracing each letter with his finger. Then he dropped his hand, bent his head, and closed his eyes.

Realizing that she had intruded on a private moment, Sammie quickly and quietly backed away from the door and tiptoed so the boards wouldn't squeak.

Wherever he was, though, she suspected that squeaking floorboards wouldn't call him back. Was the artist in him taken with the children's room? It was more than that, she was sure. Something else was happening in that room.

In about five minutes, Brad came down the stairs. The light had gone out from behind his eyes, and he was lost in some dark, inside place.

He seemed to be forcing himself into the moment. "The Treasure House is very tastefully arranged. Quality items nicely displayed." He sounded as though he were reading from a newspaper review. "I would like to hang a couple of paintings here. Shall I bring them over next week?"

She matched her response to his mood. "I'd be honored. Thanks for the kind words."

With that, he was gone. No chatting. No question about whether or not she'd come up with a title for Claudine's painting.

Brad's transformation from daylight to darkness troubled her throughout the evening. Was he suffering from private pain?

Mechiah had moved to the front of his cage and was talking indecipherably to himself, sounding, Sammie thought, like a street person in a world of his own. Taking a deep breath, she transferred him to a box. "Okay, bird, here we go." For a while, she watched him eat seeds, touched his feathers with a finger, and repeated "Sammie's good boy" and "My name is Mechiah."

Once he nuzzled her fingers, and she remembered reading in the book that parrots did that to explore them. It took every ounce of her will not to yank her hand away because at any moment he could take a bite.

Toward the end of the session, the Gray spoke. "You're a beauty," and, to Sammie's surprise, added, "Polly wants a cracker."

Sammie felt like a parent whose child suddenly showed signs of being gifted. After putting the bird in his cage and rewarding him with some carrot, she repeated the phrase back as though it contained some of the wisest words a bird ever spoke. Warmly, she wished the bird good night and turned off the lights.

The next morning, when she identified the day as Sunday, she groaned and pulled the pillow over her head. Since she'd arrived in Pineville Beach, Sammie had felt guilty on Sundays. Instead of worship in church, it had become a time to read the paper and eat a leisurely breakfast.

Then she remembered. She was going to church with Miss M. Apprehensive, she asked herself what was the worst thing that could happen. She'd cry? Be given a spiritual spanking by God? At least she wouldn't have to push her way through first-of-the-week guilt. Life was a trade-off.

As she dressed, she thought back to the day Mom had announced with delight on her face that she had embraced the Jewish Messiah. Mom had always been religious, urging that they go to synagogue, at least on holy days. It was Mom who'd told her the stories about Moses on the mountaintop receiving the Ten Commandments and Esther saving the Jewish people.

When her mother told her father that she'd embraced Jesus, he exploded. "Of all the crazy things you've done, this is the worst. Jesus is for Christians, not Jews. And Christians have persecuted Jews. I can't believe you'd do this."

But Mom had definitely done it. She'd been working as a volunteer sorting books for the public library's sale alongside Mina Bloom. "Mina showed me a New Testament with beautiful colored pictures she came across," her mother explained later to Sammie. "When we got together in her little apartment, we looked at that New Testament again. Of course, I felt guilty, reading about Jesus."

It took months, but finally her mother became convinced that Jesus was the Savior that God had promised the Jews. She already knew Isaiah's prophecy of a Messiah, and now she could see that it fit Jesus perfectly.

One noontime over a tuna sandwich and tea at Mina's kitchen table, Mom had prayed and asked Jesus to forgive her sins and be her Savior. "We knew that some Jews wouldn't understand. But Jesus was Jewish. So how could he not be for Jews?"

Mom didn't push the Messiah on Sammie like an evangelist on a street corner. But eventually, Sammie found herself with Mom at Mina's kitchen table talking about the Messiah over borscht and bagels. It took several long talks with her mother at home and lunch conversations with Mina before Sammie was ready to follow her mother by confessing faith in Christ.

Pop had insisted he wouldn't come to their baptisms at

Pastor Jim's old stone church. His own father would turn over in his grave if he set foot in a Christian church. At the last minute, though, Pop went quietly into the bedroom and changed into a suit and tie. He sat in a back corner of the sanctuary—not participating in the service, but watching intently—and he took them out for pie and coffee afterward.

Sammie heard Miss M.'s honk in the driveway. "See you later, Mechiah. Sammie's good boy," she tossed over her shoulder as she went out the door.

Miss M. had the window on the driver's side of her pickup truck open and was inhaling the fragrant morning. How appropriate that the editor would own a pickup and wear a denim jumper. As Sammie made the long step up into the passenger's seat, she was glad she'd worn a full skirt and flat heels.

Pineville Community Church met in a square wooden building painted chocolate brown with the name over the front door. There was no reader board announcing service times and the name of the pastor and no steeple on top. On the way to the front steps, Sammie paused to savor the only decoration: a bed of marigolds and petunias planted in the shape of a cross on the sloping front lawn.

Except for an unadorned white cross on the walls behind the pulpit, the wood-paneled interior was as plain as the exterior. Instead of a traditional sanctuary like the old stone church in Los Angeles, it was a multipurpose room, a kind of gymnasium. The folding chairs arranged in rows now, could be rearranged in a semi-circle for informal meetings or removed so kids could race up and down the floor, slam-dunking baskets on Friday night.

Here, people didn't walk quietly down a carpeted aisle properly attired in dresses and skirts and suits, smiling silent greetings to friends they passed. They dressed just as they had at the Merchants Association potluck, in jeans and shorts and dress-up clothes. They embraced one another or pumped one another's hand. They waved to one another across the room. They were excited and casual and enthusiastic. Sammie wondered if all this was okay with God.

A tall, slender young man with a ponytail climbed the stairs to the platform carrying a guitar. He sat on a stool and began strumming. He moved into a chorus of thanks to God and the congregation joined him. Instead of hymnals with the church's name lettered on the cover in gold, an usher offered photocopied song sheets of the lyrics.

Miss M. sang in a strong alto with her eyes closed, her face uplifted. In the old stone church, a large, burgundy-robed choir and booming pipe organ filled the corners of the sanctuary making the sound of worship full-bodied, almost professional. Here, there was the guitarist singing in a plaintive '60s tone and 150 or so unrehearsed voices singing along in a way that made her close her eyes and allow it to permeate her soul.

Sammie decided she'd better open her eyes and join her own alto to Miss M.'s stronger voice, concentrating on finding the harmony, so she wouldn't weep her way through the music. Everyone around her sang like unselfconscious children. It moved her deeply, and she wept after all.

When the pastor stepped up to the platform, Sammie sideglanced at Miss M. She'd forgotten that Jack Bishop, who'd spoken on Memorial Day in the cemetery, was the pastor here. Sammie remembered his kind eyes behind steel-rimmed glasses and his gentle words, and she breathed gratitude. This man was not a pulpit pounder who'd leave her feeling drawn and quartered.

When he announced that today was communion Sunday, her heart thumped with fear. He talked about the death of Jesus Christ on the cross between two thieves, and Sammie sorted frantically through what she remembered about taking the Lord's Supper. *I must have no unconfessed sin. If I'm not right with God, I can't participate.*

The pastor was saying that anyone who'd placed his faith in Christ could take part, but they must examine themselves first. Then he moved in front of the pulpit and stood with his hands clasped behind his back, head bowed, in the posture of silent prayer.

Examine myself? There wasn't time during this brief, silent prayer interlude for Sammie to examine her life. Should she pass up the elements when they were handed to her? She looked in desperation at Miss M. for a sign, but the editor's eyes were closed.

Ushers were passing small, round loaves of bread in baskets down the rows, and each person broke off a piece. If she passed up the loaf and cup, would people suppose she wasn't a Christian? At least those who didn't know her? Wouldn't those who did—those who'd seen the star and cross—think she was holding on to some terrible sin? But if she took the elements feeling the way she did, she'd leave feeling even more guilty than when she came in.

Miss M. took the small, round loaf, broke off a piece, and handed it to Sammie. *I can't do it. Better to be conspicuous than feel condemned.* She passed the loaf down the row to the young man in Bermuda shorts a few chairs away.

What she wanted was to run. Not just home to Mechiah. She wanted to run out of this church, out of this town, and point her car toward Los Angeles and Pop, who would enfold her in his arms and hug her against his chest. She wanted to do it now, before another chorus was sung or another Scripture spoken.

EIGHT

Fear kept Sammie pressed into her chair. And she was glad she stayed, because communion Sunday, the pastor announced, was "Service Opportunity Sunday." He read from a list of names of people who were from outside the church who needed help.

"An eight-year-old boy needs a family to stay with overnight while his mom visits another son in prison in the city." The minister looked up. Across the room, a man and woman with several children seated beside them looked at one another, then the man raised his hand. "Thanks, Bill and Elaine."

The pastor looked down at the list again. "An elderly, incapacitated woman needs someone to mow the lawn, pull weeds, and maybe plant flowers. She has no money to pay to get the job done." He waited silently. A teenage boy poked his companion who shrugged, then nodded. They raised their hands.

"A husband is caring for his wife who has Alzheimer's. He needs respite once a week." He scanned the congregation. Here and there, couples whispered to one another. A gray-haired woman a few rows ahead of Sammie put up her hand.

"A five-year-old needs a substitute grandma, someone to read stories and let her help bake cookies." After several seconds went by, Miss M. put her hand in the air.

Sammie watched the process in disbelief. Getting members of a congregation to volunteer was not supposed to be this easy. Why did this congregation act as though the pastor were giving away steaks? Had she stepped into a time warp and been transported back to an era when northwestern settlers pitched in to harvest crops or raise a barn?

The pastor read a few more needs from his list, obtained

volunteers, thanked the congregation, and asked them to stand. "If you have a personal need, put up your hand now, and several people will gather around you in prayer as I lead."

Across the aisle a skinny young woman in jeans and shirt knotted at the waist, who seemed to have trouble running down her face, raised her hand and quickly put it down. Immediately, Miss M. stepped across the aisle and held her hand; others also surrounded the girl. In the rear, in the front, and on the other side of the room, similar groups gathered. Sammie stood frozen to the floor.

The pastor's prayer was simple and fervent. Then he pronounced a benediction, and the service was over.

On the way out of the building, people pumped Sammie's hand and invited her to come back. Many told her how much they liked the Treasure House. Abby from the Tearoom appeared and gave her a hug. Sammie had to push herself to simulate warmth. She hoped it seemed more genuine than it felt.

In the truck, she turned uncomprehendingly to Miss M. "I've never seen anything like it. All those people so anxious to give their time. And you were one of them."

"Yeah. Can you imagine me wiping sticky cookie dough from a five-year-old's fingers? Cutting out shapes of kittens and puppies?"

"And the way people prayed with one another." She struggled to remain composed.

"Remember I told you this is a no frills church? We get down to the business of living for Jesus. That's all there is to it." After that, they talked about the beautiful day and the sheep in a pasture. Neither of them mentioned communion.

As Sammie prepared to step out of the truck in her driveway, Miss M. smiled. "I'm glad you came with me," the editor said. "Do it again, will you?" She hesitated, adding, "I know it wasn't easy."

Sammie looked down and smoothed out wrinkles in her skirt, thinking that the editor had a gruff exterior but a tender soul. "It gave me a lot to think about."

The yard was festooned and ribboned with pinks and yellows and was fragrant with honeysuckle. But this time it would take more than beauty to settle her emotions and unravel her thoughts.

On the way up the steps she pinched a sprig of lavender, rubbed it between her fingers, and sniffed. It reminded her of gentle English novels and country gardens and an aproned woman at a potting bench.

As soon as she opened the front door, Mechiah called out to her as though he'd been waiting all morning.

"Sammie's good bird," the bird said distinctly. In case Sammie hadn't heard, he said it again. "Sammie's good bird," and cocked his head and stared with one eye. "Well!" his look seemed to say. "Are you surprised or what?"

"Mechiah!" Sammie dropped her Bible and purse on the sofa and ran to the cage. "Mechiah! Sammie's good bird. Pretty bird. Sammie is proud of you!" She opened the cage so Mechiah could jump on her hand and transfer to her shoulder.

"Polly want a cracker?" she asked the parrot as they walked to the kitchen counter.

"Polly want a cracker," Mechiah repeated. He snuggled against her ear.

She went to the refrigerator, took out an apple, and began to cut it up. "How about this instead?"

The fact that it had only taken a few weeks for the bird to feel comfortable with her was a wonder. Still, she'd devoted lots of time most days to taming him. Gradually, he squawked less and chattered more, even sidling up to get his face rubbed.

What was it Art had said? Something about the fact that Mechiah had never been abused, so trust would come easily?

Wasn't that the way she'd been before V.J.? The thought made her want to scream out the kitchen window at the fragrant summer day.

In her mind, she pictured herself running through the yard, yanking off blossoms and trampling them under her feet, destroying the gentle beauty. It was deceptive. It was a lie. Life was not a pastoral painting.

"Sammie's good bird!" Mechiah spoke in her ear, eyeing the apple. "I can never go back," she told Mechiah as she carried bird and apple back to the cage. But would she even want to be that naive again? "No chance, big bird."

Eating a piece of apple on his high perch, Mechiah eyed her silently. Although she was probably being foolish, Sammie thought the African Gray had been waiting to speak her name when she walked in the door from church, as though it was his way of shaking hands and sealing the adoption. "I am your bird, and I expect us to live happily ever after." She'd have to tell Art Humble about it.

After eating a salad and hearing Pop say in her head that if she kept eating bird food she'd turn into a bird, she told Mechiah good-bye and headed for the back door of the Treasure House. It was nearly time to open for the afternoon. On the back porch, she stood still, distracted by a sudden distant memory of her mother's mother, Grandma Levine, lounging in the porch swing in the yard by her own back door, gently rocking back and forth.

Grandpa had known Grandma wanted a porch swing and surprised her by setting it up in their backyard one Mother's Day. Evenings after the dishes were washed, on visits Sammie made to her grandparents during her growing up years, she'd often find her grandmother on the porch, swinging gently and humming softly to herself. She'd pat the space next to her for Sammie to sit. And there was plenty of space, because Grandma Levine was as tiny as Mom and the grown-up Sammie.

They'd cuddle together and talk and sing songs, sometimes softly, sometimes boisterously. Grandma would tell her about pretty new curtains that had just arrived in the Levine's dry goods store, and about what life was like when she was Sammie's age. And Sammie would tell Grandma about being eight in Los Angeles with Mom and Pop.

Grandpa would come around the side of the yard, declaring loudly that he'd looked all over for them and what a surprise to find them in the swing. He'd wave away their offer to sit, saying swings were for girls. But Grandma told Sammie that sometimes when they were alone, he'd sit next to her and say grudgingly that porch swings weren't so bad after all.

Returning from her reverie, Sammie looked again at her empty porch. Why hadn't she gotten the porch swing she intended for this spot? To sit alone and think and swing was exactly what she needed right now.

Tomorrow, she'd order a porch swing.

Before opening the Treasure House on Monday morning, she drove to Miller's Furniture Store. The swing they had on display looked almost exactly like the one Grandpa Levine had bought for Grandma. Since the truck would be out her way that afternoon, they could drop it off then, the salesman assured her.

As she drove up to the Treasure House, she noticed a white van parked in front. Someone waiting for the store to open? When she alighted, the passenger stepped out as well.

Brad MacKenzie! Immediately she could tell that he'd recovered from whatever was bothering him when he was in the children's room at the shop last time. The gentle inner light she'd seen before warmed his face with pleasantness.

"Good morning." He glanced at his watch. "It's not quite time to open. Can we sit here a minute?" He pointed to the white wicker chairs on the porch.

Sammie was surprised at his suggestion, but settled in a

chair, a big pot of marigolds between them. "Sorry I couldn't greet you at church yesterday," he said.

She stared at him as though his words were Mechiah's gibberish. "In church?"

"You didn't see me, but I saw you. Yesterday it was my turn to work in the nursery, and I spotted you with Miss M. when parents were coming to pick up their kids."

She couldn't figure out if she was more surprised that he went to Pineville Community Church or that he was working in the nursery.

Brad seemed amused at her confusion. She pinched off a few dead marigold blossoms to gain time to recover. "I guess I'm surprised because, where I come from, it's unusual to have a man working in the church nursery. Not that it isn't a good idea," she added quickly.

He nodded, then took a deep breath. "So. What did you think of Community?"

"It's not like any church I've ever been in. Not that I'm very experienced." She looked off at the horizon. "I guess it seems too good to be true."

He checked his watch again and rose to his feet. "It's time for you to open the shop, and I don't want to hold up the wheels of progress."

She stood beside him. "Have you decided to hang a painting here?"

"I have two in the van for you to check out."

She was putting money in the cash register when he returned with a painting under each arm, each wrapped in a blanket. He lay one in a chair and the second on the counter.

When he exposed the first painting, she gasped. "It's the Secret Garden." Translucent pastel flowers blended, creating an impression of mystical beauty. "It's like a symphony rising from the earth," she whispered.

"As you found out, I don't title my paintings. Maybe that's what I should call this one—'The Symphony.' I like it."

She ran across the room and pointed to a space over the organ. "Is this a good spot? What do you think? You're the artist, after all."

He nodded and swept his arm around the room. "You're quite an artist, I'd say."

Sammie blushed. "I can't wait for Mrs. Nelson to come see the painting," she said to neutralize the situation.

If Brad noticed her embarrassment, he showed no indication of it. "I thought we could hang this one in the children's room," he said as he unwrapped the second painting.

Even before the blanket was completely removed, the picture splashed color before her eyes. How could this painting have come from the same brain that produced "The Symphony" and the painting Claudine bought? She held it up. "Brad, this is an absolute delight. It's perfect for the children's room." On nights when the blackness threatened to overwhelm her, she could sit among the toys and ponder the painting's fun and absurdity.

It was full of ridiculous images—picturing crazily mixed-up animals at an outdoor tea party. Each was perched daintily on a stool at a table set with a flowered teapot, dainty matching cups, cakes, and cookies.

The front half of one animal was a hippopotamus and the back half was a cat. The front half of another was an elephant and the back half was a puppy. "A hippokitty?" said Sammie. "An elepup? It's marvelous!"

Brad's pleasure at her enthusiasm seemed to be restrained by a certain wistfulness she'd noticed as he unwrapped the painting. Even so, she risked a question. "Are there stories behind these paintings? If there are, I'd like to let my customers know."

"The paintings tell the story," he said, and she knew he'd dismissed the subject.

She felt stricken for stepping beyond his no trespassing sign, and got busy taking out a consignment form. The trouble was he gave no indication where the signs were. They popped up suddenly like targets in a shooting gallery.

He waved the form away. "No need for that. Contracts are not for people like you here in my hometown."

Brad MacKenzie, you are a surprise a minute, she thought. A handsome package of contradictions. What she said was, "I'm honored to hang these. Thank you." Impulsively, she touched his shoulder gently. Before she pulled her hand away, he paused and looked directly into her eyes, then turned quickly toward the door and left.

Brad's warmth, she thought later, was like the sun on a partly cloudy northwestern day: now you see it, now you don't. If Pop were here, he'd grab Brad by the conversational collar and demand to know "What's going on here?" But even Pop wouldn't get away with that kind of approach with this man.

She didn't get the feeling that Brad was deliberately being difficult. Some tug-of-war was going on inside him. Instinctively, Sammie recognized the symptoms because a similar tug-of-war was going on inside her.

Late in the afternoon, as the shadows lengthened in the backyard, Miller's furniture truck pulled into her driveway, and the delivery man set up the swing for her. *One of the perks of living in a small town,* she thought. The young driver with a quick grin didn't just dump off the swing in a carton, have her sign for it, and leave her to figure out where all the parts went.

Closing time seemed to take forever to arrive, and since Jen didn't work in the shop until tomorrow, Sammie had to stay until the last minute. She paced and puttered and waited on customers and peered out the back door where she could see the swing waiting.

Finally, with the Treasure House locked up, she literally ran to her cottage, made a cup of tea, settled back in the swing, and rocked gently.

Memories of Grandma Levine snuggled around her. How she listened carefully to Sammie's story about an incident at recess. How she treated her granddaughter with dignity, an assurance that her life mattered.

God, how sweet those times were! Swinging and sipping tea, she realized how much the past was part of the present. How much those times contributed to who she was now. Mom. Grandma and Grandpa. Pop. They shaped the person she had become.

Maybe if she sat in the swing on warm summer evenings, she could reach around inside herself and find that woman. Become that woman again. But she wanted desperately for Mom or Grandma to be in the swing next to her as the voice of wisdom. *Another woman who is part of me, a woman from whom I came.*

A pang of desire squeezed her. How she ached to roll back the calendar. But she had believed V.J.; Mom was gone; and after Grandpa died, her grandmother had to be moved to a nursing home.

So Sammie rocked in her swing alone. Depressed, she poured the rest of her tea on the ground. *Why can't they find V.J. and get this over with so I can get on with my life?*

The grating caw of a crow at the top of a tall tree demanded that she make connection with her immediate and tangible world. On the lawn near the Treasure House, two blue jays squawked in battle. At the cottage door, the herb bed was spreading and bushing wildly. Beside the driveway, a seedling pine had turned brown and was dying unnoticed. Sparrows were thick on the feeder. A mother bird poked seeds down the throat of her fat baby who sat waiting for more.

A microcosm of society, she thought. Life and death. The pain of Alzheimer's and a son in prison and helplessness in old age and the blessed body and blood of our Lord.

"Sammie? Hi." She heard Autumn's apologetic voice behind her. "I saw you in the swing. Is it okay for me to come over?"

The girl stood several paces away in a pair of white shorts and a striped tank top waiting for Sammie to open the door to her space or slam it shut. She looked as though she expected it to be slammed in her face.

Sammie wouldn't do that, but she would have liked to close it gently. Of course she couldn't. After meeting Mr. Hoffman, Autumn and Jen's father, Sammie knew why Autumn expected doors to be slammed in her face.

Resolutely, Sammie turned and grinned at Autumn. "Come on over and sit down."

Autumn sat gently on the opposite end of the three-seater swing. "I think swings are neat." She hesitated. "I've never sat in one before."

Sammie treated the admission like fragile china and went on to show a piece of her own. "My grandma had a swing. It was our special place." Then, changing the subject she asked, "Where's Mike?"

"Watching baseball on TV. He usually goes to bed early because he has to get up in the middle of the night to start baking." She said nothing about his explosion.

"Autumn! Where are you?" They both recognized Jennifer's voice coming from the Le Ducs' patio.

"Over here," Sammie called back, motioning Autumn to stay seated. "Come join us."

Jen appeared between the row of rhododendron that separated the houses, her blond hair windblown. "I was on a bike ride and decided to stop by for a minute. Mike's team is losing, so he's going to bed."

Autumn motioned for Jen to sit between them. "How perfect!" Jen said, admiring the swing.

For several minutes, they swung in silence as dusk put a close to the day. Starlings strutted and a hummingbird hovered, drawing nectar from a flower. When Jen began drumming her hands on her knees restlessly, Sammie knew something was wrong.

The teenager stood up. "I've got to get back home."

"You just got here," Sammie said.

Jen flipped her hair away from her face. "Mama isn't feeling well. She might need me."

Autumn turned to her sister and drew in her breath, worry showing on her face. Sammie expressed her regret and asked what was wrong even though she wanted to slam the door on whatever was going on in the Hoffman house.

Jen looked down at her hands. "It's hard for Mama. My dad doesn't work steadily so there's always money problems. The life of a logger can be like that. Especially now that logging is mostly shut down. Especially for independent loggers like my father."

That's the most she's ever said about this. But she still hasn't told me what's wrong with her mother.

"Mama's real talented," Autumn put in eagerly. "She makes all kinds of rugs by hand. Even sells a few now and then."

Sammie's interest was kindled. "What kind of rugs?"

"Hooked and braided rugs. She even dyes the fabric herself to just the right colors. I like the heart-shaped ones best."

"Would you ask her to bring some samples by the shop when she's feeling better?" If they were as good as Autumn said, maybe she'd offer them for sale. She'd wanted some exceptional handmade rugs in the Treasure House. And these were made by a local artist.

The sisters' enthusiastic response let Sammie know that they'd guessed what she had in mind. After Jen waved good-night and disappeared through the bushes, Sammie reached beyond her reticence to get involved. "Are you all right, Autumn?"

The girl studied her bare toes. "All right?" as if they were words she couldn't make out. "Yes, I'm fine."

Sammie wanted to protest, to ask why Mike got so angry. Had he ever hurt her physically? But Autumn stood, ran her hands through her yellow hair, thanked Sammie for letting her try out the swing, and disappeared through the bushes. For several minutes, Sammie sat swinging and staring after her, remembering the girl's sobbing in the dark.

The sun rose bright on the horizon on Tuesday like a promise from God, the way it had been doing for days. Dozens of times she'd be greeted by customers with, "How do you like this weather!" But she never tired of hearing it or of answering with "Wow!" or "Absolutely great!" It was as though they were participating in an ongoing celebration.

That morning, she left Jen in charge of the shop and drove to a farm auction. A tractor and other machinery were parked around the barn, and men in bib overalls or jeans and boots walked among the pieces, inspecting them carefully. Lawn furniture and garden tools were displayed in the front yard. On the grass beside the porch, three small girls offered lemonade for sale, five cents for a paper cupful. A sign on the front door requested, *Please do not bring lemonade in the house.*

Hanging in a row on the porch were bird houses made with shingles. As Sammie sipped the cup of lemonade she'd bought, she imagined them hanging outside the Treasure House.

"Daddy made them," a freckle-faced, strawberry-blond girl

about five announced. "He used to whistle while he did it."

"Daddy did a good job," Sammie said. The girl hopped on a chair and took one down. "See inside?" she asked, opening it and holding it out for Sammie to look.

"A real bird's nest? Birds really lived in here?"

The girl grinned proudly at Sammie's surprise.

"There's a nest in every one of them. Mama said that they're for sale and the price is three dollars a piece." She cocked her head. "Do you want to buy one?

This is an item with an unmistakable history. "You are some salesperson!" Sammie said to the child. "Your daddy must be proud of you."

"He used to say he was. He used to play with me, but he can't anymore."

Pain stabbed her. "What happened, honey?"

"Daddy got hurt on the farm, and now he can't move. Mama says we have to sell the farm, and we have to move to town so she can be near her job and the place where Daddy lives now." She went on with childlike earnestness.

Bending down, Sammie looked into the girl's blue eyes. "That must make you very sad. But you're being very brave."

"Mama says I have to be a big girl now. These are my cousins and they're helping me be big."

She stroked the child's hair. "Sometimes it's hard to be big, isn't it?"

"Sometimes it's even hard for Mommy. I hear her cry after I go to bed at night."

A cousin poked her and whispered. "Ask if she wants to buy the bird house."

Sammie nodded. "I'll buy all the bird houses—except this one." She handed it back to the child. "I want you to keep it. Hang it outside your new home. Do you think that will be all right with your mother?"

"Yes, because she said I can keep a few of the things I like most. And I like this a lot because Daddy made it, and he can't make any more."

For Sammie, the brightness had gone out of the day even though the sun was still warm on her face. She was left with a heaviness in her chest.

As she browsed, she recalled the early days after V.J. left when she'd thrown herself across their bed and sobbed into exhaustion. She remembered the day she knew she had to stop. But the pain remained like an open wound in her soul. Every new misery, like this little girl whose father would probably never again hold her in his arms, made it bleed.

On a tour through the big farmhouse, Sammie selected a grandfather clock, an oak table, a trundle bed, and a white-on-white quilt several customers had requested recently. She'd contact Tom, the odd-jobs man in town, to pick up her purchases.

Sometimes it's hard to be big. She drove back to the shop and pondered that statement. Life couldn't be trusted. A woman waves goodbye to her husband when he goes out to plow a field only to find out that he'll never plow a field again.

She strained to remember what Pastor Jim had said about pain, but nothing came to mind. What had Mom said about pain and injustice?

Her mind was too confused to remember. *Mom's Bible,* she thought. It was full of the notes she'd taken ever since she'd embraced the Messiah. Sammie knew the Bible was in the trunk at the foot of her bed. As soon as she could, she'd get it out. *Mom, I hope you have answers.*

When she arrived at the Treasure House, Jen gave her a message from Claudine. "Come to dinner tonight. We've talked about it long enough. I'll grill steaks and we'll eat on the deck."

Dinner at Claudine's—even steaks on the deck overlooking

the ocean—was not what Sammie had in mind for tonight. But Claudine often tossed out a "you must come to dinner and see my new house" invitation like an air kiss, and Sammie would give her a vague response. She did want to see the house townsfolk talked so much about. And Brad's painting. So she phoned and agreed.

Claudine's new house was a split-level with a deck overlooking the ocean. Clearly it was the rich newcomer on Seagrass Road. There was no sign calling the house something like "Claudine's Castle" the way summer people seemed to name their homes. Looking at the opulent home, Sammie wished she'd brought her camera, then shrugged away the idea as getting more involved than she wanted.

Gravel spewed beneath her tires as she drove up the steep driveway. The white house looked like it had just stepped out of the pages of *Architectural Digest*. It was white-on-white, like the quilt she'd purchased at the auction.

Claudine pulled open the back door before Sammie could ring the bell. "Welcome," she smiled broadly and, with a sweep of her hand, motioned Sammie to enter.

This was the place for broad sweeps of the hand and every other dramatic gesture one could think of. Just inside the door was a basket of velvet slippers. "Choose your size, and exchange them for your shoes." Claudine wore a pair. "Would you like the grand tour?"

"Excuse my shock but I was expecting a house, not a mansion. Has Hollywood come knocking to shoot a film here yet?"

"The answer to Hollywood would be no, and I was only being polite by asking if you wanted a tour. It's required."

The interior of the house was white-on-white also. The living room was furnished with a white sofa that swept two sides of the room, mirrors the size of small storefronts, sleek chrome lamps, a thick white pile rug. The entire front of the living room was floor to ceiling windows overlooking the water, with a glass door that opened onto the deck. The sparkle of glass and white-on-white in the room was broken only by flowered pillows, plants in huge pots, a burgundy vase, a brass statue.

Sammie was too stunned to chatter polite compliments. Instead she gasped and breathed Claudine's name. She felt as though she'd suddenly shrunk even smaller than Pop's nickname of "Sample Size." She turned to Claudine who was watching her, amused, and said, "You should be wearing a satin hostess gown and ringing for the maid!"

Claudine looked down at her pink shorts and halter and laughed. "Only if I were starring in that Hollywood film you were talking about. And that's not going to happen."

Without asking, Claudine knew what was on Sammie's mind. "The painting is in the master bedroom. I'll show you."

First they toured the dining room with its magnificent chandelier over the table, the library with shelves of rare volumes, the music room with a white grand piano, and the guest rooms, each done in white with a different pastel accent.

Over the king-sized bed in Claudine's room was Brad's painting. The golden shimmer of the house on the hilltop spilled out into the room in pillow accents, flowers on the chest of drawers.

Sammie wanted to ask Claudine to go away so she could sink into the bed and gaze at the painting until it imprinted on her soul. Now she could understand visitors in art museums who sat on a bench and contemplated a painting while the clock ticked away the day.

"The house in Brad's painting," she whispered. "It's up a steep hill, like yours," she told Claudine with mist in her voice.

"But mine is not a cozy and warm, snuggle-up kind of house."

Sammie turned from the painting and whispered, "What

135

does this work of Brad's do for you?"

"It represents a place I've never been. Some days seeing it is torture, and I wonder if I'm masochistic. Other days, it warms me and keeps me from becoming the Ice Princess." Claudine headed toward the door. "Come toss a salad while I grill the steaks."

They ate on the deck at a glass-topped table, seated on white chairs, and watched a glowing sunset. "This must be the home you've dreamed of owning all your life," Sammie said.

"Not really. My original dream home was a replica of Mrs. Nelson's, furnished from the Treasure House." She played with her salad. "The question people really want to ask is: How could a bookstore owner afford such a place?"

Sammie smiled. Leave it to Claudine to cut to the chase. "My ex-husband, the famous Beverly Hills plastic surgeon to the stars, paid for it with liposuction and tummy tucks. My Beverly Hills attorney, who obtains divorces for the stars, saw to it that the settlement was all it should be."

Sammie wanted to put her fingers in her ears. She didn't want to hear Claudine's misery. Coming had been a bad idea. Until now, she'd mostly been able to avoid talk about their personal lives.

"Eleven years of Roy's affairs did it for me," Claudine continued. "This is payback for the good doctor. I deserve it. And there's not a cute or cozy inch. I may not be nice, but I certainly am honest. You've got to give me that."

They ate in silence. Then, characteristically, Claudine swept the conversational door open wide. "How about you, Sammie? Did you come here to forget a relationship gone bad?"

Sammie wanted to squeeze her eyes shut and cover her face with her hands. Instead, she simply nodded. Much as she hated the term "relationship," it fit. She and V.J. had merely been living together. He already had a legal wife.

Abruptly, Claudine ended the conversation. "How about a walk on the beach?"

They sauntered along the shoreline in bare feet, pausing to take in the pink and gold horizon and the water, now turned the same colors. Stopping, Claudine skipped stones in the water. She turned to Sammie. "You're a Jewish Christian. That must mean you believe in Jesus Christ."

Sammie dug her feet into the wet sand. "I do. I believe Jesus is the Messiah, the Savior."

"I used to be a little Sunday school girl," Claudine mused. "I even sang alto in the choir and toured with a Christian singing group. The whole bit. But then I grew up and put away child-ish things."

Questions she wanted to ask Claudine came fast to Sammie's mind, but she shushed them.

Claudine went on. "It's hard to keep believing that 'Jesus loves me, this I know,' when you feel like life is just one big emergency room."

They stood watching the surf play with their toes. "I didn't mean to depress you," Claudine said, picking up a tiny shell and handing it to Sammie.

A male jogger hugging the shoreline approached them. "It's Art Humble," Claudine said. "He runs most evenings about this time." They waved to him as he approached.

He caught up with then and ran in place, hands on hips, breathing hard. "Claudine! Are you ready for a Persian cat yet?" He turned to look at Sammie. "I keep telling her that's what her house needs. A pure white Persian sitting in the window."

"And shedding cat hair?" Claudine rolled her eyes.

Art looked at Sammie. "If it isn't the girl who eats pizza backward. How's Mechiah? Are the two of you buddies now?"

"I guess you could say that. I'm amazed that he takes to me as well as he does."

"What's not to like?"

She waved him away.

"I've got to run," he called as he took off down the beach, grinning at his pun.

Claudine narrowed her eyes knowingly. "What's going on between you two?" she asked as they headed toward the house.

Sammie shook her head. "Absolutely nothing. You know I bought my parrot from him. He's helped me a lot with Mechiah and seems to be a genuinely nice guy."

"He *is* a genuinely nice guy," Claudine said emphatically. "Hard to believe, but he's as nice as he seems."

On the drive home, her thoughts shifted to Claudine and the questions Sammie had wanted to ask. Was there a time when Claudine followed Jesus? Had she become disillusioned and turned away? Or had she merely been a churchgoer?

I put away childish things. Her house seemed to symbolize what Claudine had done to her life. Swept it clean of deep, personal attachments, including one with God. See my house, share my food, and take me as I am, cynical and thick-skinned.

Sammie was suddenly gripped with fear as though she'd seen a funnel cloud in the distance. As though she was being warned: *Cynical and thick skinned. A picture of what could happen to you if you pull away from me.*

Mom's Bible! Sammie thought frantically. *I've got to get into Mom's Bible!*

NINE

Mike was watering his front lawn when Sammie drove up. Usually she'd stop if she saw him and ask about business or baseball, even though he'd answer mostly in monosyllables. Tonight she just waved. He raised a hand halfheartedly and looked quickly away.

As soon as she opened the front door, Mechiah chattered his "hello" and began reciting his entire vocabulary. "Sammie's good bird...Polly want a cracker...You're a beauty," and ending with "Mechiah good boy." Only the way he said his name sounded more like "Miah." He simply couldn't get his beak around it.

She'd have to take time for him before she got out Mom's Bible. In fact, she enjoyed being with him. He'd grown to trust her and looked forward now to being taken out of the cage and perching on her shoulder and hopping off to investigate or play with her on the floor.

She put him on her shoulder now and stroked his feathers as he pranced down her arm, back up, and onto her shoulder again. He chattered with delight as she cut up part of a pear, and he allowed her to hand feed it to him. When he was finished, she allowed him freedom in the house.

God, you really did want me to have him, didn't you?

Kicking off her shoes, she headed for the trunk at the foot of her bed. The Bible was near the top, underneath a tablecloth embroidered by Grandma Levine. Carefully she unwrapped the tissue around it and ran her hand over Mom's name, imprinted in gold on the burgundy leather cover.

Sammie sat on the floor and read the inscription Mina had

written on the day of Mom's baptism, the day she'd presented her mother with it:

> *To Sophie.*
> *Always remember that God is your Gardener.*
> *Abide in Him.*
> JOHN 15:5.

An image of Mom in her wide-brimmed straw hat, digging the soil around her rosebushes, flashed into Sammie's mind. Mom's cheerful greeting when Sammie showed up and offered to give her a hand. Mom leaning on her shovel to think out loud. Mom saying, "When I work here, God keeps reminding me how much like these rose bushes I am. Thorny. Totally dependent on him to produce anything beautiful. Dependent on him to be *my* Gardener."

Sammie jumped to her feet, grabbed her journal and a pen, and settled back on the sofa with Mom's Bible and her own thoughts.

The Bible opened easily to John 15 because Mom had placed a photo of her rose garden in full bloom there as a bookmark. Lovingly, Sammie ran her fingers over the picture. Then her eye fell on the first part of verse four because Mom had highlighted it in yellow. "Remain in me." Sammie knew that Jesus spoke those words just before he went to the cross to die.

What had Mom written in her tiny, precise handwriting in the margin next to "remain"? *Remain means 'to abide, stay, live in me.'* The memory of a summer day much like this one drifted into Sammie's mind. She and Mom had been walking in the garden when her mother paused and pointed to one of the rosebushes.

"When I found the Messiah, my roses took on a whole new

meaning. They became an illustration of the new relationship I have with him." She had bent down to touch the bush where it came out of the ground. "See how the stalk carries the nutrients the Gardener provides to the branches?" Lovingly, she cupped one of the blossoms in her hand. "This Peace Rose is the fruit.

"Jesus showed me this picture so I'd never forget. He is the source of my peace, my joy, my patience. My part is to stay connected to him. Every day for the rest of my life, I must trust him to be my Source. No matter how things seem."

Sammie closed her eyes and buried her head in her hands. How could she do that when God let so many terrible things happen?

She picked up Mechiah, put him in his cage, and turned on the stereo because he seemed to enjoy listening to it. *Was it easy for you to learn to trust me, old bird? Or hard?*

Trust had come hard for the first woman who'd lived out her years on this ground. But she'd chosen to learn how. Claudine, on the other hand, had grown a thick skin like an armor of flesh.

Tears ran down Sammie's face. "I want to trust. Dear God, I want to trust the way Mrs. Nelson did. The way Mom did."

She wiped her eyes and wrote in her journal: *When I read Mom's Bible to straighten out my thinking about trusting God, I found the words, "Remain in me." God's words to Mom.*

I want to remain in you, Jesus. I want to trust. But I don't know how.

Was this how God worked? Ask him for what you think you need, like answers about pain, and he gives you what you really need? It reminded Sammie of when she was a child and asked mom for candy and her mother gave her carrot sticks instead. When she stamped her feet and objected, Mom simply smiled and went about her business. Pretty soon Sammie was enjoying the way the carrot sticks crunched when she bit into them and how sweet they tasted.

That night she fell into an exhausted sleep and hours later jumped awake sobbing and in a cold sweat trying desperately to extricate herself from a dream. She was in the rose garden. The leaves of the bushes were brown; dead roses covered the ground. "How could I let this happen?" she'd been crying over and over. "Mom asked me to take care of her roses, and I let them die!"

What did the dream mean? That she'd failed? That she could never be like Mom? Agitated, she turned this way and that in bed to try and shake off the memory. Finally, she fell back to sleep from exhaustion.

The next morning, Miss M. called to see if Sammie wanted to go to church with her on Sunday. Sammie involuntarily pulled away from the editor's suggestion but then her mind fastened on her prayer of the night before. "Yes. I'll meet you there." As she hung up, she wondered if she'd see Brad this time.

You're going to church to worship God, not see Brad. She studied the watercolorist's translucent burst of flowers above Mrs. Nelson's polished organ. Brad had captured the delicate colors of Pineville Beach gardens in July in one grand crescendo. If souls came in colors, what shade would his be?

A few minutes later, a plainly dressed woman past middle age who looked as though she had better things to do than curl her hair and decorate her ears came in looking for old books. Sammie sent her to the turret room and didn't see or hear from her for nearly an hour. When she finally came down the stairs again, she was carrying a half dozen old volumes.

"I'm so glad I decided to stop in Pineville Beach!" she said. "These books are treasures!"

When the woman set them down on the counter, Sammie

noted that they were all books on the subject of Christianity. "They belonged to a retired college professor who was a collector and a devoted Christian," she told the customer. "As a matter of fact, he ran out of space for bookshelves and arranged them two deep. His wife teased that he cared more about his books than he did her."

The smile on the woman's face became as bright as the summer day, and Sammie wondered how she could ever have thought of her as plain. "I wish I'd known him." She laughed and patted the bag Sammie handed her. "My friends say I don't need a husband, I'm married to my books." As she opened the door, she turned to Sammie. "Thanks for telling me who owned them. We have more than books in common, he and I."

Sammie watched the woman peek in the bag as she walked down the street. *That's my real reward. Seeing items that were an important part of someone's life yesterday embraced by someone today. Seeing continuity take place. Like my connection with Mom's Bible.*

During a morning lull, Sammie sat curled up in a white wicker chair on the front porch sipping coffee. Autumn came around the corner of the Treasure House. "Would it be okay if I bring my mother in this afternoon so she can show you her rugs?"

"She's feeling better?"

Autumn hesitated. "Than she was, yes. Besides, after all Jen and I have said about you, she's anxious to meet you in person."

A little after two, Autumn walked up the front steps carrying a large cardboard box that she set down so she could hold open the door for the woman who followed. "Sammie, this is my mother, Dossie May Hoffman." Autumn set the box on the floor and stood back waiting.

Dossie May Hoffman looked at Sammie, then slowly around

the shop, in wide-eyed amazement. When she extended her limp hand, Sammie grasped it in her own small one. But the woman kept staring around the shop as though she hadn't really heard Sammie's greeting.

Everything about Autumn's mother was long and thin. Her bones seemed to have kept growing, mindless of the fact that she couldn't produce flesh enough to cover them, so the pounds she did have were stretched too far. Her long brown hair was thin and caught up at her neck in a bun. Pop would have said she had a long face, meaning that she looked as though she'd forgotten how to smile. Even the plain cotton dress she wore that hung loosely on her body was long. Not fashionably so. More like a cover, hiding what was inside.

Autumn opened the box she'd brought. "You show your rugs to Sammie, okay?"

Dossie May looked uncertain, but obediently she took the first rug out of the box. It was braided with woolen strips of rust, forest green, beige and chocolate brown. "Mama dyed the material herself," Autumn explained proudly.

Sammie breathed her response. "It's beautiful." She took it from Dossie May and draped it in the window seat. "This is just what I've been looking for to sell in the shop."

"Show her that one," Autumn prompted eagerly, pointing in the box. Dossie May unfolded a hooked rug with a heart in the center and a farmer and his aproned wife on either side.

"Did you design these yourself?"

Dossie May nodded gravely. "I do it the way my mama taught me."

"Mother made the carpet for the center aisle of the First Baptist Church. She hooked it, like this one, in a different pattern." Autumn put in. "They even paid her for it."

"I didn't want to take money. But…" Dossie May hesitated, as though confused about what to say next. "But I had to."

"You should be paid for your work, Dossie May. You are a talented craftsperson."

Autumn's gratitude to Sammie was obvious. She motioned excitedly for her mother to show the rest of the rugs in the box, oval and heart-shaped, in various sizes and colors.

"I'd like to sell your rugs here in the Treasure House." Sammie meant her words to be the offer of a contract.

Dossie May's voice rose and fell with incredulity. "You would? You really would?"

"And more like them. I have a feeling they'll go fast." She turned to Autumn. "Can you have some tags printed with your mom's name or her business name—like Dossie May's Creations—to put on them? I want customers to know they're made by a local craftsperson. That'll help with sales."

A look of uncertainty passed between the two women. "I don't know if we should do that," Autumn said.

Mr. Hoffman? Why would he care? "Talk it over," she urged the women. "I'll take all of the ones you brought." Sammie made out a consignment form. This time when they shook hands, Dossie Mae squeezed back.

"You're as nice as my daughters said you were," Dossie May said shyly.

That night Sammie talked events over with Mechiah as she prepared to give him a bath. "Dossie May's rugs are fabulous! But the woman looks like someone from a Steinbeck novel! Mechiah…what do you suppose is going on in that house?"

Bath time had grown to be a pleasure. Her bird was a water baby at heart, unlike some parrots, according to Art. Mechiah squawked with delight as she took him out of the cage and carried him to the bathtub. The first time she bathed him, he'd tried to nip her, but gradually his trust in her grew.

Now, he turned this way and that in the water, ruffling his feathers, spraying Sammie, who sputtered at him. When she used the hair drier on him, he stood obediently on the dressing table.

"Mom would love you, Mechiah. I wish she'd known you." A wave of sorrow swept over her at the memory of her mother's death. Would she ever get over that? Ever feel at peace because Mom was with Jesus?

She turned off the hair dryer and put Mechiah on her shoulder. "Mechiah pretty bird," he announced. "Sammie's good bird."

Grateful for the distraction, Sammie responded. "Mechiah good bird. Sammie loves Mechiah."

"Sammie loves Mechiah," he repeated as she placed him back in his cage.

The next morning, as the sun rose orange on the horizon, she bicycled to her secret place by the river, taking Mom's Bible, her journal, a thermos of coffee, and a ground cloth to cover the still-damp undergrowth. The day felt fresh, and the sound of the river rippling over rocks was background music.

She began writing about the evening before. *Mechiah's trust in me has grown even more. Bath time is a blast. He knows now I'm not going to hurt him and that he can relax.* Sammie felt as though she should explore that train of thought more.

Mechiah was learning to trust her. Sometimes, if she did something that frightened him, he pulled back and squawked and even tried to nip her. But his faith in her eventually helped him overcome his fear.

My mind is running on two tracks, she continued to write. *One track believes God is communicating to me, and the other asks how that could be possible since I am so completely unworthy.*

Because she didn't want to go down that road, she quickly snapped the Bible shut and stuffed the items she'd brought into her knapsack. "Pack it away for another day," she repeated in singsong to herself as she pumped the pedals.

When she arrived at the shop, she found a message on her phone machine from Pop. "I'm going out of town for a few days to meet with some people who want to talk with me about opening another restaurant. So how is the tourist season in the north woods? Are you eating more than rabbit food? Make some chicken soup. I'll call you when I get back." He ended the message by telling her where she could reach him if she needed to.

What I'd like to do, Pop, is feel your arms around me and bury my face in your chest. But not have you tell me what to do. I want to be able to tell you what's been happening with me. Would you understand?

Later, as she dusted the organ, she thought of Mrs. Nelson. They'd talked on the phone a few times since her last visit. *But I promised to bring her to the Treasure House. Besides, I want to hear the rest of the story about Mrs. Nelson's early life with Captain and what happened after those two children went back to their father.*

On the phone, Mrs. Nelson sounded like ninety going on twenty-five. "Let's do it!" Sammie promised to pick her up as soon as she closed the shop.

Her elderly landlady was wearing navy slacks, a red bandanna shirt, and a blue denim hat with a red cloth flower in the front. She refused Sammie's offer of dinner at the Farmer's Wife, saying she'd fixed herself a cheeseburger earlier. "But I could go for an ice cream cone."

Mrs. Nelson chose banana split flavor "because it's so full of stuff. Cherries and marshmallows and nuts and bananas."

Sammie chose double chocolate delight. "The only thing better than chocolate is more chocolate," she quipped.

The two women licked their cones as they walked outside and sat on a bench. "When Captain was alive, I always saved the end of the cone for him. Then after he died, I felt guilty for a long time eating it myself. Funny the things we can feel guilty about, isn't it?"

Sammie nodded gravely.

"For a while, I stopped eating ice cream cones all together. Finally, I realized I wasn't doing anything wrong by eating the end." She stopped licking and turned to grin at Sammie. "Now I can eat the whole thing without one bit of guilt. Just watch me."

Guilt over eating the end of a cone isn't exactly the same as marrying V.J. without finding out God's will, and losing Mom's bequest, the one passed on to her from her parents. Instead of getting into that, Sammie commented about the skateboarders who careened past the shops and a blond, curly-haired boy furiously pumping his trike.

Quiet for several moments, they inhaled the fragrant evening. Suddenly, Mrs. Nelson asked what season Sammie liked best.

"Spring, I think," Sammie answered.

"I like spring best, too. The world comes to life again." Mrs. Nelson went on to ask what Sammie's favorite spring flower was. Her favorite way to relax. The kind of music she liked to listen to. The kinds of books she liked to read. Each time, she gave her own favorites as well.

Two women getting acquainted, Sammie thought. That they were twenty-eight and ninety didn't make any difference.

"I have a question for you." Sammie pointed to the river. "Why is it named Iseeyousee? My father keeps asking me, and I don't have an answer."

The old woman grinned broadly, forcing the wrinkles on her face to crowd one another for space. "The story goes that the first party of settlers were on their way from the mainland in a small boat. They'd heard that there was a river inland off the coast. One of them stood up excitedly and yelled, 'I see! You see?'

"When the second jumped to his feet, they both fell overboard. They didn't drown, but it became a joke among the settlers. All they had to say was, 'I see! You see?' Pretty soon, that's what they called the river."

Sammie rolled her eyes and shook her head slowly. "Pop will love that story. I can just hear him tell it to his friends."

When they pulled up in front of the Treasure House, Mrs. Nelson stared at the sign over the door, at the tubs of flowers in the front yard and on the porch, the white wicker furniture, the half dozen bird houses that hadn't yet sold.

Sammie's stomach felt queasy. Now that the house's owner was actually seeing it, would she resent the fact that Sammie had turned her home into a store?

Mrs. Nelson rested her head on the back of the seat and closed her eyes. When she sat up and opened them, she said, "Little girl, I knew if I prayed and waited God would show me what he had in mind for my house." She reached over and took Sammie's hand. "He did."

The words stroked Sammie's uncertainty.

On their way inside, Mrs. Nelson lingered to finger the flowers in the tubs. "'Cora's Castle,' Captain used to call the house."

As Sammie took her through the rooms on the main floor, the woman sniffed, touched, and absorbed with her eyes. When she saw the painting, she whooped. "You have a Brad MacKenzie for sale! He must like the shop. And I bet he likes you, too. Else it wouldn't be here," she added mischievously.

She ran her fingers over the organ keys. "The first evening when Captain was home, he'd ask me to play," she paused. "Winter evenings, whoever was here gathered around after dinner and sang along, whether they knew the words or not."

She moved to the fireplace. "When the rain poured so hard I thought it would break the windows, we built the fire until it roared back at the storm and sat around it telling stories. If

149

Captain was here, we all listened to him tell about his adventures at sea." Her face was painted with remembrance.

In the kitchen, her landlady stood back and shook her head at the cookstove. "You've got it so clean and polished it looks like the day Captain bought it. Let me tell you, that's not the way it was when I lived here. It was a working stove then, loaded with canning kettles in summer and fall. Pots of beans and stew in winter. Bread in the oven. Wet shoes drying around it. Baby chicks keeping warm.

"When my mother and father visited they asked why I wouldn't rather choose to live where I could have creature comforts and servants." Mrs. Nelson was silent for a few moments while she examined the memory carefully. Then she turned to Sammie. "Can you imagine me supervising servants and having tea with society ladies? I told my mother and father, 'This is where God wants me. This is the life I was created to live.' Till the day they died, they never understood."

She scampered through the downstairs rooms as though she were on a treasure hunt. First, she looked out the back window. "A porch swing! I always wanted one right there!"

I'm actually watching a ninety-year-old woman scamper! Sammie tried to imagine what this tiny dynamo must have been like when she was twenty-eight.

Her landlady picked up a flat iron and said she liked the kind that plugged in and had a well of steam much better, but these made good decorations. At the sink she said, "When we first moved in, we had a pump instead of running water. That was the latest thing—water in the house instead of outside."

On the way to the dining room, she stopped to pat a pie safe. "Blueberry. That was Captain's favorite." Of a portable blue kerosene heater, she remarked, "I wouldn't have those. They were too dangerous around children. Besides, they smelled awful."

She pointed to a kerosene lamp. "We had lots of those, of course. It was the older children's job to polish the chimneys every Saturday."

In the dining room, she admired the table and chairs, glassware, china, and silver. "Captain made our first table. It had to be big, I told him, and easy to scrub. He made benches to go with it and not a splinter in any of them."

Upstairs, she popped into each bedroom, stopping to remember how it was. In the children's room, she sat in a tiny chair that fit her perfectly. Sammie sat cross-legged on the floor beside her and fingered a rag doll with a cloth face and button eyes.

"How my children would have loved this room!" Mrs. Nelson breathed, as though it were a secret. "They didn't have many toys, and most of what they had were made by Captain or me." She looked at Sammie when she spotted the painting. "Another Brad Mackenzie!"

"I secretly hope no one buys his paintings. I'd hate to part with them," Sammie told her.

Instead of showing amusement at the comic animals, Mrs. Nelson rose and walked out of the room. "No amount of money can pay what it cost for him to paint that picture."

She started to ask Mrs. Nelson what she meant, but as they walked into the turret room, thought better of it. Her remarks did confirm the fact that behind the curtains Brad kept pulled was a tragedy.

There wasn't time to think more about it. "Your photographs were good, but nothing like being here." Mrs. Nelson circled the room, inspecting the books, then sat looking out at the water. "I had to see if it still felt the same." She breathed deeply and folded her hands in her lap. "It does."

"When I first came here, I sensed something special about this room," Sammie said. "Besides the view, I mean." She looked questioningly at the older woman and waited.

"It's where I came to pray when my heart was so heavy I couldn't carry it around by myself any more. When I was so full of joy it seemed as though I was going to explode. Nights when Captain was gone and I couldn't sleep, I came up here and looked out at the sea and begged God to keep him safe. In this room I remembered that I was not alone with my problems." She patted the arm of the rocking chair in which she sat. "I had a chair like this one, a kerosene lamp, and my Bible."

Sammie spoke hesitantly, measuring each word. "Sometimes I come up here to think and pray."

Mrs. Nelson turned to Sammie and squinted in the brightness. "We use flatirons or electric irons, kerosene lamps or electric lamps, but life doesn't change that much, does it? We feel wonderful and terrible, and we pray a lot."

Sammie vowed to herself that before the day was over, she would bring up a kerosene lamp and put it on the table next to a Bible open to the Lord's Prayer.

She leaned forward eagerly. "Tell me. What happened after the children went back to their father? What did you do then?"

"We bought this house and moved in. When Captain was home, we'd come into this room and pray together for God to show us what to do next. Then early one fall when he was out hunting, he found a family living in a tent in the woods. They were living on fish and game and whatever grew wild. They'd been taking baths in the river all summer, and that's where the woman had been washing their clothes.

"They were a sorry looking sight. The parents were barely grown themselves, with three young ones of their own—all under six. Sarah Ann, the baby, was still in diapers. Joe had gotten sick, and they lost everything. He got to feeling more and more miserable about himself and life and just plain lost hope. I guess these days, you'd say he was depressed. He wouldn't let his wife ask for help. He was so beaten down that, when Captain said he was taking them home with him, Joe didn't argue.

"The family moved in here and filled up the bedrooms. Joe was real good with his hands so Captain and I gave him jobs to do around the place. When folks saw what he could do, they hired him to do this and that. Annie and I sewed clothes for her and the children. She helped me can, and I saw to it that we set aside part of it for her family to take when they went on their own.

"After a while, Joe made enough to get a place for them, and they moved out." She punctuated the end of the story with a smile of satisfaction. "They got along fine.

"While they were here, sometimes Matthew—he was four then—would wake up in the night and cry real soft because he'd dreamed he was in the woods again. We'd come in this room, and I'd rock him back to sleep before Annie, his mom, heard him. It was like she'd never get back all the rest she lost."

Sammie could only shake her head slowly in disbelief. "What I didn't know when I opened my shop here was that this was a treasure house long before I ever came along."

"It's the people God brought to Captain and me who were treasures," Mrs. Nelson said. "Aimee and her daughter, Faith. Aimee was beaten black and blue by her husband." Fire flared in her eyes. "Would you believe he took stove wood to her? No shelters for women in those days. Yes, and when he came here yelling for Aimee to come home—he didn't care about the child—I met him in the front doorway with my rifle. Couldn't call 911 in those days. Aimee got a job in the city, and she and Faith boarded with a nice family until they could get a place of their own.

"Whoever stayed with us, I told about God. I held them while they cried. We'd come up here and pray. Mostly, they blossomed. Except for a few, of course, who stole from us and took off."

"It must have been hard. But you had such faith."

Mrs. Nelson smiled. "I don't know about that. Remember I said I wanted a blueprint from God?"

Sammie said she remembered.

Mrs. Nelson laughed. "That's why I spent so much time in this room." She squinted out at the water. "It got harder. An awful lot harder. To trust God, I mean. Some days, I screamed at him, I was so desperate. Especially when God took Captain."

Sammie waited for her to go on. Instead, she glanced at her watch and held it up for Sammie to see.

"Mickey Mouse? You have a Mickey Mouse watch?"

Sammie grabbed the near-century hand, "I love it!"

"Yes, and Mickey says it's past my bedtime."

When they reached Mrs. Nelson's door, she invited Sammie in. "Remember when you asked to see more pictures in my album? There are some of Annie and Joe and the kids and Aimee and Faith, too."

In the first photographs, both families looked as though the life had been squeezed out of them, and they were dry to the bone. In later pictures, they were greening again.

Saturday and Sunday were unusually hot for the Northwest, and vacationers in short shorts and skimpy tops made people-watching an Olympic sport. Residents stood in knots on their way to the post office and the hardware store, grinning and shaking their heads knowingly when tourists passed by.

After coffee and toast spread with cream cheese and marion-berry jam in the porch swing on Sunday morning, Sammie changed to a linen-look ivory-colored dress with a lace inset at the V-neck and sandals and drove to church. Miss M. was waiting, and her smile became one hundred watts when she spotted Sammie.

The worship glowed like stained glass and Sammie found herself soaking up its sacred sounds and responding from some deep place that had only recently been stirred. During the offering, she scanned the sanctuary for Brad and spotted him on the other side, tieless like most of the men and wearing a short-sleeved white shirt. He caught her staring at him and smiled and nodded. Miss M. did not miss the exchange.

When the pastor announced that Brad MacKenzie had an announcement, Sammie's eyes popped open wide.

"Through 'Helping Hands,' we provide for unwed mothers during their pregnancy and arrange adoptions," Brad began. "At the Pineville Beach Harvest Festival next Saturday, we'll have a booth selling bagel sandwiches and beverages, and the proceeds will go for that ministry. We still need people to help out. If you can do that, let me know after church."

She thought of Claudine's statement at the Memorial Day celebration that Brad kept to himself, and she realized that wasn't completely true. But his activities were mostly through church, and apparently Claudine wasn't aware of that.

Another activity that involved children. Should she volunteer? After all, it was a bagel booth, and she knew her bagels. During the sermon, she kept shoving the question back so she could pay close attention, especially since the title was "Finding Faith."

The pastor read about Peter stepping out of the boat at Jesus' bidding and walking on the water until his faith failed, and he began to sink. "Did you realize that Peter—and every one of us—already has the ability to believe? That we're born with it?"

No, Sammie responded silently. *I did not.*

"God created us with the ability to trust. We do it all the

time. A baby instinctively trusts the one who cares for him. We grown-ups trust others every day. Think of those you trusted this week: the short-order cook who grilled your hamburger, the dentist who drilled your teeth, the pharmacist who filled your prescription.

"As we grow up, we learn who is trustworthy and who isn't. The short-order cook, the dentist and pharmacist have proven themselves capable at what they do.

"Jesus was challenging Peter to use the ability to trust that he already had. Only this time to place it in God. 'Take courage,' he said. 'It is I. Don't be afraid.' What he implied was, 'I am the Son of God. Your Messiah. I created and sustained the universe. You can trust me.'"

Sammie felt as though the sun had risen after a very dark night. Of course. Why hadn't she seen that before?

After service, she sought out Brad. "Put me down to help in the bagel booth."

He looked pleased and consulted the schedule in his hand. "How about 10 A.M. to 2 P.M.? That's when we'll need help most." She wanted to linger, to ask what he'd thought of the sermon, how "Helping Hands" worked. But others were waiting to talk with him.

As they walked to their cars, Miss M. invited Sammie for a quick stop at her place for coffee. "I know you have to open the shop soon."

Sammie accepted the invitation. As she pulled in the driveway, she was amused because it certainly was "a place." A big black lab bounded to greet them. A few chickens pecked in the yard. An orange cat meowed and rubbed against her legs.

"The place is in process, just like me." Miss M. grinned. Lumber was stacked at the back of the house, new windows had been installed. "I pretty much live in the kitchen." Red-checkered oilcloth covered the kitchen table that sat in a windowed alcove. "Before I go to work, I drink my coffee, read my Bible and pray, and enjoy the mountains."

The copper kettle Miss M. had bought at the Treasure House gleamed on the wood stove. A wash boiler for wood sat beside it. The cabinets were new and without smudges. Rag rugs that looked like the ones Dossie May made were splashes of color on the floor.

The living room was sparsely furnished with unfinished walls. "If I didn't insist on doing most of the work myself, it would go faster. And I get sidetracked planting a garden, getting chickens, and other projects—like running a newspaper."

And being a grandmother to a little girl who needs one.

"You must get satisfaction from every door you hang, every wall you paint," Sammie commented.

Miss M. nodded slowly. "I have to settle for small signs of progress. In the house and in me."

They drank coffee at the kitchen table, and Sammie admired Mount Ashley on the horizon. "In the winter, with snow on the top and the sun shining, it looks like an ice cream cone." Miss M. sighed and leaned back in her chair, at peace in the midst of chaos.

The phone machine was flashing when Sammie returned home. Pop's was the first message, letting her know he was back home and asking her to call.

The other was from Dave Vivano: "Sammie, my man! Raise the flag! We have V.J. in custody! What a relief, huh? Call as soon as you can."

T E N

O h, God!"
Even though it had beeped its last beep, Sammie
stood staring at the phone machine.

Instead of a grand, overwhelming sense of relief the way
she'd fantasized she'd feel the moment the call came that V.J.
was behind bars, she felt as though tiny explosions were taking
place in her body like fireworks on the Fourth of July. But
without brilliant colors or celebratory sounds.

Now that the time had actually come, she couldn't even
wrap her brain around Dave's words: "V.J.'s in custody." No
sense of solid satisfaction. No *Yes!* with hands raised in the air.

Never mind if you can't feel the way you expected. Figure out
what you need to do first.

Call Dave, of course. Would he expect her to respond with
loud cries of "Whoopie!"? There was no "whoopie" rising from
her bones.

Numbness turned to nausea. She stood erect and took deep
breaths slowly.

Her parrot intervened. "You're a beauty. Mechiah good boy.
Sammie's good boy." The bird had moved to the front of the
cage and and was eyeing her in hopes she'd take him out.

"Thanks, Mechiah." When she didn't take him out, he
began ringing a bell fastened to a hanging, multicolored cord.

Because her hands were shaking, she had to punch in
Dave's number slowly and carefully so she wouldn't get the
wrong number.

"Vivano here." His take-charge voice. His mother said he
didn't know how to say "pass the sugar" without sounding like
a cop.

"It's Sammie, Dave."

"Sammie, my man!" His voice softened. "We've got him. And we're going to nail him." Dear Dave. He knew how she'd feel and tailored his response to fit.

"I thought I'd feel vindicated," she told him. "Or at least a sense of relief. But right now, all I feel is sick."

"Yeah. It's not real to you yet, and it probably won't be for a while. Sammie..." he hesitated. "Sammie, we need you to come down and identify the bum. We've turned up a third woman he 'married' and fleeced. She's on her way here. Who knows, there may be more."

Sammie tried to click through the arrangements she'd have to make. Book passage on a flight. Call Pop. Ask Jen to work in the shop and stay in the cottage to take care of Mechiah. See if Autumn would come and help Jen once in a while so she could get an hour off here and there. "I could probably get there day after tomorrow."

I promised to work in the church's bagel booth! But that wasn't until Saturday. She'd be back in time. Not that selling bagels seemed important now, but she had made a commitment to Brad, and it seemed important to do what she promised. Besides, she didn't want to miss being with him.

Two days later, she was fastened in seat nine by the window with her journal on the fold-out table in front of her, open to a blank page. In the next seat was a woman dressed in purple pants. She had lacquered gold-and-silver hair.

She put her hand on Sammie's. "I'm scared to death to fly, so I popped a pill and I'm going to zonk out. Sorry not to be more company. But believe me, you'll like me better this way."

Sammie was secretly glad.

The first time she'd flown, she'd been fascinated to see that the earth below looked like a series of Playskool towns. Since then during trips in the air she'd only glanced down occasionally at the familiar scene, then buried herself in a book. Now, though, she stared at the miniature scene, aware of her separateness from earth.

She remembered reading once that God saw the whole of what we call "life", and we only see the tiny moments in time that we're living. *I can only see the mess I'm in—flying to Los Angeles to identify V.J.,* she wrote on the blank page. *God sees the whole picture. I have the ability to trust. God gave it to me as part of my original equipment.* Next to the entry, she drew a happy face.

She looked out the window at the ground again, watching tiny tin cars move along ribbon roads. Then she continued her entry. *We learn that some people are trustworthy and some are not. That we can trust some people in particular ways but not in others.*

The sleeping woman next to her moaned and shifted. *My seatmate is unable to trust this plane to hold us up. Trust is something we learn.*

The stewardess was coming down the aisle with breakfast trays so Sammie put her journal under the seat in front of her and accepted the tiny omelet and muffin in a tiny dish with tiny compartments to eat in a tiny space. "Meals for midgets," Pop called them.

He'd be horrified that she was savoring every bite. But it wasn't from the food that she obtained comfort. It was the feeling of safety because she was in the air out of reach of the trouble that awaited her on the ground.

With her carry-on bag over her shoulder and a smile pasted on her face, she deplaned, asking God to keep her calm. Pop met her at the gate. Letting the bag slide to the floor, she opened her arms. Instead of what her father called his "ten-dollar hug," he gave her one worth no more than twenty-five cents. *Preoccupied with V.J.,* she thought. The little girl inside, who still wanted to believe that Daddy could make it all better, withered.

He guided her out of the airport and did his best conversationally. "Was the flight okay? Did they give you a greasy midget omelet and dried-up muffin?"

Sammie smiled. "It makes me appreciate your meals more." As they walked to the car, Pop hummed a melody of his own invention, revealing that his inner discord level was threatening to go over the top.

He was dripping with anger. "They finally got the bum, Sammie. They should lock him up and throw away the key. And for good measure, he should be castrated. Better still, leave the fathers of the women he ruined alone with him for fifteen minutes."

It would be all she could do to keep her father from exploding. She wished she was as good at that as Mom had been.

Traffic on the freeway was bumper to bumper. "I'd forgotten how bad it is," she said. "Back in the north woods the worst we have is some congestion on weekends during the tourist season."

He wasn't into small talk. Sammie gritted her teeth and stared straight ahead when he honked at the car in front of him and yelled at the driver. She gritted her teeth as Pop changed lanes and honked and slammed his fist on the steering wheel. She had to remember that since they'd caught V.J., her father had probably been lying awake nights reliving the whole event, frantic because he hadn't been able to protect her.

"One of the junk newspapers has been calling since V.J. was arrested. They want to know where you are," he said. "I hang up on them."

"Pop, I'm sorry they've been bothering you."

Since Pop was a well known restaurateur, local papers covered the story when it first happened. The headline was, "Bigamist-con man fleeces Sophie's daughter." If there was a follow-up story now, she could only pray that someone in Pineville Beach didn't get their hands on it.

As they pulled into the long driveway past Mom's rose gar-den and up to the house, she felt as though she were revisiting a dream that had been both sweet and painful.

Sammie looked at her father. *He shouldn't have to go through this. It's my fault for letting my emotions shut off my brain. For not listening to his warnings about V.J. It's my fault that he's ready to blow. So now it's my responsibility to take what he says and not do battle.*

The Sternberg's mist gray house didn't have a spot of chipped paint or a single unclipped hedge. As always, it looked spiffed and polished and ready for company. Mom had kept it that way to please Pop. He wasn't the kind of person who would let it go now that she was gone.

"I don't make much of a mess," Pop told her during one of their long-distance phone conversations. "Tilda still comes in a couple times a week to clean and do the laundry. Jessie still keeps the grounds and cleans the pool and does general main-tenance."

While Pop went to the den to return some phone calls and look at the mail, she wandered through the rooms. This was definitely not a "place." When they had it built, he insisted it be expansive and have an east and west wing.

For the son of Rumanian immigrants, that was a symbol. A visual reminder that the kid who started with a hole-in-the-wall eatery now owned a restaurant rated four-star that was fre-quented by celebrities. That the kid from the tenements who ate bread rubbed with garlic for dinner had arrived.

Mom was everywhere in the house. Sammie had forgotten how gifted she was at giving each room her personal signature. "It must hurt," Sammie had suggested to Pop once, before she moved to the northwest, "to be reminded of Mom everywhere you turn. Why don't you sell and get something smaller?"

He'd looked long and heavily at her. "This is my home. And

162

I don't want to forget your mother." Still, she wasn't sure whether living here gave Pop comfort or kept him mourning.

Like Claudine's, the house was large and airy, but instead of being sterile, it was warm and soothing. Mom had strewn roses in every room: lush pink ones in the sofa pattern, tiny yellow ones in the master bathroom wallpaper, needlepoint ones on the dining room chair seats, embroidered ones on white organdy pillows in the guest room.

Sammie walked into the large, gleaming kitchen, one appropriate for a photo layout of a movie star's home. This room had been designed and furnished completely by Pop. Mom had just smiled and stepped aside and let him do it. "You're the chef. Whatever you decide will be wonderful." He'd chosen the best of everything, and Mom had said that it made this daughter of a dry-goods store proprietor feel like Alice in Wonderland. But then she'd said that of the whole house.

One day when Pop had come home with the painted wooden sign that still hung over the sink, "Sophie's Place," Mom had laughed at the ridiculousness of it. "It should say 'Sam's Place.'" Often she teased that one day he'd come home and find "Sam's Place" hanging over the sink instead.

Sammie glanced at her watch. Nearly two. Pop would insist they have lunch, and if she objected he'd argue that the tougher the day, the more important it was to eat well. But she'd have to call Dave right away and find out when he needed her for the lineup.

On the phone, Dave said he'd schedule the lineup for four thirty and asked how she was doing. She answered that she didn't know how she was doing but that Pop wasn't doing well at all.

"Understandable. My advice is that your father stay home. It will only make things worse for him to be here." She sighed in agreement.

"It'll be over fast. Park in the back of the station. I'll be waiting."

So I won't have to walk through the outer offices, she thought. *And maybe see people I know.*

Pop did insist she have lunch and promised he'd fix something quick. "You'll need strength to look at that dirt bag again."

The matzo ball soup and bagel with cream cheese he fixed did settle her queasy stomach. He understood when she couldn't finish it, but he fussed that she eat as much of the soup as she could. As she sipped the hot broth, she wondered how she was going to convince him not to come to the station with her. *Dear God, show me what to say.*

She decided to be direct. "Pop, I need to go to the lineup alone. To prove to myself that I can do it. That V.J. hasn't licked me." What she said was true.

It must have been from God because her father amazed her by letting her know that he understood. "Yeah, Sammie. Okay." He wilted, though, and she knew he was feeling helpless.

As she turned down familiar streets to the station, stopping at a red light that always had taken too long to change, she thought longingly of the time in the air when she'd been able to separate herself from problems on the ground.

Checking her hair in the mirror, she was relieved that the Los Angeles summer only made it more curly. That the yellow shift she was wearing didn't wrinkle easily.

The yellow shift. She looked down at it and felt as though she was going to burst into tears. How could she have been so stupid? It was the dress V.J. used to say proved that she liked butter because the color made the sun come out on her face. How could she have forgotten?

Wait a minute. Calm down. Your mind was on other things. Chances are he won't even see you today. You'll identify him through one-way glass, and he'll probably be led away right afterward.

But I'll know. Wearing it makes me feel like a fool for believing him. It makes me feel dirty.

There was no time to go back to Pop's and change. Maybe she could take the next exit off the freeway and find a store where she could buy a dress that had no personal history. But a glance at her watch told her she'd just have to go the way she was. Wearing the reminder, "I was taken by V.J. Magellan."

Dave was waiting on the steps of the rear entrance to the station and hurried toward her. Taking her arm, he hustled her through the corridor to room twelve and introduced her to two other officers who were waiting in the room, Kelly Monahan and Brian Adamson. The former was a stocky female with short, curly auburn hair who'd make any perpetrator think twice about trying something. The latter was tall and slender, nearing retirement, with a scar down the right side of his face.

Dave picked up the mike and spoke into it. "Bring them in."

She wished Dave would take her hand, put his arm around her shoulder, but of course that wouldn't be professional. What had she told Pop before she left? *I have to do this myself to prove that V.J. hasn't licked me.* Yellow dress or not.

The men marched in. Her heart pounded in her chest, making it hard to breathe. Dave called for a side view. "Pick him out Sammie. Take your time."

She scanned the lineup. *There he was. Number two. V.J. the Irresistible.*

A wave of weakness swept her body. Determined not to give in to it, she willed herself to push past her feelings. Yes, the other men had similar characteristics—tall and slender with dark hair. But time would never erase V.J.'s image from her mind. Hadn't she given him her heart and her body?

Don't forget this moment, she ordered herself. V.J. standing in a police lineup. The bored look on his handsome face as he stared straight ahead. The hint of a sardonic smile.

"Do you see him, Sammie?" Dave's voice was the pat on the shoulder that Pop couldn't quite muster.

She took a deep breath and spoke firmly and with assurance. "I see him. V.J. Magellan is number two." Suddenly the yellow dress she was wearing no longer mattered.

"Are you sure that's him?" Brian asked.

"I'm sure. Positive. That's him."

"Good work, Sammie." Dave opened the mike again and instructed the men to leave.

"This guy is nailed," Kelly commented as she left the room with Brian. "He didn't even try to change his looks. I guess he thought all he needed was an alias and he was home free. How sure of yourself can you get?" After words of thanks to Sammie, they walked off down the hall.

Dave pulled her aside. "Sammie, I have something to ask you. What you decide is entirely up to you. V.J.'s third 'wife' is here. Would you like to meet her? You already met wife number one. Maybe you want to meet this one now and maybe you don't. I thought I should give you the opportunity. It would be all right with her."

"Oh, Dave, I don't know...." Would it make her stronger to meet another victim? Could she help the other woman?

Her meeting with angry, tenacious Billie, wife number one, the attorney who vowed to pursue him to the ends of the earth for disappearing, stealing from her, and taking another "wife," had stiffened Sammie's spine. "It was big of him to live with us one at a time." Billie had spat out the words.

"You'd like her, Sammie. But it's still up to you."

"Let's go, Dave."

He led her into a room used for interrogation, with bare walls, high windows, furnished only with a table and chairs, then left to get V.J.'s third "wife." *Sounds like the title of a novel. V.J.'s Third Wife.* She wondered what name he went by when he married her.

Minutes later Dave ushered in a willowy woman perhaps a few years older than Sammie. The first word that came to mind was "feminine." V.J.'s third wife wore a black jumpsuit in a silky fabric, a gold pin at her throat, matching earrings, and high-heeled black pumps. Her short, jet black hair was styled in soft waves around her face, and her skin was milky white.

"Sammie Sternberg, meet Loralee…err, Sweet." Dave turned to Sammie and shook his head. "Sweet was the name V.J. used. Timothy Sweet. Can you believe it? That guy has more nerve than brains!" He excused himself to make some phone calls.

Loralee breathed her words softly. "I can't believe it's true. But it is, isn't it? He's a bigamist, and we were never really married. I have to keep saying it over and over to myself."

"I can honestly say I know how you feel," Sammie said. "He was such a good liar. He had us convinced that he loved us."

Loralee looked past Sammie to some scene from yesterday. After moments, she spoke. "He stole from me, you know. He took all my jewelry, fine pieces my mother left me."

Her voice had grown softer until it wasn't much more than a whisper, and Sammie had to lean forward to hear. *God,* she prayed. He must have searched hard to find someone as fragile and trusting as Loralee, who looked as though she should be wearing crinoline and carrying a parasol.

"My story is pretty much the same," Sammie said. Sammie took Loralee's hand.

"I waited, you know," the woman went on. "For the right man. I wanted to give myself to one man for the rest of my life." Her green eyes filled with tears.

Sammie found herself whispering, "Me, too, Loralee." *The lowlife must specialize in virgins! Make that past tense. His days of specialization are over.* "Do you have family, friends, a pastor to help you through this?"

"Oh, yes. But I just want to hide. I'm so ashamed. I feel so…so terrible."

"Hide?" She put her arm around Loralee, who was blotting her tears. "Yes, I understand that, too." Speaking as much to herself as Loralee, she went on. "Taking time alone to heal is a good idea. But hiding?" She gave a rueful smile. "Not a good idea. I know." She hesitated, unsure whether or not to say more, then decided she must. "God can help."

Sammie waited as Loralee blew her nose delicately. "I'm a little farther down the road in all this than you are," she continued. "One thing I've learned is that we must not let this destroy our ability to trust those who deserve it. Not everyone is like V.J."

Dave caught the end of Sammie's sentence as he walked in the room and took in Loralee's wan face and smudged mascara. Both women rose to leave. Loralee smiled sadly and reached down to hug Sammie. "Thank you. Seeing and hearing you gives me the first ray of hope that I can make it, too. I'll try to take your advice."

After Loralee left, Dave gave Sammie a high five. "Sammie, my man, you've got what it takes!"

"Actually, I'm stunned that I could say what I did. Dave, I'm so angry I could go in his cell and tear V.J. apart. That poor woman. Without God, she doesn't have a prayer."

"Hey, kid! You're doing exactly what Uncle Dave said you should. Getting angry instead of blaming yourself. Even if you have to be angry about what V.J. did to Loralee instead of you."

"Dave, my thoughts have been such a mess, some days I've wanted to tip my head upside down, empty it out, sort through the thoughts piled on the floor, discard the irrelevant ones, and organize and put back the rest."

"Sorry. There are no shortcuts. While I'm thinking of it, Mama wants to know if you could come for dinner tonight."

"I wish I could. But I'll only be in town a short time, and I feel as though I need to be with my father as much as possible. Especially for dinner. You know how he is about that."

He nodded and looked at his watch. "It's just about quitting time. How about coming to Mama's now for coffee and some of her cake? You could still get back to your father's for dinner."

She followed him in her car to the neighborhood Mama vowed she would be carried out of feet first. There on the corner was St. Ignatius Church, across the street the bread store with crusty loaves piled in the window. The aproned, mustached produce man stood under the awning of his place, and a white cat guarded the butcher shop with salamis hanging in the window.

They climbed to the third floor of the brownstone where Dave grew up. "Mama huffs and puffs up these stairs, but she'd never admit they're too much for her."

He hadn't bothered to call ahead. Mama was always ready for company. He knocked and called her name and immediately the door swung open. Mama took one look at Sammie and enfolded her in her arms.

"Bambina! My little bambina." Pulling Sammie inside, she led her to the sofa. "Sit. Dave, get coffee and some of my cake from the bread box. I stay here with my little girl."

How I love this room, Sammie thought. The silk lampshades, the taffeta pillow with a poem about mother, the china cabinet crowded with every memento her children and grandchildren ever gave her. It told the story of Mama Vivano.

"You see him, that bum?"

"Only in the lineup, Mama."

"Maybe you should go see him in jail and shake-a you fist in his face. Nah, maybe not. Father Ryan would say not a good thing to do."

Mama drew back to get a good look at Sammie. "You shrunk. You little girl, now you littler. You need Mama's cooking. You stay and eat? The family is coming."

"I can't stay, Mama. I need to be with Pop. This is hard on him."

"I want to say no, you stay. But you right. You need to be with you poppa. So tell me all about the place you live now."

Sammie loved listening to the cadence of Mama's speech, like the rhythmic rocking of a boat. She described the shop and cottage as Mama sat holding her hand and nodding.

When she was finished, the three of them sipped coffee and ate the rich cake Mama had baked. Sammie asked about the family and exclaimed over photographs Dave brought out at his mother's bidding. Eventually Sammie glanced at her watch. "I have to go pretty soon. Pop will be getting home from the restaurant and looking for me."

Dave rose and carried their dishes to the kitchen as Mama opened her arms again and drew Sammie close. Buried in the soft, ample breast where dozens of children and grandchildren had been, Sammie felt safe. "You been hurting bad. And all alone, too." She rocked Sammie in her arms gently and crooned. "Mama's bambina. Mama loves you. It's gonna be all right."

Mama's love soothed and salved and melted. Months of unspent emotion poured down Sammie's face and onto Mama's blue cotton print dress. For minutes she sobbed as Mama rocked and crooned. When Sammie finally became quiet again, she wiped her face. "I'm sorry. I didn't mean to fall apart."

Dave entered the room again. "You needed to, Sammie." He smoothed his mother's graying hair, pulled back in a bun. "It's all Mama's fault."

After Sammie washed her face, she left for home with instructions from Mama to call and write, because mamas worry about their little girls.

Pop arrived hot and unraveled from the restaurant shortly after she got home. She suggested a swim before dinner, which was his favorite way to unwind, next to cooking. They floated and treaded water and talked about the lineup and his day at the restaurant and even splashed one another the way they used to.

About an hour later, he called her to dinner. The table had a centerpiece of pink roses. Pink candles were lighted and two places set with Mom's china. He brought in a platter of cheese blintzes, string beans with lemon, and cucumber and dill salad.

"Not too fancy, but the blitzes you can't get in the north woods, I bet." Afterward they drank iced tea on the patio.

Swimming and cooking had calmed him. Over dinner, she told him about the porch swing and that she'd volunteered to sell bagels when she returned. Just before they said good night, he made her promise to be home for dinner the next night.

For a long time she sat by the pool, letting "used-to-be" settle around her. How it was before V.J. and before Mom's death. How her life had been influenced by Mom's persistent goodness and faith. Her mind drifted to the present. Dave had known she needed to see his mama.

She felt exhausted. As she climbed in bed, she wondered what Brad would have thought about the events of the day and was glad he didn't know. But she was looking forward to working in the bagel booth with him on Saturday.

The next morning there was a note from Pop on the refrigerator. *Dinner at 6:30. Sorry I wasn't here to cut up your orange for breakfast. EAT! There's plenty of food in the refrigerator for breakfast and lunch. Rest yourself.*

For once she decided to obey her father. Instead of running all over the city to try and see this person or that, she'd make some phone calls. Besides, she had no desire to be cross-questioned.

Maybe I should go visit V.J. Face-to-face, she could ask him "Why?" and "Did you ever really love me?"

No. I no longer have a desire to spin a romantic fantasy that he loved only me. That he is terribly sorry for what he did and begs forgiveness. Even in custody, Dave had told her, V.J. was contemptuous of what he called "these sick women making false accusations because they don't have a life."

Aunt Tessie was glad to receive her call but she was on her way to B'nai Brith. Friends she called at the radio station wanted to know how she was and said how glad they were that V.J. was behind bars. Mina wasn't home, and Pastor Jim's secretary said he would be away all day attending a ministerial conference. That, she decided, was enough contact with the outside world.

When Tilda came to clean, she gave Sammie a Mama Vivano hug and remarked at how puny her girl was looking. Sammie remembered Pop's warning about the media and said, "If anyone comes looking for me that you don't know, ask for identification. If they're reporters, I don't want to see them."

After breakfast and a dip in the pool, Sammie felt an urge to sink into something soft and feel old times around her again, to walk through the garden, listen to Mom's worship music. She hadn't had a whole day with nothing to do since she'd opened the shop.

The hours were luxurious, and when she felt rested, she pored over the notations in her mother's Bible. Once, the doorbell rang and she could hear Tilda telling the caller in icy tones that Samantha Sternberg would not see him.

When Pop returned from Sophie's, she felt gentled by her day. V.J.'s trial was down the road, but at least he was behind bars, and what's more, he was not out on bail. And her day at home had reminded her that she'd had a good life before he came along.

She stuck her head in the kitchen, and Pop waved a wooden spoon at her. "Out! Can't you see that the chef is chefing?"

A few minutes later, he hunted her down in the den reading one of Mom's books. "Sammie, I need you to run to the store and buy me a pound of butter. It's an emergency, so go now."

It wasn't like Pop not to check and see if he had all the ingredients before he began cooking, but he hadn't exactly been himself lately. Quickly she slipped on her sandals, brushed her hair, applied fresh lipstick, grabbed her purse, and smoothed out her Tahoe print skirt. This was not a good time to keep Pop waiting.

In the supermarket she picked up a bag of tiny jelly beans because she'd noticed that his jar in the den was empty. Keeping it stocked with any color but black was one of Mom's thoughtful acts. *Ask Tilda to keep it full for him*, she wrote on her mental list.

The driveway was full of cars when she returned. What could have happened?

On her way to the back door, she looked more closely at them. A black Honda with a clergy sticker on the windshield. A white Chevrolet that looked suspiciously like Aunt Tessie's.

The moment her key was in the lock, the door flew open and a group of familiar faces appeared, yelling and whooping, and Pop was in the center of them. They burst into a loud, off-key rendition of "Happy Birthday."

Pastor Jim and his wife, Allissa, were there; Aunt Tessie, Sammie's cousins Lou and Rebecca who'd been best man and maid-of-honor at her wedding, Dave, and Mina. Obviously Pop had brought this particular group together to please her, since he merely tolerated Pastor Jim and Allissa, and Mina, too.

She poked Pop on the arm. "You old phony!" The next several minutes there were hugs and laughter and explanations.

"We were waiting down the street out of sight for your

father to give us the high sign that you were gone," Lou said.

"You think we'd let you get away without celebrating your birthday as soon as we had the chance?" Pop shook his head. "No way."

Aunt Tessie chattered breathlessly, and Dave grinned with obvious pleasure. "Mama wanted to be here, but she promised my brother Sal she'd baby-sit his kids so he and Maureen could get away to celebrate their anniversary."

The guests stacked gifts on the buffet in the dining room, and Pop had the table set with all her favorite foods. "I fixed them at Sophie's so you wouldn't know," Pop said. There were plates piled high with potato knishes and chicken livers with mushrooms, mini bagels and sliced turkey, buffalo wings, pizza, a watermelon basket of fresh fruit, and slices of rich, moist honey cake.

Giggles and guffaws filled the room. Those who hadn't seen it insisted she tell them all about the north woods and the Treasure House. She talked about Mechiah.

The food soon disappeared. She opened their gifts and was so touched her voice broke when she thanked everybody. The charm bracelet Pop sent on her birthday dangled from her wrist, and as she showed it around, Pop tried unsuccessfully to hide his delight.

Just when she thought the evening was about over, Pop disappeared into the kitchen and returned with a huge layer cake that read "Happy Birthday, Sammie."

She threw her arms around him, and he balanced the cake precariously. With one deep breath, she blew out all twenty-eight candles. Instead of making a wish, this time she prayed silently, *Teach me, Lord, what I need to learn.* The group applauded, and after he sat the cake in the center of the table, Pop responded with a big hug.

The idea of leaving tomorrow suddenly stabbed her. But it

was reassuring to know that she had roots and relationships here and nothing had severed them. What was even more astounding was that she didn't have to live here for the relationships to remain alive.

Before the guests began making moves to leave, she wanted a few moments of private conversations with each. Aunt Tessie and cousins Rebecca and Lou she invited to come for a vacation so she could show them the sights. When she cornered Dave, she let him know she was onto his motive for taking her to Mama's and thanked him. He answered with a birthday hug.

Mina took Sammie's hand. "You need to talk to someone when you're up there in the north woods? Call, Sammie dear. Call and we'll talk. I'm always here for you."

Sammie looked into Mina's honest face, grateful for the day she showed the New Testament with pictures to Mom in the library.

The last to leave were Pastor Jim and Allissa. Jim leaned forward on the sofa and got right to the point. "Have you been talking everything over with God?"

"More now. I'm studying my mother's Bible, too. She has all these notes in it."

Allissa clapped her hands together. "All evening I've been thinking about Sophie. She felt so privileged to be a Jew who had found the Messiah!"

Jim looked earnestly at Sammie. "Remember, God will take you through this time. You keep drawing near to God, and he'll draw near to you."

Pop, who had been carrying the leftover food into the kitchen, came in and sat on a straight-backed chair. "Yeah, Reverend, Sophie drew near to God and look what happened to her. She dropped dead in the rose garden."

Everyone remained silent, then Jim spoke softly. "I'm sorry, Sam."

Pop shrugged. "I have to admit that God did have a good week when he created the world. After that?" Humor was her father's way of neutralizing a conversation.

"You're not alone in how you feel, Sam. Maybe at a time that's more appropriate, we can talk."

"Thanks, Reverend, but talk doesn't change anything. God did what he did." He slapped his knee. "Right now, I want to talk about this daughter of mine. Maybe I should get out her baby pictures…"

"It's *my* birthday, and I say absolutely not."

Laughter broke the tension, but inside Sammie was very still.

My dear, sweet father is angry with God.

ELEVEN

Pop drove to the airport subdued after his outburst at Pastor Jim the evening before. She could almost hear him chastising himself that he'd really done it this time. From the moment he parked the car and headed them for the elevator, he guarded a mysterious brown paper bag about which he entertained no inquiries. Only when the boarding clerk announced that Sammie's seating section was boarding did he remove a gold gift box from the bag and hand it to her.

She sniffed it. "You didn't!"

"Oh, yes, I did."

She removed the lid. "Cheesecake!" Sophie's was famous for Pop's rich, delectable version. "If I share it with Mike and Autumn, he'll want the recipe, you know."

"You don't know the recipe. No one knows the recipe. Why do you think I make it at two in the morning when no one else is around?"

Sammie put down her packages, smoothed her father's gray hair, and then opened her arms. He loved so deeply and hurt so badly and tried to be both poppa and momma.

"Thanks, Pop. I promise to gain five pounds." She gave him a big hug, and they exchanged small smiles and waved good-bye before he turned and walked away.

Jennifer had worked as though she'd been trying for an A-plus while Sammie was gone. Every teacup was dusted, every deposit slip filed. "And guess what Mechiah did last night? I turned on the radio so he could listen like you told me, and he sang along with the commercial for Oscar Meyer. Honest!"

Sammie smiled, more at the change in Jen than at the idea of Mechiah singing along. *See what trust can do?* From a girl who was scared silly that she'd make a mistake, she's becoming a confident young woman. At least here, in the Treasure House.

Saturday, the day of the Bagel Booth, was a perfect end to August. She chose cool pink slacks and a white knit shirt Mom had decorated with pink roses for her. Always before, she'd taken it out, held it indecisively, then put it back. Today, it looked right and felt right, she decided as she stared at her reflection.

Brad was opening the booth when she arrived a little before ten. He laughed as he handed her a blue and white striped apron like the one he had on. "I'm afraid it'll fit you six times."

She lifted it up at the waist and wrapped the long ties around and around, making a bow in the front. "How do I look?"

He stepped back and surveyed. "You look good, Sammie," he said with a seriousness that startled and flustered her. "And I'm glad you're here. And not just because you're our resident expert in bagels."

Fortunately, at that moment a red-haired, freckle-faced teenage boy who obviously lifted weights came in the back door of the booth. "This is Cameron," Brad handed him an apron. "He worked here last year. Cam knows as much about this as I do." The boy blushed, and she smiled at the contradiction of a body builder who blushes.

Soon after the festival opened, a line formed at the Bagel Booth for breakfast sandwiches. Sammie took orders, Brad worked at the sandwich board, and Cameron served beverages and acted as cashier. Customers took their food and found places on benches or the grass to dine.

Merchants had set out tables of items for a sidewalk sale, and people had begun strolling and browsing. In addition to bagels, other booths served Chinese and Mexican food, fried chicken, elephant ears, donuts and scones, strawberry short-cake, and cotton candy. Each was to benefit a charity.

One of several musical groups scheduled to play today was assembling in the gazebo. A clown would create balloon animals for the kids, and firemen would demonstrate the drop-and-role fire safety technique. At the opposite end of the square, kiddie games were set up, and Sammie could see a small boy tossing a bean bag in hopes of choosing a prize from a plastic bucket.

When the next customer stepped up to the counter, Sammie nearly choked on her, "May I help you?" It was Harry who had verbally attacked her at the Merchants Association potluck.

"Well, well, if it isn't Sam Sternberg's daughter, Sammie. You're giving the Bagel Booth authenticity, I see."

She forced herself to smile pleasantly. "Can I get you a bagel sandwich? It's for a good cause."

"Me eat Jew food? I guess not. As a matter of fact, why can't your church sell some American food?"

"Do you have a problem with that, Harry?" Brad swiveled, stepping in front of Sammie, and looked unflinchingly at him.

Harry clenched his jaw. "You bet I do."

"We love Jews, Harry. Jesus was a Jew, you know."

"So you're defending your little star of David, here. Is she something special to you? Don't let your guard down, Brad. Keep your eye on the cash register. She might want a little something off the top for Sternberg."

Cameron stepped alongside Brad to help shield Sammie from the gathering crowd. His face was flushed and his body tense, as though he was ready to use some of the muscle he'd worked so hard to build.

Surprisingly, Brad's voice softened. He spoke gently but

firmly like a parent taking charge. "I know why you hate Jews, Harry, and I'm sorry for what happened. But it's wrong to base your ideas about a group of people on one terrible experience. You're not evening the score this way. I'm sorry for you. You're sick, and you need help."

Harry uttered an oath, turned, and walked across the green and out of the village square.

The crowd of people who'd gathered were murmuring and shaking their heads. Several spoke appreciatively to Brad and sympathetically to Sammie. Brad put his arm around her shoulder. "I'm sorry, Sammie."

She couldn't stop shaking. With a word to Cam to take over, Brad led Sammie out the back door of the booth. As he did so, Miss M. appeared as if by magic and offered to help out.

Brad led Sammie down Main Street and stopped in a quiet place down a side street under a shade tree where his van was parked. After he had her safely seated, he slid beside her in the driver's seat. Even though the temperature was rising fast, Sammie was still shivering as though an arctic blast had managed to seek and find only her.

Brad reached into the back seat, retrieved a plaid woolen blanket and covered her with it, then leaned against his door.

"Maybe if I explain what happened to Harry, it'll be easier." He stared down the quiet street. "When he was a teenager, his father went into partnership with a man who was Jewish. The partner kept the books, and Harry's father trusted him. But the man was secretly skimming money, and eventually he milked the business dry and took off. The business failed and Harry's father was left with enormous bills he couldn't pay. He left a note saying he was too ashamed to go on. Harry found him hanging in the garage.

"Harry had to quit school and help support the family. Life was hard for him after that. Instead of becoming a doctor the way he dreamed, he worked his way up in the wholesale grocery business. Harry has blamed all Jews for ruining his life. His wife left him. His grown kids won't have much to do with him."

Sammie closed her eyes and rubbed her forehead. Finally, she opened them and stared out at the street. "Thanks for telling me." She looked at him gratefully. "And thanks for standing up for me back there...and for protecting me." Her voice broke. The shivering had stopped, and now she felt very, very tired.

"It's not like this hasn't happened to me before," she went on. "It is easier knowing why." She glanced down at the shirt her mother had decorated with roses.

They sat quietly, listening to their thoughts and the background sounds of the autumn harvest festival. "All those people who heard what Harry said..." she began and turned to look Brad in the face. "They were *for* me...they supported me..." Tears came to her eyes and she brushed them away quickly.

Seeing her tears, Brad reached for her hand and held it. *The natural thing to do,* Sammie told herself.

"Do you want me to drive you home? I could come get your car later and bring it to your house."

"No. Sternbergs have never been quitters, and I can't change the tradition now. I want to finish my shift."

Cam seemed surprised and pleased to see her, and so did Miss M. For the next three hours, Sammie took orders almost steadily, joining Brad to make sandwiches when another volunteer came on board. At two, when she left, there wasn't time for more than a quick "so long" because of the customers who had waited late to have lunch and were hungry.

Jen was definitely ready to be relieved when Sammie got to the shop. "We may not be on Main Street, but the crowds came anyway."

By closing time, Sammie was bone weary. At home, she kicked off her shoes, tuned the radio to a station that played Christian music, and collapsed on the sofa with a glass of iced tea. Dinner would have to wait. Doing nothing was what she wanted most right now.

When the inspirational chorus "Something Beautiful" began playing, Mechiah cocked his head. What he did next made her want to run to the phone and call Art Humble. For, true to Jen's words, he was actually trying to sing along. When he stopped, she applauded and praised him with, "Mechiah sings pretty." Art would say that this proved not only that he was one smart bird but that he was happy with Sammie.

It was while she was applauding that the doorbell rang.

Brad stood on the step carrying a large box. "I came to see if you're too sick of bagels to eat some for dinner. We had left-overs with all the makings for super sandwiches."

Mechiah answered before she had a chance. "Polly wants a cracker."

Brad looked startled until she explained about her parrot. At her invitation, Brad spread the sandwich makings on the kitchen counter and went to work. "You just relax."

As they ate, she raved. "My father, who owns a restaurant, would be impressed." She liked being with Brad, but she'd liked being with V.J., too. Brad was a Christian; V.J. only professed to be one. He'd convinced her, though. But then, she wanted to be convinced.

Mechiah chewed on his rope, ringing the bell and chattering insistently like a spoiled child, wanting attention. After they ate, Sammie took the gray out of the cage. Brad gave the bird time to feel at ease with him before he stroked him.

"You want to be his friend for life? Get an apple from the refrigerator and cut pieces for him."

"Any bird friend of yours is a bird friend of mine."

Brad watched with amusement as Mechiah went to his high perch to eat his food. "How about teaching him to say, 'Mechiah loves Brad?'" he teased.

"Give him treats very often and I may not have to. He'll come up with it on his own."

They stood awkwardly for a few moments, and he suggested he should probably go and let her rest. As they walked out the front door, he commented on the swing. "It's one of my favorite places," she confessed. She asked if he'd like to try it out.

, They sat on opposite ends and quietly swung, each enjoying the evening breeze and greenery. She reminisced to him about Grandma and Grandpa Levine. Then, taken by the mood, she asked, "Do you have a family?" As soon as the words were out of her mouth, she called herself stupid for getting personal with a man who'd made it clear that his life bore a "no trespassing" sign.

He rubbed his ear, a gesture she hadn't realized he repeated when he was tense, then said, "I have a sister who teaches school in Ohio, where I came from originally. That's my family."

"How did you come to choose Pineville Beach? I was looking for a place to open the Treasure House and knew I'd found it when I drove across the bridge and into town."

He shifted. "About the same for me. I was looking for a place to live and paint, and this was it."

She had a feeling they were both edging their way around secrets. "Do you have a studio with a skylight and lots of windows like in the movies?"

He laughed. "I built a house on the river, and yes, my studio does have lots of windows and the proverbial skylight." No invitation to come see it, she noted.

After a few more minutes of swinging, he rose to go. She stood and offered her hand, but instead of shaking it, he held it. "I just wanted to tell you again that I'm sorry about Harry," he said. "You were a credit to the name of Sternberg the way you handled it."

"If it weren't for you and Cam…" She walked him to his car. "You know? I'm sorry for Harry. He's throwing his life away."

He settled behind the wheel. "Ever since I met him, I've been praying for him."

"I…I'll pray for him, too."

After Brad left, Sammie took a walk through the neighborhood and measured the words she'd spoken that evening as though they were distances and she'd gone too far. By initiating the visit, hadn't Brad made himself vulnerable? The question was: how vulnerable did she want to allow herself to be?

Miss M. called the next morning while Sammie was getting ready for church. "I can't believe how clumsy I am. Yesterday, I fell off the ladder while I was working on the house and sprained my ankle. So I won't be at church today." No, she didn't need anything, she insisted, except to practice getting around on crutches, a feat that so far had escaped her.

The service was about to begin when Brad slipped into the pew beside Sammie. At first she felt pleased and flattered that he sought her out. But during worship, she kept having flashbacks of V.J. beside her, head bowed, reaching to hold her hand. Why did the past keep invading the present?

Before, she'd been able to keep her thoughts carefully concealed beneath a placid exterior. This morning, though, she felt as if they were storming the gate and threatening to push it down.

After the store closed, she went for a long walk on the beach, hoping the salt air would purge her mind. However, while the exercise tired her body, an hour later her mind was still an unsorted jumble.

Monday, Tuesday, and Wednesday mornings she rode her bike to her secret place before opening the Treasure House. For a long while, she sat thinking her thoughts in God's presence.

Brad's quiet strength made her feel secure. He had a depth of soul that she knew she hadn't begun to plumb.

In this protected place where nothing interrupted but a chirping bird, she prayed for Harry's pain and wasted life and asked for his healing and for Pop in his spiritual struggle. "Help Pop to believe in the Yahweh of his people." All she could pray for V.J. was that justice would be done. Sensory impressions of the tiniest wildflower and the tallest pine sang glory to God like an earth choir.

Each day, she studied Mom's Bible. On Monday, she rejoiced in Psalm 147 with her mother over the fact that the Creator of the universe also sustains those who are humble before him. On Tuesday she praised God with her mother that they'd embraced Jesus as the Christ of God the way Peter did in Luke 9. On Wednesday, she prayed to receive Jesus' attitude of humility in Philippians 2.

Wednesday evening was perfect for puttering in the yard. Sammie filled the bird feeder and put out peanuts for early-morning squirrel visitors, pulled stray weeds, and removed dead blossoms. She would water in the morning. Before too long, the squirrels and flowers would be gone and steady rain would replace the sunshine.

After a leisurely bath, she cut a piece of Pop's cheesecake and sat at the table eating and trying to convince Mechiah that birds didn't like it. He was squawking back objections when she heard a loud clattering crash, like baking pans thrown to the floor, coming from the Le Ducs'. It was followed by a smashing sound she couldn't identify.

Autumn's pleading voice was the one she heard first. Then, Mike's roar. A door slammed. Autumn called Mike's name.

Sammie began to shiver the way she had on Saturday after the encounter with Harry. What should she do? Close the door and windows and turn up the radio? Call 911? Mike was yelling about Autumn's stupidity, and Autumn was crying.

God? Sammie prayed.

Immediately, she had a clear impression that she had to go next door and help Autumn. Making her way through the bushes, she found Autumn crouched on the ground the way she'd been last time, only now Mike was standing over her, cursing.

As Sammie knelt and put her arms around Autumn, Mike turned the force of his anger on Sammie. "Get out of here! Go on, get! This is none of your business."

She stood up and faced him the way Brad had done with Harry. "Back off! Leave your wife alone! Do it now, Mike!" she said with steel in her voice. "I'm taking her home with me."

Sammie hoped he couldn't see her shaking. Terrified, she turned her back on him and led Autumn through the bushes to her house. Mike ran after them, yelling for her to come back. Without a word, the two women stepped inside the cottage, and Sammie closed the door behind them.

Sipping hot tea, Autumn explained through chattering teeth. "Mike did a wedding cake, and the people didn't come to pick it up when they said they would. He asked me to call, and I did. But I couldn't reach them. Then he asked me to help him finish a tray of Napoleons for Margie's Catering. I forgot to call again about the cake.

"When the people did call, they were mad because they thought Mike was going to deliver it. They're influential, and Mike thinks they'll ruin him, and it's all my fault."

Autumn began to sob again, and Sammie spoke soothingly. "No more talk now. Come on, I'll fix you a bath. You soak and relax. You're staying the night." Autumn was reluctant, but when Sammie insisted, she finally acquiesced.

While she was in the tub, Mike came pounding on the door. "Let me in. Who do you think you are? Autumn's my wife, and I want her home now!"

Be calm and take charge. Sammie spoke forcefully and deliberately "Go home and cool off, Mike. If you don't, I'll call the police. You can see Autumn in the morning."

That moment, Autumn burst through the bathroom door with a towel draped around her, dripping water and fear. Mike hit the door with his fist. Then there was silence.

She turned back to Autumn. "It's okay. Go soak some more. I don't think he'll be back tonight."

As they lay side by side in bed, Sammie wished she felt as calm as she forced herself to sound as she handed Autumn Mrs. Nelson's bear. "He's perfect for hugging."

Autumn scrunched under the sheet and wrapped her arms around the bear. "Mike didn't used to be like this. Not this bad, anyway. He's so afraid the bakery will fail. We've only had it for a year and a half. I think Mike figures someone like him could never make it work."

She sat up in bed, still hugging the bear, and looking younger than Jen. "Mike's folks were drunks. His older brother left home as soon as he could and Mike took off at fifteen. He knocked around, surviving however he could. Then he got a job as a baker's apprentice. He got jobs in donut shops and small bakeries for minimum wage to get experience, barely managing to make it. When he came into Pineville Beach broke and out of work, Mrs. Nelson gave him a place to stay and helped him find a job. A year and a half ago, she loaned him the money to open the bakery."

Learning that Mrs. Nelson had been his savior didn't surprise Sammie. Autumn lay back down and turned on her side to look at Sammie in the moonlight. "The bakery was his

187

dream. Mrs. Nelson was the first person in his whole life who ever believed in him. He thinks he doesn't deserve anything good to happen to him. By nighttime, all the worry builds up—especially now, when business slacks off. He gets to the place where he can't handle it any more."

She shook her head. "He doesn't get drunk or use drugs. It's not that. His folks always told him he'd never amount to anything. He believes them, I guess."

Dear God. Are there secrets behind every door?

Autumn's words came more slowly now. "No matter how good business is, he's sure that it's only temporary and that tomorrow, he'll fail. I love him, but I don't know how to help him." Soon, her voice trailed off, and she fell into an exhausted sleep.

Minutes ticked away on the bedside clock. Sammie feared that if Mike didn't get help, he might do more than yell or pound the wall. Next time, Autumn might feel the physical force of his wrath. As she drifted off, Sammie thought of Mrs. Nelson at the door of her house, shotgun in hand, defending Aimee against an abusive husband.

At sunrise, Autumn was out of bed and getting dressed. "Mike needs me. He has several big orders to bake, plus all the regular stuff." She pushed back her blond hair, then sat on the edge of the bed to put on her shoes.

Suddenly, she wilted. "I'm scared to go home, Sammie. So scared of what's going to happen when I do."

Sammie jumped out of bed and reached for a pair of jeans. "I'm going with you. Chances are everything will be okay."

They found him in the bakery kitchen rolling dough for pies. He looked up and nodded slightly to acknowledge their presence. "I have a dozen pies to get ready by ten," he told his wife and gestured to pans of donuts cooling on racks. "I need you to ice and glaze them." As though nothing had happened.

Autumn put on her apron and went to work.

Jen came to work later that morning balancing a large cardboard box on her bike. "More rugs!" she grinned between breaths. They spread out a heart-shaped yellow one in the window seat and a red, white, and blue one on a chair in the dining room. Draped on chairs and laid over tables, the woolen hooked rugs beautifully displayed their authentic, early American patterns. Sammie and Jen stood back, pleased at what they saw.

"See?" Jen held out a tag on one of the rugs. "We got them printed the way you said. Mom's so proud. My father said absolutely no to the tags at first. But when we told him what you said about increasing sales, he changed his mind."

Jen evidently didn't know what had happened next door the night before. Sooner or later, though, she would.

On Thursday evening, Mina Bloom called. "You've been on my mind so much the last few days, I just had to find out if everything's okay."

Sammie recounted her experience with Harry and Mike and Autumn and the mornings she'd spent in her secret place with God. How she seemed to be hearing from God during those hours. How she wished she'd hear from him more the rest of the time the way other Christians said they did.

Mina chuckled. "God doesn't just speak words, like 'Go here, do this, go there, and do that.' He guides us all kinds of ways. Trust him. He'll make something beautiful out of your life."

Something beautiful, Sammie mused. "Oh, Mina, I'll never be the Christian Mom was."

"Sammie, learn from what Sophie wrote in her Bible. But don't try to be Sophie. God made you a unique person. Find out who he created you to be."

Until V.J. came into her life, she thought she knew. But

because of him, she'd redefined herself as a fool and a failure. A fool for believing a liar and a failure for allowing V.J. to steal the money her mother had inherited from Grandma and Grandpa Levine. Money they'd worked thirty years in the dry-goods store to save. Even God couldn't change that.

On Friday, when Jen came to work after school, Sammie drove to an estate sale and picked up some oak furniture to refinish during the winter months. When she returned, Jen put on her backpack. "Autumn told me about the other night. Thanks. If anything happened to her… Autumn always tried to protect Mom and me when my father got like that."

Before Sammie could comment, the girl was out the door, on her bike, and gone. *More secrets behind closed doors.* Only this one, she had to admit, was probably not very secret around Pineville Beach. And Jen's father did more than yell.

Things had been quiet next door all week. Sammie watched and listened, stopping in the bakery three times and talking briefly with Mike and Autumn when they were outside. On Saturday, she went next door on a mission—to buy coffee cake for Sunday breakfast and to invite Autumn to church the next day. There wasn't much chance that Mike would go. But would he keep Autumn from going?

Autumn was boxing pastries for a customer, and Mike was sitting at a table drinking coffee. After the woman left, Sammie and Autumn made small talk about the weather and how they had to appreciate every nice day they had from now on.

Sammie took a deep breath. "Miss M. took me to Pineville Community Church, and I really like it. Would you like to go with me tomorrow, Autumn?" Surprising even herself, she turned to Mike. "And you, too?"

Mike rose from the table and walked into the kitchen. "Not me." Before he disappeared, Autumn asked permission as if he were her father. "Can I go?"

"Suit yourself," he called over his shoulder. "As long as you're here to open up at one."

On Sunday morning, Autumn appeared at her door wearing a sherbet green dress with pearl buttons down the front and a matching band on her hair that set off her delicate coloring. Brad wasn't among the congregation, and Sammie decided he must be building towers with toddlers in the nursery. Miss M. came slowly down the aisle on crutches and plopped into the pew beside her with a grunt and a greeting.

Autumn sang the choruses and hymns in a sweet soprano that matched her personality. She seemed to absorb the pastor's sermon on love through the pores of her skin like sunlight.

Periodically, he recited his key verse from First John. "This is love: not that we loved God, but that he loved us and sent his Son as an atoning sacrifice for our sins." Jack Bishop offered God's love as a soothing balm, an ointment for the soul, and Sammie could almost see the Holy Spirit gently applying it to Autumn Le Duc.

Autumn looked as though her soul were still in the sanctuary when she got out of the car in front of the bakery. "Can I go with you next week?" Sammie said that she'd like nothing better.

~

Fall had dripped its way into Pineville Beach. Mornings the pines were often gauzed in fog, and when it cleared, huffs of it remained in the treetops. On some partly cloudy, partly sunny afternoons, Pineville Beachers rushed outside, they claimed, to dry off their feathers.

Most days Sammie decided, God must have set his sprinkler on permanent drizzle to keep the Northwest green. When tourists came into the shop, women shook the rain from their hair, and men asked if Sammie thought it was going to rain.

They bought wreaths and pottery pictures and pillows for their grown children and confided that they were going south.

Merchants in Pineville Beach who opened only for the tourist season had closed their doors until spring came to dry out the sopping terrain. Others pulled up the shades in their shops on weekends. Many, though, determined to make it through with the open sign visibly displayed and merchandise polished and ready.

Permanent residents provided enough business to keep open those stores which sold necessities. Enough people considered books a necessity to include Claudine. They seemed to think of Mike's bread and rolls and donuts as necessities, too. But he refused to believe he could make it through the winter. Only now, instead of yelling and cursing, he had grown sullen again.

Townspeople came and went through Sammie's doors to buy a birthday gift for a neighbor or to look for a dry sink to put in the kitchen they'd just remodeled. Late in October, after Sammie had refinished the furniture she'd bought at estate sales and inventoried it, she cleared a spot in the Treasure House kitchen to set up a table where she could make jewelry.

Not that she knew how she'd distribute it. The only outlet she had was the shop. But she had to have a sideline to keep going.

She organized her supplies on the table, starting with tubs of single earrings and necklaces with missing stones she'd purchased by the pound from jewelers. Alongside she spread out pin backs, linoleum samples for backing, glue, paper towels, and a soft cloth.

Her pins had caused a stir of excitement among her circle of acquaintances in Los Angeles. "I love the fact that every pin is unique," women would say. "I may go to a party and find someone else wearing my dress, but no one will ever have a lapel pin like mine."

Customers loved the fact that she made pins to order as well. "My sister loves Victorian things and her favorite color is teal," one would say. Without a plan in mind, Sammie played with the jewelry findings, eventually selected one that seemed right, and glued it to the backing. Lost in the creative process, she created an overlay of stones, gold, silver, and other material and produced an art object that would make the customer exclaim, "That's just right! My sister will love it!"

God had decided the northwest needed a good drenching on the October day she sat to work at the jewelry-making table in the Treasure House for the first time. This was the season Pop warned her about. Should she have listened? With the Treasure House empty of customers and her life empty of intimates, she was feeling desolate. Was this the way Noah's wife felt on the ark?

From the tub of jewelry findings, she grabbed handfuls, spread them on the table in front of her, and stared at them.

Broken pieces, she thought.

The chorus she and Mechiah heard on the radio and that Mina mentioned began singing in her head.

Something beautiful...

Her eye fell on a pendant with the center stone missing.

God, is that why you brought me to Pineville Beach? To make something beautiful out of the broken pieces of my life?

TWELVE

October continued to drip and drizzle, shower and pour. Birds chirped their gratitude for seeds in the feeder and pushed and shoved one another with a flurry of feathers for the right to feed. Sammie stood at the kitchen window and scolded, commiserating about hostility in the family of birds. Mechiah chattered defensively in the background, "Mechiah good bird."

On weekends, late vacationers came through town and drove away with candle sconces, Amish dolls, a foot warmer, a glove chair, linens, baskets, and china. "What a treasure!" they remarked delightedly and then laughed at their own joke when they realized that was the name of the shop.

Pop called at least once a week, or Sammie called him. "Are you getting moldy up there from all that rain?" he'd ask. "Growing moss? Down here the sun is shining." He asked every time if she was starving to death because business had dried up, and she assured him she was doing just fine.

After those conversations, she worried, then reminded herself that she'd saved money during the summer season and her rent was so low, thanks to Mrs. Nelson, so she should make it through. *If I figure out a way to sell my jewelry.*

When business was slow, she worked at the jewelry-making table. Wednesday afternoon, she was combining several small hearts and searching the bin for other pieces to complete the arrangement. *Lord, what am I going to do with these when I finish them?*

Even though she wore one of her pins every day as an advertisement, she knew she couldn't depend on enough customers coming in the shop through the winter to see the pins.

Would the Treasure House become one more shop with a closed sign hanging in the door?

She set the pin down and shut her eyes. *God, if you really did lead me here to Pineville Beach so you can make something beautiful out of my life, you'll have to help me make enough money to stay here.*

Immediately, Sammie felt guilty for telling God what to do.

Mom's Bible was on the drop-leaf table at her elbow where Sammie placed it every morning so she could read when she had time during the day. She turned to the Sermon on the Mount, where she'd stopped reading the day before.

"Your Father knows what you need before you ask him," she read in Matthew chapter 6.

I needed Pineville Beach. Mechiah. Birds to build their nest under the eaves. God knew I needed these things.

"This is how you should pray," Jesus went on. Did his voice soften with gentleness as he taught the Lord's Prayer? Or did he speak the words with eternal authority?

"Our Father who art in heaven, hallowed be your name, your kingdom come, your will be done on earth as it is in heaven. Give us this day our daily bread…"

Give us this day our daily bread. Jesus taught us to ask for daily essentials. Making enough money to survive was an essential.

She looked around for someone to tell. "Guess what God just showed me! He wants me to trust him for my daily needs."

Maybe Brad would drop into the shop. If he did, should she tell him?

That afternoon while she was arranging dried flowers in baskets, the bell jangled. A woman with a smile like the pot of gold at the end of the rainbow stood dripping on the rug just inside the front door. She removed her wire-framed glasses to wipe them dry on a handkerchief and shook her rust-colored wash-and-wear curls like a spaniel after a bath.

"Wow! I thought of the Northwest as pleasantly damp but this is unpleasantly sopping! Not that I'm complaining. I'll take it any way I can get it." Her eyes looked like they were responding to some internal applause sign.

As she surveyed the room, she raved. "Can I spend a week just browsing?" Then she caught sight of the black and gold pin that Sammie was wearing on her vest. "Stunning!" Sammie showed her the display case of pins next to the cash register, each resting on its own black velvet bag, and she handed the woman a brochure.

The customer gasped and looked at Sammie. "Where do you sell them besides here?"

"Nowhere right now." Sammie hesitated. *Not a good idea to tell a customer my business problems,* she thought. Then, for a reason she couldn't explain, she went on. "Just this morning I prayed that God would help me sell my pins this winter during the off-season."

Instead of looking blank, the woman exploded. "God, you did it again!" She extended her hand. "I'm Mollie Holly. Not made up. It's my real name. My mother has a sense of humor. My business is to represent artists and craftspeople by selling their work at shows and to help get them in the marketing mainstream." She shook her head slowly. "You know, as I drove into Pineville Beach, I asked God to show me if he had something here for me to do. Why am I always so blown away when he goes ahead and does it?"

Mollie handed Sammie a business card. "I realize that for all you know I could be some kind of flake, but I can supply references. I'll be in town until tomorrow. May I come back this evening so we can talk?"

Sammie's mind raced. What was she getting herself into? But because she'd prayed earlier and God had brought to life, "Give us this day our daily bread," she agreed and offered to make dinner. "Only around here we call it supper."

Mollie Holly arrived promptly and energetically and told Mechiah that he was beautiful. The bird promptly gifted her with his entire vocabulary.

She rubbed her hands together when she saw the poor man's stroganoff Sammie had prepared. "At my age and with my genes, pounds move in and settle down without an invitation." She looked Sammie up and down. "A problem you'll never have. So hold me accountable. One helping only, and I'll savor each bite."

When they sat, Mollie asked permission to return thanks. Her words to God were as alive as her eyes.

When she lifted her head, she said, "I'd like to represent you and take your pins to shows. I'd also like to come up with a plan to get you broad exposure. For example, I know women in the public eye who would wear your pins. If I send you a list of names and information about each, could you make pins tied to their special interests?"

"Well, sure, but I can't believe you just walked in the shop the way you did and now here we are...."

Mollie's laugh was as rich and thick as melted chocolate. "We both know I didn't just 'walk in' by accident, honey." As she went on to explain how much she loved to help people find exposure for their talents, Sammie marveled at the woman's enthusiasm, which was a yard long.

Instead of shaking hands on the deal, Mollie suggested that they pray. "I'll send you a formal contract when I get back to the office." She took Sammie's hands and talked to the Lord as if she could see his face.

Brad stopped in on Friday and immediately admired the seashell motif pin she was wearing. His eye caught the display of pins, and he looked at each in the case for a long time, saying nothing, then read the brochure describing them.

"This is good, Sammie. This is just what I want for my sister's birthday. Could you make an 'Originally Yours' for her centered on a teacher theme?"

Brad MacKenzie, the artist, wanted her to create a special pin for his sister? Suddenly, Sammie felt uncertain. Her voice wavered. "I'll do my best."

"Your best will be perfect." He had a way of turning ordinary moments into intimate ones, she thought.

As always, Brad wandered the downstairs rooms to see the new displays she'd created. "There's a big blank spot over the organ," she reminded him pointedly. Weeks ago she'd sold his painting and had been waiting for him to bring a new one.

"Ummm" was all he said in reply. Summoning her courage she did tell him about her prayer and God's answer. He nodded slowly as she spoke. "Sammie Sternberg. You are a kosher blessing."

She snickered. "There's nothing kosher about me, except the dill pickles in my refrigerator."

Never, she noticed, did he go upstairs on his inspections. Not since the first day, when he'd come down shaken and left abruptly.

Now that the season had slowed, she had to cut Jen's hours but was determined not to let her go. On Friday, when Jen drove her mother to town for groceries in the family pickup, they stopped in the shop. Sammie handed Dossie Mae a check for rugs sold the previous month and gave her a hug of congratulations. The woman sucked in a gasp of pain.

"What's wrong?"

Jen watched her mother with ancient eyes. "Oh, my back is hurting today. It's nothing." She looked at the check. "Jen, maybe I can buy you ice cream before we go home."

Another ailment? Sammie thought after they left. Or was

she hiding bruises beneath her cotton housedress? The look in Jen's eyes seemed to tell the story.

After closing, Sammie walked next door to see how the Le Ducs' off-season business plans were going. They'd begun serving homemade soup and chili daily, along with Mike's bread, rolls, cakes, and pies, and it brought in a lunch crowd. The Bakery was also becoming the morning meeting place for people who worked this side of town, and they came away with desserts for dinner too time consuming to make at home.

Since the standoff when Autumn spent the night with Sammie, Mike had come pretty close to exploding a few times, Autumn told her privately. "He's been getting in the van and taking off when he becomes angry. Sometimes, he's away for a long time, and I don't know where he goes or what he does. When he comes home, he's quieted down."

She looks so fragile, Sammie thought.

"I get so tired of it," Autumn went on. "It's like I'm on one of those roller coasters at the carnival that comes to town. It goes up and down, then goes along smooth and even and next thing you know it's climbing and going down so fast your stomach does flips."

Each week Autumn went to church with Sammie and basked in God's presence. On "Service Opportunity" Sunday in October, they raised their hands to take a birthday cake to a nursing home once a month. Mike grudgingly agreed to contribute the cake and the two of them led singing and games with patients and came home pleasantly satisfied.

Sammie grinned to herself as she dressed for church on the first Sunday in November. *Communion Sunday and I'm actually looking forward to it!* She recalled her first experience, when she nearly walked out. Now when the trays reached her, she took the elements with great care, thinking only that they represented Calvary.

From her personal collection of lapel pins, she'd chosen one to wear with a cross in the center surrounded by star bursts. It looked as though the message of the crucifixion was exploding into the world. When Miss M. slid into the pew next to her, no longer on crutches or using a cane, she admired the pin.

"You have talent to burn, girl," Miss M. whispered, and Autumn smiled in agreement.

As the pastor walked to the pulpit to begin the service, Miss M. added, "How about if I do a feature article on 'Originally Yours' for the paper?"

Sammie nodded.

After the service ended, they made arrangements for Miss M. to come to the shop after closing time the next day for an interview.

———

"I have to control myself," the newspaper woman began when she arrived, giving Sammie a start. "Keep my mind on business, I mean, when what I'd like to do is wander around and find a lamp and maybe a hutch for my living room. It's getting close to done, finally."

In answer to Miss M.'s questions, Sammie explained that sometimes a customer gave her old jewelry that belonged to a deceased family member. No one wanted to wear the pieces because they were out of style, so they commissioned her to make pins from these to wear in memory of the loved one.

Miss M. held up a pin. "I hadn't made the connection between the jewelry and the rest of the items for sale in the Treasure House." She fingered through the tub of findings and held up a necklace with stones missing, then leaned forward and looked Sammie square in the face. "Does your passion have anything to do with the fact that you're making something beautiful out of broken things?"

"I...I didn't think of it that way when I started." With more certainty, she went on. "But, yes, I guess I do like resurrecting things that no one wants." She pointed to a discarded wooden window frame on the wall that she'd refinished and decorated with fish hooks and flies. "Like that, for instance."

Miss M. set her notepad and pen down, ran her fingers through her gray hair, propped her elbow on the table, and leaned her face on her hand. For several moments, she stared into space.

"I know, Sammie. I know why you left California. I know what happened."

How many times had Sammie fantasized this moment? Manufactured responses to every possible scenario? And now that it was here, she couldn't think of a thing to say.

Awkwardly, Miss M. took Sammie's hand. "I'm not good at this. I just want you to know that your secret is safe with me. I won't publish it in the paper; I won't tell anyone in town. I've known for quite awhile."

She let go of Sammie's hand, stood up, and began pacing. "You're not the only one who was hurting when she came to Pineville Beach. Who wanted to start over. I used to be on a big-city newspaper. You knew that. I'd been there a long time and was getting a reputation in the news business. I loved getting the big stories and the big headlines. Having been in the news business, you know about that, too."

Sammie nodded.

"Then our paper was bought out and the new owners had a tabloid mentality. Sensationalism, never mind the facts. It meant compromise my ethics or get out while I still had some.

"It was about that time that a journalist friend told me about Christ. I gave him a hard time with my questions, the way you might expect I would. He simply showed me the answers in the Bible, and I respected the Bible because my mother taught me to.

201

"About that time, it all came down at the paper. I did decide to resign, and for the first time in my life I actually prayed for God to show me what to do. When he seemed to be leading me to buy a small-town newspaper, I was stunned. How could I ever be happy in Podunk writing about city council meetings and selling advertising to feed stores? It was a matter of faith."

Heavily, Miss M. sank back in her chair. "My city reporter friends made fun of me, Sammie. They still see me as a failure. It's been years, but I still hear about it. Word is that I'm a nobody in a place where nothing happens."

Looking in Sammie's eyes, she leveled each word like a soft-ball at a target. "But…God…was…right. I've never been happier. Right here, with my one-horse newspaper in my mess of a house."

Minutes later, she left. As soon as she'd driven away, Sammie walked out the front door and down the steps. It was dark now; shops were closed and people on the street had retreated to their private lives. Still she stepped into the shadows.

How had Miss M. found out? When did she first know? Right after Sammie came to town because she'd read stories in the Los Angeles papers? Or recently when Sammie returned to Los Angeles to identify V.J.?

Because of two words, she now felt naked. *I know.* She wanted to sink to the ground in a heap and have someone wrap protective arms around her. Pop. Mama Vivano. Brad. Yes, Brad.

Miss M. said she wouldn't tell. But wouldn't she be tempted to whisper her secret to just one confidant? Wouldn't that person be tempted to whisper to just one other?

The following Sunday in church, Miss M. made no indication that their conversation ever took place. Still, Sammie was uncomfortable joining hands for prayer and made excuses about why she couldn't stop by the house after church.

Thanksgiving was less than three weeks away when Pop called asking her to fly down and spend it with him. "You know I cook the best turkey west of the Mississippi."

"I can't. That Friday and Saturday I have to open the shop."

The truth was she didn't want to fly to Los Angeles. She changed the subject by telling him about Mollie Holly and promising to send him a copy of the newspaper article.

"Hey, maybe I can get some of the women I know through the restaurant to wear pins. You know, the ones who are written up in the columns." He named several prominent women they both knew.

"I'd design pins especially for them," Sammie said.

Pop let her know he wouldn't have much to be thankful for if she was in the north woods and he was in California for Thanksgiving. She tried to placate him by promising to call on that day.

That same evening, Brad called to talk about Thanksgiving as well. "I'll be helping with the Thanksgiving Day dinner the church is having. Do you want to join me?"

"Strange that you should call right now. I just turned down Pop's invitation to fly to California for Thanksgiving." Would Miss M. be there? Part of her wanted to say thanks but no thanks and spend the day with Mechiah.

On the other hand, at the church she could be with Brad. And keeping busy would be better than spending the day replaying the soap opera of her life. "I haven't inherited my father's talent for cooking, you know. But I'll do what I can."

"I thought you could head up the group that decorates the tables. Give it the Treasure-House touch."

Why couldn't he add that he'd like to be with her? Was it reasonable to read that into what he'd said? Or was he just prompting her to be more active in the church?

Sammie, don't you realize that if Miss M. could find out about

V.J., Brad could, too? Brad has all kinds of contacts. You could be just as naked before him as you are with Miss M., only he hasn't said anything.

The next couple of weeks, she lived in fast forward. Gulping morning coffee as she dressed, straightening the cottage, making "to do" lists, throwing in a load of laundry, putting seed in the bird feeder and peanuts out for the squirrels.

Days in the Treasure House she refinished furniture, cleaned the shop from top to bottom, and made jewelry for Pop's society friends and for Mollie to sell at shows. She ordered inventory and paid bills and cleaned files and scheduled Jen in order to get away to auctions and estate sales. After work, she rode her bike or walked the beach. Twice, she ran with Art Humble.

Some evenings and weekends she met with the Thanksgiving dinner decorating committee of which she was appointed chairperson and worked on centerpieces and banners. One evening, she went to the Farmer's Wife for dinner with Claudine, scrupulously avoiding personal conversation.

She took Mrs. Nelson for tea and crumpets at Abby's and celebrated monthly birthdays with Autumn in the nursing home. She dropped in at the bakery to check on Autumn when she saw Mike take off in the van. The girl looked worn, a junior version of her mother, and Sammie wondered how long she could go on this way. Mike needed help, but Autumn said flatly that he wouldn't agree to get it.

To cap off the evenings, Sammie collapsed with a cup of mint tea on the sofa and hand fed Mechiah a treat. If he became too curious afterward and knocked over a vase of flowers or got into the candy dish, she put the offended bird back in his cage for the night.

Wednesday evening before Thanksgiving she had just stepped out of the shower, toweled her hair, and slipped into her robe when the doorbell rang. Cautiously she called out, "Who is it?"

"Special Thanksgiving delivery!"

Emotions that had gone to bed for the night jumped alert and sounded in a cacophony. "Pop? *Pop?*"

It couldn't be, but she knew it was. She threw open the door to see his grinning face. He pointed to the handmade sign he wore on the front of his navy waterproof jacket. *Deliver me to Sammie Sternberg, the Treasure House, North Woods, U.S.A.*

They yelled each other's name as they hugged long and fiercely. "You wouldn't come to me, so I came to you," he said matter-of-factly when they finally quieted down and she pulled him inside.

"Thanksgiving by phone is no substitute for turkey and mashed potatoes and gravy and stuffing across the table," he said. "Even if we do have to go to the Farmer's Wife to get it, since there's no time to buy and cook for tomorrow. And that's some compromise, let me tell you!"

But she had to be at the church for dinner! Even though the decorations were all in place, she'd agreed to help Brad in the kitchen. *Pop, you didn't even consider that I might have plans.* His face was shining the way it had the evening he surprised her with a birthday party.

She explained about the dinner Pineville Community Church was serving and her commitment to help. *It couldn't be worse.* The last place her father would want to be on Thanksgiving was in church with a bunch of Christians.

"Oh." It was a tiny puff of a word. She hadn't seen this deflated, defeated version of her father since the early weeks after Mom's death.

He sat woodenly in a chair. "To surprise you was stupid. You have a life here...." He rose and picked up his suitcase. "I'll just go to the bed-and-breakfast. I called ahead and reserved a room."

"Pop." She put her hand on his shoulder and gently pushed him down. This was no facade to make her sorry and change her plans. He had reached out for used-to-be and found here-and-now instead.

"It's just that I have a commitment. You know you taught me to keep my word. So how about you come with me? These are nice people. I'd like you to meet them."

Without enthusiasm, he agreed. She suggested that, since he'd be in town until Saturday, maybe they could have their private dinner on Friday. His face brightened slightly. "How about if I cook? I could get everything Friday morning."

She made tea and sliced applesauce cake she'd baked during her whirlwind of work and uncovered Mechiah who'd gone to sleep for the night. He blinked and stared, then clucked a scolding at her thoughtlessness.

Pop shook his head. "I still say why couldn't you be like other daughters and get a puppy or a kitten?"

Mechiah interrupted. "Kitty, kitty, kitty…"

They laughed and talked about Sophie's and the Treasure House and "Originally Yours."

After one more slice of cake that he pronounced not half bad, Pop kissed her and left for the night.

Thanksgiving dinner was scheduled for 1:00 P.M., but Sammie had to be there by 11:30. She offered to return home for Pop just before mealtime, but he insisted on going along early. All morning Sammie had been breathing prayers for God to use Pop's presence at the meal for good in his life.

Sammie inhaled the aroma of turkey as they entered the church building. Brad was in the kitchen preparing sweet potato casseroles, a towel tucked around his waist. Christa and Harry Matthews, a middle-aged couple from the church, were peeling potatoes next to him, aprons around their ample waists.

Still praying, Sammie introduced her father. At the sight of the food-laden kitchen, Pop came to life. "You didn't know you'd have help imported all the way from Los Angeles!" He inspected Brad's sweet potato casseroles. When Sammie explained quickly that her father was a chef and restaurant owner, Brad stepped aside. "Be my guest."

She tucked a towel around her father's waist and nervously left to check on the tables she and the committee had set the day before.

It looks like a banquet hall, she thought with satisfaction. White tablecloths, candles in holders borrowed from the Treasure House, cornucopias spilling with miniature pumpkins, gourds, polished apples, and tiny dried ears of corn. On the walls hung the banners they'd made. Each celebrated God.

THANKS BE TO GOD FOR HIS INDESCRIBABLE GIFT
GIVE THANKS TO THE LORD
ENTER HIS GATES WITH THANKSGIVING AND
HIS COURTS WITH PRAISE

Back in the kitchen she worked on relish trays, breathing a prayer of thanks that her father was occupied with two of the things he liked most: preparing food and talking with people.

By one o'clock, families dressed in finery put away for special occasions had entered the sanctuary-turned-dining room and stood in knots, moaning with pleasure over the aroma of turkey and stuffing.

Hostesses urged them to find seats at the tables and provided booster seats for toddlers. "No separate tables for the children," the committee had decided earlier. "We'll sit as families and make sure singles aren't left out. After all, it's the family of God

207

who'll be gathered to give thanks. So we're all related."

Assisted by high schoolers, the kitchen crew carried out platters of succulent turkey, bowls of dressing, sweet potato casseroles, vegetables, sparkling Jell-O salads, rolls, relish plates, and cranberry sauce. When the tables were laden with food, cooks and servers removed aprons and towels and sat down. Sammie arranged for Pop to sit between Brad and her.

The pastor stood and sounded a fork on his water tumbler for attention. "Welcome to God's Thanksgiving table. Let's bow and pray."

Sammie stole a nervous glance at her father. Eyes open, he stared straight ahead.

As the meal started, Brad bragged to others at the table about Pop's expertise in the kitchen, then looked at Sammie. "Talent runs in the family."

After the meal and before pies from Le Duc's bakery, the pastor rose. "It's customary to thank God for something he's done for us personally this past year."

Across the room, Miss M. raised her hand, and a lanky teenager scurried to her with a microphone. "I'm thankful I finally learned how to walk on crutches." Seriously, the newspaper editor went on, she would be ending the year in the black, and only God could make that happen.

Brad whispered that he was going to the kitchen to get dessert ready and see to the coffee and tea. When he rose to slip out, Pop followed. Sammie decided she'd better go, too.

Pop probably didn't realize that loudspeakers in the kitchen carried the testimonies. The three of them made more coffee and lined up pies and serving plates on the counter while they listened to a testimony about a child saved from terminal illness.

Pop turned to Brad. "And what about all the times a child dies? Or an innocent person is shot dead in a drive-by?" He looked at Sammie, "Or a wife who is one of the truly good people drops dead before her time?"

Slowly Brad put down the knife he was using to cut pies and leaned close to Pop so he'd be heard over the voice on the loudspeaker. "I struggled for years with that question myself, Mr. Sternberg."

Pop stared at Brad curiously. "And?"

Instead of answering, Brad remained silent so they could listen to the new male voice that came through the loudspeaker say: "I was out of work for seven months and humiliated at first because my family and I had to accept help from the church. God didn't bring another job right away, the way I prayed he would. But we're stronger for what we went through."

"Hearing people talk about how good God is used to make me angry," Brad went on. "If there was a God, and he's compassionate, how could he stand to let so many tragedies happen?"

Sammie thought she saw tears glistening in Brad's eyes. "Mr. Sternberg, I don't always know why God allows things to happen."

"So how do you stand it?"

Brad began slicing a pumpkin pie. "I know God, and that's enough."

THIRTEEN

Until the last testimony was over, pie was served and eaten, children rounded up, and good-byes tossed like kisses, Pop stood silently at the sink scraping dishes. On the way home he asked if Brad was the new man in her life.

"No." She felt guilty about the sharp edge in her voice. "He's just a friend."

"It wouldn't be so bad if you two did have something going." Before she could object or make a joke, he changed the subject. "The turkey was good, but a little dry."

"Is that your official opinion?"

He ignored her jab. "But Mike's pies were nearly as good as mine. Not quite. Not enough cinnamon in the pumpkin. But pretty close. That kid is a good baker. Too bad he's hidden away up here."

"Why don't you tell him how good he is? He needs to hear it."

So before they went home, they stopped at the Le Ducs'. Without a hello or remember me, Pop spoke what was on his mind. "Kid, you bake some pies! You ever want to move to Los Angeles, let me know. Sophie's could use you."

Mike, whose demeanor when they entered had made it plain that he wasn't going to let anyone keep him from watching the football game, jumped to his feet and offered his hand. "Thank you!" He offered the two of them seats on the sofa, and they talked about spices in pumpkin pie and the best kind of mincemeat.

While Sammie worked at the Treasure House the next day, Pop shopped in the morning for Thanksgiving dinner number two and spent the afternoon cooking. The air was happy with the smell of turkey as she walked back to the cottage after closing.

Pop had covered Mechiah's cage. "I heard about enough from that bird. More than once I threatened to roast him along with the turkey." They sat at the table with a perfectly browned turkey in the center, a mound of stuffing seasoned with the fresh sage that was still growing outside the door, mashed potatoes with nary a lump, tiny peas and pearl onions, fresh cranberry dressing, sweet potato soufflé, and a tray of sliced fresh fruit with Pop's special dip. "I cut down, seeing as how there's only the two of us." He took warm rolls from the oven. "And I cheated on these and bought them from Mike."

He lit cinnamon-scented candles, then turned out the lights and sat down across the table. As inconspicuously as possible, she closed her eyes and began silently to tell God thank you when her father interrupted.

"Thanksgiving was the one time when your mother insisted we say a blessing. 'You cook, I bless,' she used to say. Remember?"

Sammie nodded slowly.

"So I say it to you," he said. "I cook, you bless."

There's no trying to figure you out, Pop. Her mind raced for the best way to handle this fragile moment. Then it came to her. "How about if I read verses from Mom's Bible as a blessing?"

"Yeah." His voice trailed off.

As Sammie got her mother's Bible from her nightstand, she searched her mind for Old Testament passages that might be appropriate and remembered Psalm 103 that Mom had been memorizing before she died. By candlelight she read.

Praise the LORD, O my soul;
    all my inmost being, praise his holy name.
Praise the LORD, O my soul,

and forget not all his benefits—
who forgives all your sins
and heals all your diseases,
who redeems your life from the pit
and crowns you with love and compassion....

After a few silent bites of dinner, Sammie began to talk about family Thanksgivings when she was growing up, and Pop chimed in with ones he remembered when he was growing up. "If we had chicken, it was a feast."

He left for the bed-and-breakfast, and she finished cleaning the kitchen which, she'd insisted, was her contribution to the dinner. Then she took Mechiah out of his cage. After she stroked his silken gray back and told him what a strange holiday it had been, he hung upside down from her hand.

That night, instead of praying in bed and perhaps falling asleep in the middle of a "God bless," she fell to her knees. "Work in Pop's life, Lord. I don't know what he needs, God, but you do. Provide it for him."

Pop left the next morning beaming over the lavish breakfast Amy served and condescended that some good things did happen in the north woods after all. He hugged Sammie long and hard, and Sammie whispered heartfelt thanks in his ear for coming. He tossed a "mazeltov" to Mechiah and drove off in his rental car for the airport .

Sammie tingled with anticipation later that soggy Saturday, when Brad called inviting her to see his studio after church. "There's something I want you to do when you get here," he added mysteriously.

Wheedling would obviously get her nowhere, so she told him, "I'll come after I drop off Autumn."

Sunday morning dawned thick with fog after a night of hard rain. Even old-timers shook their heads about the steady downpour since the season changed. But the cheerful radio announcer promised it would clear off by noon and be cool and sunny.

Sammie chose a cherry A-line dress that made her skin rosy and a white woolen jacket with a print silk scarf at her neck. As she walked to the car, she hugged Mom's Bible to her chest.

Autumn's eyes had widened the first time she'd seen the Bible. "Your mother wrote all those notes?" Now, seated in the pew, Sammie saw it as a legacy from her mother. Wasn't it more important than the financial inheritance she'd lost? Was God trying to tell her something?

As she drove along the river after church, she felt like Little Red Riding Hood on her way through the woods, and sang about going to Brad's house, amazed at how many different emotions could be going on inside her simultaneously.

The friendly weatherman was right this time she realized as she drove along the river. The fog had burned off and, though the trees still dripped, the sky was beginning to look like a depressive on a good day. Suddenly, in a clearing and surrounded by the stateliest of evergreens and backed by the mountains, was Brad MacKenzie's place.

Now the Red Riding Hood analogy of going to grandma's house no longer seemed appropriate. The only similarity between the house in the fairy tale and his was that both were in the woods. Instead of a quaint cottage with window boxes of geraniums and a thatched roof, Brad's house was a large, two-story, gleaming log house, so much a part of the landscape that it seemed to have grown there.

The studio, which was separate from the house and also faced the river, lived up to her ideal of everything an artist's studio should be. As she got out of the car, Brad appeared in the doorway and waved.

"Stunning!" was the only word she could think of when she

entered, because she did feel stunned. The room was bursting with light from the wall of windows facing the river and the skylight overhead. It was spacious with no knickknacks. An easel with a partly finished painting stood in the corner, captain's chairs and a love seat faced the window wall. A huge table was spread with art paper, paints, and brushes. Lamps and a bookcase with a shelf of art books completed the furnishings.

Along the two walls hung Brad's paintings. Overwhelmed, her natural instinct, as always, was to sink to the floor. Once, she might even have done that. Instead, she stood and stared.

Brad waited silently. Her mind didn't generate a mouthful of congratulatory words to heap upon him. Instead, Sammie was soaking in the artistic images. There wasn't a garish element in any of the paintings. The tones of every flower, every seascape, every landscape, were the subtlest. Each painting shone with mystical translucence.

And in every one was a child—picking a flower, digging a hole in the sand, climbing a hill, running with arms flung wide.

"I feel as though I should whisper and walk on tiptoe." She surveyed the room again. "You haven't wanted to sell these?"

He was silent. "No. I've decided to put one for sale in the Treasure House, though. It'll be the first."

He smiled wistfully. "I don't invite many people here," he admitted. He looked like a little boy showing his box of treasures.

When words came again, she said, "I'm speechless. And like my parrot, that doesn't happen too often."

He laughed. "I want you to pick out a painting to hang for sale in the Treasure House to replace the one that was sold."

"Me?"

"Why not? After all, you'll have to look at it every day. And you know your customers best."

He was trusting her? "I can't decide."

"Look them over and think about it while we have coffee on the patio," he said. "I think it's warm enough out there today."

He went through the connecting door to the kitchen of his house. She walked out the back door of the studio to the kitchen patio, and he joined her, carrying mugs of hot coffee. She wrapped in a blanket on the chair, and they sat side by side watching the river rush by.

"You could almost cast out from here."

"There's a better spot where the bank is lower just down river. Have you done any fishing?"

"Pop took me when I was growing up. The first time, I got a trout bigger than any he'd caught, and he threatened never to take me again. Of course, he did."

She thought of her secret place, and a shadow of the old spontaneous Sammie wanted to let Brad into that intimate chamber of her life. But what if one thing led to another, and she told more than she meant to? Or maybe she was being a fool because it was possible he knew all about her already but hadn't let on.

The old Sammie grew bolder and gave her a shove, but she still felt as vulnerable as a little girl when she spoke. "I discovered a place on the river where I go frequently to journal and meditate and pray." She hesitated the space of a breath. "I call it my secret place." Laughing ruefully, she added, "I guess it's not a secret any more."

He reached over and took her hand. "If you tell a secret and the other person promises to keep it, then it's still a secret. And I do promise to keep it."

Was there more behind his words about secrets than what met the eye? *Let it go. Enjoy the moment with this handsome, gifted, quietly-strong man holding your hand.*

They watched the river rush by and felt the breeze on their

faces and talked about inconsequentials. Not daring to look at Brad, Sammie let the moment wash around her and through her.

Finally, he squeezed her hand before he let it go and stood up. Taking his signal, she stood next to him. "Thanks for being so kind to my father," she said. "You made a profound impression on him."

Brad answered simply. "I'm glad. We're all just a bunch of walking wounded, after all."

That he had no intention of stepping any farther into that mine field she could tell by the change in his voice as he led the way back to the studio. "Have you decided which painting you want?"

She hadn't, of course. But when she entered the studio, her eyes fell on a seascape with the sky in gradations of the gentlest pink. A tiny girl ran down the beach to her father who was waiting with open arms.

"This one. With the father and child."

Without a word, he removed it from the wall and wrapped it, then loaded it into her car. She slid behind the wheel. "Thanks for coming, Sammie Sternberg," he said. "I like sitting with you on my deck watching the river run by. Come back any time."

For days, the memory kept her chirping like a sparrow on the feeder even though the entire Olympic Peninsula was as wet as a sopping sponge. Relentlessly, rain pounded the windows, then let up to a pleasant drizzle, only to pound some more. Sturdy tourists who traveled, rain or no rain, stood on the rug inside her door, shaking and stomping and asking if it was always like this.

Still, the business side of Sammie was optimistic. Not long after Mollie Holly's visit, the woman had called for an order of jewelry to have on hand and to take to pre-Christmas shows. "Send me a variety—from funky to classic to antique."

"Now there's a challenge I'll enjoy!" Sammie told her.

"Remember the pin you gave me? I sold it right off my body! I wore it when I was shopping, and a woman asked me where I got it. When I told her I represented you, she asked if I had any to sell right then. I took the pin off my lapel, and we made a deal."

Sammie stayed up late filling Mollie's orders. Then Mollie sent a list of women in the public eye she knew who would wear pins and tell inquirers where they could get one themselves. The list began:

Savannah Buchanan—professor in a private college. Hobby is playing the harp. Favorite color is lilac, favorite period is Victorian. Gentle and feminine.

Cara Duncan—state legislator. Intellectual, dramatic, wears bold colors. Hobby, amateur theater.

Pop also called requesting pins to give longtime, newsworthy customers. "This way I can brag about my talented daughter and maybe keep you from starving to death at the same time. If these women wore feedbags, they'd start a fashion."

His descriptions of customers was less focused than Mollie's: *DeDe Petrie always orders blitzes and would stand on her head to be the center of attention, but her beauty salon is where all the rich women go.* Sammie managed to sift through his statements to a personal profile of each.

Mid-December, he'd called excitedly from Sophie's. "I'm in my office celebrating over a piece of chocolate cheesecake. Too bad you can't have one with me."

"What are you celebrating?"

"The reaction to your pins. Women are talking more about them than our raspberry tarts. You need to get a fax so I can get orders to you fast."

Shops in Pineville Beach were decorating for Christmas with swags and wreaths of pine and fir and branches of holly. Main Street twinkled with tiny lights, and the week before Christmas, churches would take turns putting on a live nativity scene in the bedecked village green.

Teams from the community church spread through town giving parties in nursing homes, distributing baskets, toys, and clothing to the needy. Wearing rain gear and carrying umbrellas against the recurring downpour, teenagers caroled every Friday night in neighborhoods. Swathed in her aqua raincoat with the hood pulled down to her eyebrows and sloshing in boots, Sammie accompanied them along with Autumn and Abby.

In front yards with porch lights on, the carolers called widows and widowers, single mothers with children hanging on their jeans, couples who'd spent Christmas together for decades, to give joy to the world. Doors flew open as people left TV programs and stood wreathed in light,

Sammie set up a hand-carved nativity scene in the Treasure House and wondered about Christmases when the Nelsons lived here. She imagined a giant Douglas fir in the living room decorated with strings of popcorn, stockings hung on the fireplace by the children who were living with them at the time, baskets of giant pine cones on the table, Mrs. Nelson reading the Christmas story from the Bible.

Is that how it was? Resolutely, she phoned Mrs. Nelson. "You promised me a bowl of Captain's favorite clam chowder, and I haven't collected yet. If you're up to it…"

"Am I up to it? Just say when!"

"Friday I go caroling with the kids. How about Saturday night?"

"Yes. I'll see you right after you close the shop. Will you pick up a loaf of sourdough bread at Mike's on the way?"

During lulls in business that week, Sammie created an

"Originally Yours" pin for Mrs. Nelson. From her bin of jewelry findings, she selected antique silver filigree curved in the shape of a life path. She gave it dimension by layering other antique pieces, and finally she dangled silver fruit along the path. It was small enough not to be overpowering on the tiny lady.

When she arrived at Mrs. Nelson's, she paused to read the giant letter written in red and tacked to Mrs. Nelson's door.

Dear Friends,
Smile!
Sing!
Celebrate!
God has come into the world.
His name is Jesus.
Say the word
And he'll move into your life.
The word is "Yes."

Mrs. Nelson answered her knock looking like Santa's grandmother, wearing a red eyeshade and red jumpsuit. Sammie greeted her warmly. "I love your letter on the door."

The old woman's response was a grin so wide it accordion-pleated her face with wrinkles. "Come on in, the chowder's ready."

She ladled steaming bowls of creamy clam chowder thick with clams, potatoes, and bacon and cut slabs of the sourdough bread Sammie brought. After a few spoonfuls, Sammie took time to look around the tiny apartment. On a table in the living room was a miniature nativity and in a corner in front of the window was a Christmas tree about as tall as Mrs. Nelson. The most unusual holiday decorations were children's crayoned pictures of Christmas scenes that filled nearly every available wall space.

"Wow! Were these all drawn by your kids? The ones who lived with you, I mean?"

"Every one. It was a tradition that they make me pictures for Christmas. 'Course, they didn't have anything else to give. And I didn't want anything else. Besides, a picture drawn by a child captures who he or she is that moment. Even after they moved out, they kept sending me pictures."

When the meal ended, Mrs. Nelson took Sammie on a tour of the wall gallery. Ellie, who was two when her mother died in the fire, did multicolored scribbling. Her brother Billy showed himself in bed heaped with covers and grown-ups cooking at a stove.

Pictures signed by Matthew, who'd moved to Nelson's from a tent in the woods, included one of a giant Christmas tree with red and green circle ornaments and a long table loaded with food. In another he drew a fire in the fireplace and stockings hanging from it.

Sammie remembered Faith as the little girl whose mother was abused. In her picture, she was a tiny figure surrounded by towering grown-ups. Outside a window leered a huge, scary face. Scattered about the page were tiny Christmas trees.

Other pictures were signed by children she didn't know. Lettered across some of them were lines such as "I love Jesus" and "Happy Birthday, Jesus." Stick figures baked cookies and decorated Christmas trees and hung wreaths and read from the Bible, much as Sammie imagined.

Mrs. Nelson turned out the lights, and the two women settled on the sofa in the apartment lit only by the Christmas tree. "The last thing you told me was how desperate you were after God took Captain," Sammie began. "Was it an accident at sea?"

Her landlady squeezed her eyes shut. Was she praying? Composing herself? The woman opened her eyes and stared straight ahead and began speaking. "I had a bad feeling because the weather had been so unpredictable."

For a few moments, she rocked back and forth. "The parents of the family staying with me were lazy, and the teenage boy, Tim, was caught stealing from places in town. I had to put them out and was trying to convince myself I'd done the right thing when the storm hit." Her voice fell to a whisper. "Everyone on board drowned."

Sammie felt as though she'd barged into a place of private mourning. "I'm sorry. I shouldn't have…"

Mrs. Nelson came back warm and reassuring. "Yes. You should have. God wants you to know Captain's and my story. It's love that makes me choke when I tell it." She tilted her head and squinted beneath her eyeshade. "Love brings pain along with joy."

Mrs. Nelson blew her nose on a Christmas handkerchief she took from the pocket of her red jumpsuit. "Not three months later, God brought another family. When that one was ready to leave, he brought another.

"Sometimes I came across a teenage girl whose parents didn't want her. Missionaries from all around the world who were on furlough came to stay in the cottage. You've probably seen their names in the guest book. Then three years ago, Mike came.

"He needed a place to stay. Ed who owns the hardware store gave him a job and couldn't get over what a hard worker Mike was. Only thing was, Mike had a bad temper."

Sammie nodded. "He still does." She recounted his explosions at Autumn. "I intervened once, and Autumn stayed with me overnight."

The old woman rose and began pacing the floor with stiff legs. "Can't sit in one position too long." She sat again. "I know about what you did. When Mike gets ready to blow up, he comes here. We talk. He calms down. I tell him to come before he blows up."

Reaching desperately for a piece of information to brighten

the conversation, Sammie told Mrs. Nelson that Autumn was coming to church with her.

"God is going to use you in that family's life. He has already." At the bookshelves, she stopped pacing, removed a photograph album, and turned on a lamp. "As I said, Mike's story isn't finished yet. But you might like to see its beginning here in Pineville Beach."

Flipping to the back of the album, she opened to a page of snapshots of a beanpole youth in jeans and white T-shirt. His face was drawn and his eyes as scared as a doe Sammie had caught in her headlights one night recently.

"The boy was always serious. His folks never gave him any reason to believe in himself. But Ed kept telling him what a great job he was doing and gave him a raise.

"He was scrawny. I made sure he ate right, and he started lifting weights. He repaired things around here, kept the yard up, and was a stickler for details. The one time he did smile big was the day I baked a birthday cake in the shape of a star and wrote his name on it in icing. No one ever made a cake just for him before, he said. Then he met and married Autumn."

Sammie filled in. "And you loaned him money to open the bakery."

Mrs. Nelson nodded slightly. "But he still feels like the little kid who had to listen to his father say every day, 'You'll never amount to anything.'"

After her landlady closed the album, she leveled one of her frighteningly direct questions at Sammie. "Are you learning to trust, little girl?"

Sammie hesitated. "I…I trust you." She rubbed her forehead. "And I'm beginning to trust God…just beginning…especially after a sermon Pastor Jack preached on faith." She frowned because she didn't know how to say what she meant without revealing too much.

"Now you need to learn to trust yourself."

Trust herself?

"God brought you to me just the way he did all those others," said Mrs. Nelson. "I feel as though you're one of my kids." She opened the album, this time to the page after Mike's. "I've already begun my Sammie section." Mrs. Nelson had mounted the photographs of the Treasure House. "We'll both have to wait and see what comes next."

From her purse, Sammie took the small gift-wrapped package with Mrs. Nelson's name on it. "I made this for you."

The old woman looked as though she'd been plugged into a wall socket. "Get the one for you." She pointed to a green foil-wrapped gift under the tree. "I'll open mine first," the woman announced, "because I can't wait."

When she drew the pin from the velvet bag, she choked up. "It's beautiful. It's like one of those lifetime achievement awards they give." She opened her arms for an embrace. Holding her was like hugging a bird, Sammie thought. Bright plumage and underneath tiny, fragile bones. *Ninety years of miracles.*

"Thank you, Sammie Sternberg," Mrs. Nelson whispered before she moved away.

Next, Sammie opened her package and drew from it a small, hardbound volume. Opening the yellowed flyleaf, she read the title: *My Savior: or Devotional Meditations in prose and verse on the names and titles of The Lord Jesus Christ.* It was authored by the Reverend John East, and the publishing date was 1860.

"It's one of my favorites, and I want you to have it."

The fifty-two short chapters covered names of Christ from Alpha and Omega to Wonderful. "An old book about Jesus—and with a history! What a perfect present for me!" Sammie whispered her thanks.

"Open to page 153 and read the first sentence in the last

paragraph," Mrs. Nelson instructed.

Sammie obeyed. "All that my Savior has and is, he has and is for me," she read.

"It's true, little girl."

Solemnly, Sammie nodded. They embraced one more time, and Sammie went home where she set Mrs. Nelson's gift alongside her mother's Bible.

This was a special December, a special Christmas, she believed. How could she capture its memories? Write about it in her journal? Yes, but that wasn't enough. In earlier years, her first response would have been to take pictures of the holiday.

Running to the closet, she lifted out her photo equipment and then retrieved film from the refrigerator where she stored it. Tomorrow, between the daily torrents of rain, she'd take photographs of Pineville Beach in December. Not quick snapshots to use up a roll. She'd take her time the way she used to so she'd get pictures that said something.

Sunday in the wintertime, merchants kept their shops closed. At home after church, she ate a baked potato with sour cream and chives and eyed the sky hopefully. About one thirty, the rain stopped and the sun stepped from behind its cloud curtain and took a bow. She tossed a quick "good-bye" to Mechiah, stowed her camera gear in the backseat, and drove off to her first location: her secret place.

The undergrowth and trees were wet, but she was wearing her aqua raincoat and black boots. Stooping, she took shots of her spot from several angles, then turned her camera to the river, which was dangerously high and rushing angrily downstream.

As she drove past Brad's she made a mental note to ask if she could get shots of him painting in his studio. The pictures would tell the story of her life in Pineville Beach this Christmas.

That reminded her to also ask Miss M. when she could get

a portrait of her behind her cluttered desk at the *Pineville Herald* and Mrs. Nelson sitting at her kitchen table sipping industrial-strength coffee wearing her "I don't do mousework" sweatshirt and an eyeshade.

The photograph of Claudine's house with a huge, green wreath on the front door, would emphasize the home's regality— a potentate standing aloof, waiting to be honored.

At the village green, she took pictures of laughing young people stuffing straw down each other's shirts while they set up the nativity for the live reenactment. To her mental list, she added, *Return to photograph the live nativity.*

One more picture. Dossie Mae working on her rugs. *Probably not many signs of Christmas at her house,* Sammie warned herself. *I'll just drive by and if the logging truck is gone, I'll know Paul Bunyan isn't there. If it's in the driveway, I'll keep going.*

Only the pickup was in the driveway, so Sammie pulled in behind it. Jennifer answered her knock and stood silently in the doorway, her eyes wide with fear. Behind her, Sammie saw Dossie Mae dart from the kitchen, through the living room, and into the hallway that led to the bedrooms. Sammie shuddered, for Dossie Mae's eye was blackened, and ugly red bruises covered that side of her face. Too late, Jen's mother tried to shield her injuries with a hand.

Anger at the world's victimizers made her seethe. "What's going on, Jen?"

Jennifer still stood in the doorway. "What do you mean?"

Protective to the end, she thought. "Your father beat your mother, didn't he? And I'm pretty safe in saying it's not the first time."

Jennifer took a long, deep breath that Sammie knew was a silent admission. "I want to come in, Jen."

The girl stepped aside and Sammie entered. "I want to talk with your mom."

"She can't come out. She's sick." Tears filled Jen's eyes.

Sammie put her arms on the girl's shoulders. "I know. She's sick to death of being beaten up by your father. You don't have to pretend anymore. I've suspected this has been going on for a long time."

The life went out of Jen, and Sammie hugged her Mama Vivano style. Jen's head fell on Sammie's shoulder; the girl heaved wracking sobs.

"It's too much for you to carry, Jen. I'm here. I'm your friend. I want to help."

FOURTEEN

Jennifer's tears made a trail down Sammie's neck.

"Let it out," Sammie encouraged, patting the girl's back and wishing hugs would make it all better.

The girl took deep, shuddering breaths and struggled to regain control, when they heard a faint call from down the hall. "Jen? Honey, please come here."

Jen jumped. Sammie could hear the girl's mind working as she frantically wiped her eyes and blew her nose.

"Coming, Mama."

Sammie lay a hand urgently on Jen's shoulder. "I want to talk with your mother."

"Mama's too ashamed to talk to you."

"Ashamed? Of what? Being beaten up? Your father's the one who should be ashamed!" Her words had more passion behind them than she meant to be there. Sammie took a deep breath. "Listen, Jen. You need a friend right now, and so does your mother. She knows me. Maybe she'll trust me."

Resigned, Jen nodded and motioned Sammie to follow her. "Mama?" She called through a curtain that hung where the bedroom door should have been. "Sammie's coming in with me." To make a statement instead of asking a question took courage, and it was probably born out of desperation.

The double bed Dossie Mae sat on with her face turned to the wall was covered by a plain patchwork quilt. Like the living room, the bedroom was also drab, the walls covered with ancient, faded tan wallpaper with a blue geometrical design, stained shades pulled down at the windows, a scarred dresser in the corner, a kitchen table along one wall stacked with miscellany. The only cheerful touches were the quilt and some of

Dossie Mae's rugs on the linoleum floor.

Sammie sat on the bed next to Dossie Mae. It took all the self-control she could muster not to cry out at the sight of the woman's swollen, discolored eye and cheek.

"Get some things together and come home with me, Dossie Mae. You can't stay here. And you, too," she told Jen. "You need to get out of here."

Was she sure she wanted to harbor an abused woman and her daughter? Hoffman wasn't nicknamed "Bull" for no reason.

But hadn't God led her to the Nelson house that had long been a refuge for desperate people? She thought again of tiny Mrs. Nelson standing at the door alone confronting another angry husband.

"I can't go." Dossie Mae's face was stark. "Anyway, he's okay now. He's sorry."

"He may be sorry, but has he changed? You're not safe here." She turned to Jen. "Does he ever hit you? Did he ever hit Autumn?"

"Only Mama. He yells at me, makes threats. But he takes it out on Mama."

Dossie Mae was eager to explain. "He hasn't always been like this. Only now he can't make a living in the woods, and he doesn't know where to turn. He's very proud and independent. Then, when his truck broke down several days ago, it was more than he could take."

Sammie tried to reason with Dossie Mae, but it was useless. And Jen wouldn't desert her mother.

When Sammie stood up and looked down at that beaten woman, her anger turned to compassion. "Next time, he could kill you," she said softly. "Please think it over. There is no women's shelter in Pineville Beach, but my house is always open to you two. Any time of the day or night."

She thought of the reason she'd come—to take photographs.

228

The picture she now saw of two generations of abject women standing in the front doorway belonged on the cover of *Life* magazine. Of course, she wouldn't shoot it.

Fear gripped her as she drove back through a new torrent of rain with her windshield wipers chanting rhythmically. What would Mrs. Nelson have done in a situation like this?

As she pulled into her driveway, she wondered what Christmas would be like in the Hoffman house. It was only a week away. Could she do something to make it better for the Hoffman women?

With Mechiah perched on her shoulder, she set about making hot cider with a cinnamon stick, then lit Christmas candles, careful that Mechiah's curiosity didn't get the better of him. Curled up on a corner of the sofa as the rain pounded on the roof, she'd read the book Mrs. Nelson had given her for Christmas. That would be a perfect respite from the day. Except for the picture in the back of her mind of a skinny mother and daughter huddled together against another kind of storm.

An idea jumped center stage in her mind. Why not make "Originally Yours" pins for Jen and Dossie Mae for Christmas? And one for Autumn. It wouldn't solve their problems, but it might remind them that they were each someone special.

When Sammie yelled her excitement, Mechiah awakened, took off across the room, and lit on a chair back. After she captured him and apologized while she smoothed his feathers, she secured him in his cage. "Sammie's sorry. Mechiah good bird."

Self-pityingly, Mechiah agreed with her assessment. "Mechiah good bird."

Why not go to the shop and start on the pins right now? She dashed through the rain and settled at her jewelry-making table. Even though Mrs. Nelson's house was silent as midnight, it didn't feel empty or frightening now, for around her were her treasures, symbols of the life God had helped her build.

What kinds of pins should she create for Dossie Mae, Jen, and Autumn? In her mind she dug for an identifying characteristic for each woman as she roamed with her fingers through the jewelry findings.

For Autumn and Jen, she'd create pins that symbolized their tender, inner beauty. A jeweled hummingbird on a cluster of flower for Jen. For Autumn, an intertwined wreath.

Dossie Mae would probably be pleased with a pin that depicted her talent as a craftsperson. A silver spool of thread, a sewing machine, scissors, a thimble.

As she worked, she planned other gifts she wanted to give. For Mike, something to do with sports, maybe a trivia book. Miss M. would like the copper candlesticks for sale in the shop to go with the kettle she'd purchased. Cookies for Art Humble, perhaps. In the shape of cats and dogs? Sammie giggled to herself as she wondered if she could find a cookie cutter in the shape of a parrot.

Then there were Abby and Claudine to figure out. Maybe she'd make a pin for Abby; the woman had many interests to capture. For Claudine, a gourmet food basket would suit her.

Shopping in her head was exhilarating. She loved to surprise people, something she'd gotten from Pop who used to come home from Sophie's hiding presents behind his back when she was a little girl. Every time she tried to get a peek, he'd twist and turn and tell her he absolutely didn't have anything.

But she wouldn't send him a present or even a card.

"I don't believe Jesus is the Messiah, so why would I do all that Christmas stuff?" he used to ask. He didn't even celebrate Hanukkah. Mom had made sure Sammie knew that the holiday marked the rededication of the Temple in 164 B.C. after it had been desecrated. Mom always lit candles during the holiday.

But Jesus' birth Sammie and her mother celebrated by

themselves. Together they attended Christmas eve service, then came home, read the story of Jesus' birth in Luke 2, and exchanged presents. Very early Christmas morning, they loaded the car with brightly wrapped gifts and stealthily crept up to front and back doors of families where a father was in drug rehab, a mother had taken off, a child was in the hospital. After each delivery, they imagined with glee the expressions when someone opened the door.

Pop always worked late Christmas eve and long hours the next day because Sophie's was packed. She and Mom had agreed to make him "King for a Night" when he finally did come home. No holiday decorations in the house to make him uncomfortable, just candles everywhere bathing the rooms with their warm glow, his favorite beverage next to his favorite chair and the footstool ready for his feet.

"I know. You're buttering me up because you want something," he'd bluster. But he'd settle comfortably and come obediently when they called him to dinner. This was the one holiday where he didn't cook. And he fell in line easily because, as far as he was concerned, it wasn't a holiday. Not his holiday, anyway.

By midweek, four days before Christmas, the lapel pins were finished and Sammie's shopping was done. The holiday excitement was running down, and she awakened sick over the fact that it was still raining hard. For the first time since she moved to Pineville Beach, she wished desperately for California sunshine. Nothing sounded good for breakfast. Mechiah's calls for attention made her want to cover his cage. The rest of the week stretched out like a bleak weather forecast.

The holiday blues that all those magazine articles warned against, she thought dully. No more Christmases with Mom. The home she and V.J. had decorated lavishly was now inhabited by others. What she wanted was to pull the covers over her head and wait for spring.

She mustn't let herself slide back in the pit again. *Live in the here and now and not in the used-to-be. You can't live life looking at yesterday.* She remembered when she was a little girl, she rode on the train in a seat that was facing backward and got sick to her stomach. *That's what happens when you look at where you've been instead of where you're going,* she reminded herself. She'd better get with the program or she'd become a Christmas casualty.

The Treasure House was busy with shoppers, but during lulls she brainstormed ways she could create her own holiday traditions. Yes, she'd go to Christmas eve candlelight service the way she and Mom did. Should she have people without families over for a potluck on Christmas day? Help with the birthday party for Jesus at the church? She'd definitely read the story of Jesus' birth in Luke 2 the way she and Mom had done.

About noon, Pastor Jack Bishop's wife Tracy phoned. "We're having a potluck open house Christmas afternoon. Please feel free to drop by if you don't have other plans. We'd like to have you."

Sammie brightened and thanked Tracy, saying she wasn't sure of her plans yet. She promised to let her know.

Midafternoon, Brad called. "Do you have plans for Christmas day?"

She hesitated. "I do have an invitation, but I haven't decided whether or not to go."

"I wondered if you'd like to spend the day with me."

She caught her breath as he went on, carefully choosing his words. "The past several years, I've spent it alone by choice. This year, I'd like to spend it with you." There it was, spoken plainly. He wanted to be with her. What he was waiting to hear was, did she want to be with him?

This was the invitation she'd hoped for but hadn't been willing to let herself imagine. There was no one she'd rather spend Christmas with. No question. "I'd love to spend Christmas with you, Brad." As plainly spoken as he.

"I thought we could drive to Mount Ashley and have brunch at the ski lodge. I don't plan to ski. Just relax and enjoy."

"Pop used to say that anyone who strapped boards to their boots to see how long it would take to break a leg had something wrong with them. So obviously skiing wasn't something I learned growing up. It's on my list of things to do someday, though."

Two days before Christmas she helped with the church's birthday party for Jesus. When she returned home, she wrote about it in her journal. *Mom would have loved to see the children's faces as they blew out the candles on Jesus' birthday cake and sang "Happy Birthday dear Jesus." I took some photos and plan to give each child one after they're developed.*

The next morning, a small package came from Pop with shocking instructions. *Do not open until Christmas!* But he had never before even acknowledged the holiday! She tucked it away making a mental note to call him Christmas day and open it then.

That afternoon, she gave the lapel pin gifts to Jen. "How are things at home?"

"My father feels badly about going off the deep end. He even cut a Christmas tree for us in the woods and brought it home. It's the first time in years we've had a tree. We're going to stop in at Mike and Autumn's Christmas day for a little while, even though he and Mike don't get along." She shook her head. "You probably guessed they wouldn't."

That same day, Claudine ran across the street with a wrapped gift, and Sammie gave her the basket of gourmet foods she'd put together. Claudine investigated the contents and smiled with approval. "Papaya salsa, chocolate truffles, herbal vinegar, chocolate macadamia cookies, mini toasts, orange honey."

When Sammie opened her gift and found a book of photographs of paintings by Georgia O'Keefe, she hugged it to her chest, then put it down and hugged Claudine.

Summoning courage, Sammie changed the subject. "How about coming to Christmas eve service with me?"

Claudine looked amused. "I know all about Christmas eve services. They're all candlelight and passion about the baby in the manger. Invite me to something less intense at your church sometime, and I might take you up on it. Who knows?"

On Christmas eve, Sammmie dressed in a softly-pleated raspberry skirt and white silk blouse and pulled on black boots. The sanctuary was nearly full, and as she stepped inside, she felt immersed in the holy day. Velvety-red poinsettias were banked on the platform. A banner across the front announced in gold letters: AND HIS NAME SHALL BE CALLED IMMANUEL. Soft carols sounded like angel voices on that long ago night. It was as though someone left the door to eternity open.

Jackson Jones, a young black man who'd recently started to attend the church, stood center stage, clasped his hands behind his back, raised his head to heaven and sang "O Holy Night" in a pure tenor. Of all the Christmas songs, this one had stirred her even before she found the Messiah. His glasses glinted with reflected light, and his face shone in a way that stirred and filled her spirit.

Joy spilled down her face as she took the bread and grape juice during Communion. Her first Sunday she'd passed up those elements. Now she bowed her head in gratitude because of how differently she felt.

Later, propped in bed wearing powder blue flannel pajamas

with feet, she opened Mom's Bible to Luke 2 and the story of the birth of Jesus that she and her mother always read aloud on Christmas eve. Suddenly, she felt unsettled and uncomfortable.

I should be reading my own Bible.

But why? Why did it matter?

You need to depend on God to teach you, not your mother.

At first, the idea puzzled her. Gradually, though, she realized that what she needed to do was study the Bible for herself and then use her Mom's notes to amplify what she'd learned.

She padded across the floor and retrieved her Bible from the bookshelf, propped herself up in bed again, and began reading the story of Jesus' birth.

"And there were shepherds living out in the fields nearby, keeping watch over their flocks at night...."

Prayerfully she reflected on those first words, then wrote in her journal: *God revealed Jesus to ordinary people—ones like me.* She imagined how stupefied they were. How their lives were never the same.

Sammie hugged the stuffed bear and listened to the rain on the roof. Right now, she felt safe. *Like Noah must have felt in the ark,* she thought as she drifted off.

Very early Christmas day, she called Pop because she knew he'd be leaving soon for Sophie's. "I was good and waited to open your package even though it almost killed me." She decided not to call attention to the fact that he'd never given Christmas so much as a friendly nod before.

"So open. I've got two swallows of coffee and one bite of Danish left and then I'm out the door. But don't expect me to sing 'Jingle Bells.'"

"That's okay. My ears aren't ready anyway."

She tore off the brown wrapper and a layer of silver gift paper. Inside a bigger box was a tiny velvet one, and she snapped it open.

When she saw the contents, she gasped, "I don't believe it." All she could do was repeat herself. "I just don't believe it.

"You like it?"

"Like it? I love it!" A tiny gold charm gleamed on its velvet backing. "You knew about my necklace just like it, a star of David and a cross."

"Sure. Wear it in good health, Sammie. It's from Mom and me."

There was so much she wanted to ask him, so much she wanted to tell him, but this was not the time.

"Got to go to the salt mines," he told her.

"Thanks, Pop. If I were there, I'd spoil you rotten tonight, the way Mom and I used to."

Brad came for her at eight o'clock on Christmas day. He was wearing café au lait slacks, a brown leather jacket, and black boots. Laughing, she showed him her own black boots, then pointed to the blue jeans, red turtle neck, blue denim jacket with red plaid lining she was wearing. "I've never been to a ski lodge before. Is this appropriate?"

He studied her carefully and drew out his words. "You'll do just fine."

Flustered, she bustled around the cottage, doing a last minute check, and said good-bye to Mechiah who stared at her stonily. "I didn't spend time with him this morning and he's sulking. 'Good-bye' is a word he refuses to learn." She picked up her camera case that was sitting next to the front door, and Brad took it from her.

As they drove out of town, Brad commented that she was wearing her star and cross necklace, and she showed him the new charm on her bracelet from Pop. "You talked to him in the church kitchen, so you know this gift is totally out of character."

Temperatures were falling, and an ice storm was predicted for the day after Christmas. As they drove along the river, they talked about how turbulent it was and how dangerously high. "In the sixties, it went over the banks and destroyed homes," Brad told her. "I guess you've heard that the weather bureau is warning it could happen this year if this rain doesn't stop. And there's so much snow in the mountains." She had heard, and the idea frightened her.

A gentle rain washed the countryside, but they hadn't gone far on the winding road up the mountain when it turned to snow that made cat's paws on the windshield. The peaceful silence between them, interrupted by comments about the scenery, was one that never existed with V.J. She realized now that she rarely relaxed with him because he always had a new idea, a new plan, a new demand. His way of maintaining control.

Soon the road became snow-packed, and Brad pulled over. "You keep warm and enjoy the scenery while I chain up."

He performed the job expertly, stomped the snow from his boots, and got back behind the wheel. They continued their climb. Sammie shook her head in wonder as she surveyed the roadside forest layered with white. It reminded her of a wooded scene inside a glass globe that Pop had once given her, the kind you could shake to make it snow. The snow fell silently, and they grew quiet again, as though speech would spoil the moment. But as they climbed higher, she yelped at a sheer drop-off on the passenger's side. He laughed and took one gloved hand off the wheel long enough to squeeze her own reassuringly.

They talked about the Christmas eve service. "How did you spend Christmas when you were living at home?" he asked.

She told him about Hanukkah and how things changed when she and Mom found the Messiah. "I'm searching for my own traditions now." She braced herself as he made a hairpin turn, then looked down through a break in the trees. "But I'm not sure this is one of them!"

"That's exactly where I'm at," said Brad. "Searching for my own traditions." Before she could decide whether or not to ask him why, he punched up a tape. "Maybe we should sing some carols." He led in a clear, firm baritone. She joined in a timid alto because she was always unsure she was hitting the right notes. Mom used to say she got her musical ability from her father.

Traffic slowed, and the snow deepened as they got closer to the top. At another break in the trees, she looked fearfully down the cliff again.

The road circled and twisted one final time before they drove into a clearing. "Here it is," Brad announced. He pulled into a large parking area in front of the sprawling, natural log lodge.

"It's a king-sized version of your house!" She jumped out of the car and ran to a spot where she could take it all in, and Brad followed. They stopped and stood side by side, holding hands. All around them, snow-capped peaks dominated the skyline. Majestic firs and pines were draped with white. It was gigantic and expansive and pure and completely overwhelming.

She shook her head slowly. "All I can think of is what David wrote: 'When I consider the work of your fingers, what is man that you are mindful of him, the son of man that you care for him?'" Brad tucked her arm in his and hugged it to his body.

Soon, they became aware of groups walking to the lodge and skiers heading for the slopes. "Pictures!" Sammie announced. "Got to get pictures." She and Brad raced to the car so she could get her camera. Using a wide-angle lens, she took several shots of the lodge as snow fell. Brad watched her move to different positions, stoop and stand and lean and straighten and snap the shutter. When she was finished, they walked to the lodge.

In the great room, floor-to-ceiling windows spread across one long wall and a great floor-to-ceiling stone fireplace spread across an adjoining wall. Long sofas faced windows or fireplace and invited skiers to sip hot beverages and talk about their day.

Christmas brunch was being served in the main dining room, and a waitress escorted them to their table. "It looks like they've been shopping at the Treasure House," Sammie remarked, looking around at lanterns and wash boilers and antique kitchen tools displayed along the walls. She ran her hand over their table top made of split logs varnished to a high sheen.

"That is without a doubt the biggest, most grand indoor Christmas tree I've ever seen," she breathed when she saw the one in front of the windows decorated in a Victorian theme.

They groaned their way through the buffet line, complaining because they had to choose between cinnamon rolls the size of coffee cakes and muffins the size of soup bowls. When she encountered herring in sour cream, she laughed. "When I tell Pop about this maybe he'll be convinced that the north woods is civilized after all!"

In the fast-filling dining room, they bowed their heads while Brad spoke a simple prayer of thanks for the meal. Sammie studied the old black-and-white photographs on one wall as she ate, and Brad explained that the lodge had been built during the Great Depression largely by the Civilian Conservation Corps.

When they'd emptied their plates, Sammie groaned. "My mind insists that I'd better get more to eat because the food looks so good but my stomach says, 'Uh-uh, I'm full.' Guess I'd better listen to my stomach."

She settled back in front of the fireplace in the great room where they could also see the panoramic view out the window while Brad went for coffee. He handed her a mug and settled beside her. "Thanks for coming with me. Except for Bethlehem, this may be the perfect place to spend Christmas."

She leaned forward to get a better view. "It puts us humans in our place, doesn't it, seeing ourselves as part of something so much larger?"

Brad took a sip of his coffee. "I reminds me that God didn't stay on his mountaintop and look down on us and say, 'Too bad you're in such a mess.' He came down and became one of us." He shifted and leaned back. "In spite of your yelps on the way up, this could become a new tradition." He stopped short of calling it "our new tradition."

He reached out and pushed back a curl from her forehead. "You're easy to be with. Thanks."

"For what?"

"For not asking questions."

She returned his steady gaze. "I'm sad that something has been making you unhappy."

"I know you are. I've come to trust you, Sammie. One day soon I'll tell you about it. But not today. Today we celebrate."

Brad had come to some kind of decision, and he clearly had a measure of relief. With carols playing on the speaker system and the heat from the leaping flames in the fireplace warming their faces, they embraced the moment and settled back holding hands.

Finally, Brad consulted his watch. "If you want to tour the lodge and take a few more pictures, we'd better get going."

After they'd seen the rustic sleeping rooms with patchwork quilts on the beds, the upper level dining rooms, and the gift shop, and after she'd taken pictures using her cable release of both of them playing in the snow, they headed down the road toward the valley.

She stole a glance at him as he focused on the road ahead.

His strong, even features, the hardness of his body, his quiet directness, his spirituality, combined to give an image of stability V.J. never had.

V.J.'s Christianity, she knew now, had been prepackaged like the trays of fresh fruit her father was always complaining about in supermarkets. "Big fat-face strawberries on top and not much worthwhile underneath." Brad's Christianity came from deep within. *All the more reason why he'd expect you to be honest. To be genuine.*

In her handbag, she had a gift for Brad but thought that if he didn't have something for her, it might embarrass him. So she was relieved when they climbed in his van to drive home, and he reached in the glove compartment and handed her a tiny, wrapped package.

Inside was an original watercolor, small enough to hold in the palm of her hand, of a dark-haired girl sitting beside a gray-haired woman in a porch swing.

"Brad!" Her eyes filled. "It's Grandma Levine and I!" What she wanted was to reach out and hug him. What she did was crowd the air with a series of "Thanks!"

Her gift to him was a five-by-seven-inch framed print of the photograph she'd taken of a driftwood cross rising from a pile of driftwood on the beach. For a long moment, he stared at the photograph, then turned to look at her. "It's perfect. You don't know how perfect." He looked deep into her eyes. "Thank you for giving me the best Christmas I've had in a long time."

The ice storm hit, and the community church canceled its New Year's eve service. New Year's Day the temperatures rose, and the ice melted. In the morning, Brad called asking if he could take her for a drive that evening. "I waited to see what the weather would do, and it looks as though the roads are okay."

When he arrived to pick her up, his forehead was creased with wrinkles. "The river is beginning to wash across the road in some places, and the melting ice is making it worse."

They drove along the Iseeyousee so she could see for herself how high it was and how angry. Here and there, water covered portions of the road. Brad slowed and water sprayed from their tires.

A few minutes later, he pulled in at Fort Barker and parked. She turned to him, startled, feeling suddenly unsafe in this dark, completely deserted place under a starless sky, with the surf pounding on the shore.

He shifted in his seat so he could look directly at her, and she changed to the same position. The glow from a street lamp illuminated his face. "I want you to know why I had trouble in the children's room at the Treasure House. Why I am the way I am."

"You don't have to..." she began, thinking that if he remained silent, she could, too.

He held a finger to his lips. "It happened six years ago on Christmas day back east. My wife Vonnie and I had been married four years and had a beautiful daughter. Her name was Betsy, but we called her Bitsy.

"Vonnie had been seriously depressed for months. She was a Christian, but a very troubled one. She was seeing a psychiatrist. She started drinking, and some nights she kept at it until she passed out. Nothing I did seemed to make any difference.

"On Christmas, though, she was bright and cheerful. We opened our presents Christmas morning and played with Bitsy for quite a while. I cooked dinner and late in the afternoon, as we planned, I left to visit my mother in a nursing home about an hour away. She was terminally ill.

"I took Mom out for a ride to see the Christmas lights. When we got back to the home, there was a phone message that I was to call the state police. That's when I got the news.

Over the phone." He struggled to continue. "Vonnie had taken Bitsy with her in the car. I figure she might have been looking for more to drink because I found an empty bottle at home."

His voice broke. "She was driving under the influence and went over an embankment. The car caught fire and they were killed."

Brad buried his face in his hands, and when he took them away, his face was etched with agony. "My wife and my baby were gone."

Sorrow pumped through her body with every heartbeat. *My God. My God. My God.* She wanted to throw her arms around him. Instead, she began to shake the way she had after Harry's verbal attack at the autumn festival.

He took his hands away from his face and clasped them tightly in his lap. "I should never have left them alone. I should have known that holidays would be hard for Vonnie. And Christmas worst of all.

"For years, I was angry with myself and her. She killed our baby. She killed Bitsy and I was partly to blame. That's why I moved here to Pineville Beach. To withdraw from the world." His face softened. "But God came with me."

He looked around at the darkened stone walls. "I drove to the fort to tell you this because it's the place I came to through the years. It's the place where God broke through to me, when I finally started to listen."

She could see years of unspent emotion on his face as he stroked the back of her hand. "The photo you gave me for Christmas of the driftwood cross raised up from a pile of drift-wood says it all."

His body convulsed with dry, wracking sobs. The tears she'd been struggling to contain began streaming down her own face.

Awkwardly, she reached out and took him in her arms.

Quietly, they wept.

FIFTEEN

Sammie had never held a man while he sobbed. V.J. never wept, and although she and Pop had clung to one another in sorrow following Mom's death, he'd done his sobbing in private.

Brad had removed his "No Trespassing" sign and exposed his soul to her. She actually felt his woundedness and came away with the imprint of his pain.

The more she thought about his story, the more ashamed she felt. Compared to his, her experience was minor. Sure, she was conned and ripped off. But Brad lost his wife and his baby in an accident so horrible it must be carved in his memory in blood. The pit into which Brad had fallen was far deeper and blacker than her own.

Knowing that didn't remove the sting of her own experiences. Her pain wasn't lessened because his was deeper. But it did make her think less about herself and more about him.

They left Fort Barker and drove to Sammie's where they dashed through the heavy rain to her front door. He said goodnight, then took both of her hands in his and kissed them. "I'm glad you know." He looked exhausted.

"I wish I'd been there to make the last six years easier," she told him.

"So do I. But depending only on God has given me a closeness to him I probably wouldn't have otherwise."

In the seconds it took for him to put her key in the lock and open the door, she made a decision. "I'll call you, Brad. Soon. There's something I have to tell you."

Three days later, before opening the Treasure House, she did call Brad. "Can I pick you up at three thirty and take you for a drive?" She knew that he painted until early afternoon, and she could get away then because Jen came to work in the shop after school.

He didn't try to find out on the phone what she wanted. But his voice did have a lilt in it when he agreed. "I'll be ready."

Tuesday was cold and overcast and the threat of rain that could turn freezing again hung in the air. On her way to pick up Brad, Sammie realized that she'd unconsciously chosen daylight instead of darkness to talk to him. Maybe it was because both times Fort Barker had played a significant role in her life had been in the daytime: when she first arrived in Pineville Beach and when Dave visited.

Few tourists visited the fort in January, and it was deserted. She parked in the same place Brad had, shifted behind the wheel to face him the way he'd done, and he shifted to face her.

God, if ever I needed your help, it's now.

When she began to tremble, he took her hand and held it gently. "There's no easy way to say this, I guess. You see, I was married, too, Brad. Or at least I thought I was. The name he was using was Vincent James Magellan. After he forged my name and stole the money my mother left me that was a bequest to her from my immigrant grandparents, I found out that he already had a wife. The police finally caught him. By that time, he'd taken another so-called wife. We don't know how many others he's fleeced."

"My poor Sammie!" His voice was as gentle as the hand that still enveloped hers.

Then, dropping her hand, his expression darkened. His voice sounded like the rumbling of thunder. "That guy makes me so angry I'd like to…"

Instead of being shaken by his anger, she felt relieved. He wasn't blaming her. He wasn't asking, "How could you let yourself be taken in?"

"At first, I was numb," Sammie went on. "Then furious.

Then overwhelmed with guilt. I thought I'd drown in it. You're one of the few people I know who can really understand."

She looked him full in the face and spoke with passion. "I should have known better."

"All those shoulda, woulda, couldas, right, Sammie? They move in and take over."

Why didn't he move from his side of the front seat and hold her in his arms? Then she could just bask in his sympathy. Anyway, he didn't need to know the rest.

But a sense of urgency pressed her to tell it all.

So softly that he had to lean forward to hear, she whispered the words. "He stole something else from me. I was a virgin when he married me."

He reached out and enfolded her in his arms. While the sea pounded the shore and seagulls circled, he held her gently and whispered in her ear. "My poor Sammie…"

She wept.

Finally, reluctantly, she pulled away and wiped her face on the clean handkerchief he handed her.

"The day I arrived in Pineville Beach, I came here to Fort Barker. I saw it as a ruin that symbolized my life. Quite a while later, I brought a detective friend who's been working on my case to see the fort. Dave saw it differently than I did. He said that to him the fort symbolized victory, that it's still standing because of victories. He said I would win too."

On the drive back to his house, Sammie told Brad that Miss M. had found out about her past but kept her word not to tell anyone. Brad raised his hand as though taking an oath. "I solemnly promise not to tell anyone, either."

"Keeping it secret doesn't seem to be as important any-more," she mused aloud, amazed at the idea. Hastily she added, "Of course, I wouldn't talk about Vonnie and Bitsy and what happened."

"I don't care if people know. I just wasn't ready to talk about it before. And I hadn't met the person I wanted to tell it to."

As she drove him home, they commented about how dangerously high the Iseeyousee was. "It's not at all the picturesque place I saw when I first drove across the bridge," Sammie said. Limbs broken off in windstorms were floating downstream in the brackish water.

When they pulled into Brad's driveway Sammie suddenly remembered Claudine's painting. "After hearing about Vonnie and Bitsy, I think I understand what you put on canvas. The perfect cottage on the hilltop with the little girl in front. That's the life that ended on Christmas eve, isn't it? To an outsider the painting looks idyllic, but it could be titled 'Broken Dreams.'"

When Brad only looked silently out the window at the rain that had begun to fall, she wondered if she'd said too much. "I'm sorry...."

He turned to her and shook his head. "No, you're right."

She leaned forward, hoping he'd go on, but he only sat and rubbed the back of his neck thoughtfully. "What I'd like us to do is to sit in front of the fireplace with mugs of hot coffee and comfort one another. But what I think we should do is take some time apart to pray. It was God who led me to open up to you and you to me. Now we have to wait and see what he has next."

Was he saying that this might be the end? It was entirely possible that he's just a very caring man, she thought as she drove off, and she was reading too much into his honesty and tenderness. It was also possible that he was too scarred to have another relationship. Or that she was too scarred herself.

Would she be able to accept God's will if it was different from her own? She was afraid it would be.

For the next three weeks, she did pray as Brad requested, but that didn't keep her from being nagged by uncertainty.

Sundays, after she saw him in church and they talked casually, she kept asking herself why they couldn't just be normal, like every other couple. Go out for burgers, or sit in front of the fireplace with mugs of hot coffee.

But wasn't it a lack of caution that got her in trouble with V.J? She certainly hadn't prayed to find out if that relationship was God's will. Instead, she'd insisted God give her what she wanted.

Business in Pineville Beach had slowed to a near stop due to the time of year and the flood warnings. Daily, as she made "Originally Yours" pins, she thanked God for sending Mollie Holly who had brought more business than she could handle alone. Shop owners her father contacted through Sophie's were asking to stock her pins, and she'd turned the requests over to Mollie. To keep up with demand, she was teaching Jen how to craft them, and the girl was demonstrating her mother's creativity.

The third Sunday after she told Brad her story, Sammie invited Miss M. to stop with her at Hotcake Heaven after the church service. They each ordered one pancake and coffee.

Sammie got right to the point. "I wanted you to know that I told Brad about V.J."

"I knew that if you told anyone in town, it would be him."

The waitress brought their pancakes topped with bright yellow scoops of melting butter that they each began to spread. Miss M. bowed and thanked God for the food, then looked up. "How do you feel now that you've told him?"

Sammie thought hard. "What I feel isn't just relief, I guess. It's freedom. Not 'Whoopie, everything's great,' mind you. But I'm not as obsessed by thoughts of the experience as I was. I guess what's happening is that God is helping me put it in perspective."

When she'd finished her last bite, Miss M. spoke reassuringly. "I said I wouldn't tell anyone about V.J., and my promise still holds. Telling is not my place."

Sammie responded with a look of gratitude.

As they sipped their coffee refills, they talked about local flood warnings. "I know you're good with a camera. Have you gotten pictures of places in Elk Creek where the river has already gone over the bank? Some roads are out, and people on the North Iseeyousee have already had to be evacuated."

She hadn't taken pictures, but when Miss M. said she'd like to use some in the *Pineville Herald*, Sammie promised to do so as soon as possible. In her mind, she was already sorting through the kinds of film she had stored at home.

Early the next morning she packed her camera case with film and headed for the North Iseeyousee. After half an hour, the road narrowed and was so heavily wooded that the trees grew like a bridal arch overhead.

Elk Creek, a sparsely populated logging town dominated by a once-thriving mill, looked as though it should have been named "Sorrowful" even before the flood. Its one general store had flaking white paint, a sagging porch, and gas pumps with no gas. The houses that sprang up in clearings like a few remaining teeth reminded Sammie of the Hoffman place.

Here, the river had flowed over its banks, creating a man-made lake in which the haggard homes seemed to float. Up ahead the road was closed where water had washed it out. On the river side, a man was rowing a small boat toward the store in a field where, not long ago, someone had kept cattle or grown hay. Elk Creek looked like a ghost town going down for the third time.

Backing up to the driest ground she could find, Sammie parked her car and alighted carrying her camera case. On the porch of Pete Peterson's General Store, still safe because it was on the opposite side of the road from the river and on high ground, stood a man she presumed to be the owner, hands on hips, wearing a slicker and boots. Sammie got off a few quick shots of him.

"Terrible," he said as he surveyed the scene. He didn't introduce himself. "I was here for that other one. We had to evacuate then, but I'm hoping and praying and staying as long as I can this time. People around here depend on me."

"Have they been evacuated this time?"

"Yeah. To the emergency center set up in the schoolhouse down yonder." He gestured with his head toward the closed road. "'Course people had to be taken there by boat. Daisy Pietre won't leave, though. She's out there." He pointed to a small yellow house surrounded by water.

The man she'd seen in the boat had rowed to dry ground and was walking across the road to the store. When he arrived, Sammie introduced herself, explaining that Miss M. from the *Pineville Herald* had asked her to take pictures.

"Will you take me to the Pietre place?" He looked her up and down slowly, shook his head at the stupidity of the idea, and motioned her to follow him to the boat.

He wasn't going to volunteer his name, so she told him hers. When that elicited no response, she asked what she should call him. "Will." And clearly, that was all this wiry, gray-bearded old-timer was about to offer. He'd be perfect for the role if they made a movie version of the flood, she thought.

Sammie shot pictures of houses submerged to their window frames as Will rowed by. A dog, perched on the roof of his doghouse, howled in terror, and she got off a shot. "Can we go by and pick him up on our way back?" she asked. Will grunted in what she hoped was agreement.

At the Pietre place, Sammie climbed out, held her camera over her head and waded through the flooded first floor. She found Daisy Pietre, who looked as though she'd dug stumps for forty years, bundled in a red plaid jacket, black twill pants, and navy watch cap, sitting on the top step looking down on the water on the main floor. "I'm not leavin', so go away."

"Mrs. Pietre, the river hasn't crested yet," Sammie said. "The water could come even higher than it is already. You're not safe here."

Will's voice thundered right behind her and made Sammie jump because she didn't know he'd followed her inside. "Daisy, you old fool. Get outa here while the gettin's good."

She scowled down at them. "I ain't goin', Will, and that's all there is to it."

Will shook his head in disgust. "Next time it'll be the firemen who'll come. They'll get you outa here." He turned and waded out the front door, waving and muttering in disgust. Before she followed, Sammie backed off at the foot of the stairs and took shots of the lone holdout at the top.

On the way back, Sammie snapped pictures of Will rescuing the drenched dog from his house. Once in the boat, the big black animal waggled in ecstasy and shook his sopping coat.

On land, Will deposited the dog with the store owner who went for a pie tin of food and set it on the porch. "Poor old Blackie. Your folks will be glad to see you alive." Blackie wagged his tail furiously and kept on eating.

Twenty-four hours later, Sammie picked up her prints at the store, and when she thumbed through the stack, a smile spread slowly across her face. The shot of Pete Peterson on the porch of the general store, of Blackie, nose in the air, howling, on top of his submerged dog house, of Daisy Pietre on the top step inside her house, of Pete rescuing Blackie were good. Very good.

Miss M. rewarded her with an enthusiastic "good job" as Sammie laid them out on her desk. "I want to run these on the front page. Okay if I use your byline and a blurb so folks will know you used to be a reporter in Los Angeles?"

At the mention of newspaper publicity, for once Sammie's heart didn't sink into her stomach. "Sure, no problem."

The next afternoon, Claudine breezed into the Treasure House and laid the front page of the *Pineville Herald* in front of Sammie. The huge, black headline read, "Flood Hits Elk Creek." A layout of her photographs nearly filled the page. A sidebar read, "Photographs by Pineville Beach resident Samantha Sternberg. Miss Sternberg worked as a reporter for radio station KTWI in Los Angeles."

Sammie felt a first shiver of fear as she read the words. Claudine studied her reaction carefully. "I just wanted you to know I think these are great."

Every hour, the flood was the top story on local radio, and news bulletins interrupted regular programming. Television news ran video of homes and businesses along the rapidly rising river that were being flooded. The Iseeyousee was expected to crest the following night, and townspeople would be warned when to evacuate. Sammie kept the radio playing, and Mechiah preened himself and repeated like a mantra, "Mechiah good boy."

Fear nibbled at her soul early Friday morning as she sat sipping coffee, so she opened her Bible to Psalm 91:

He who dwells in the shelter of the Most High
will rest in the shadow of the Almighty.
I will say of the LORD, "He is my refuge and my fortress,
my God, in whom I trust."

The Holy Spirit made the passage personal:

"He is my refuge and my fortress, my God, in whom I trust."

The words were an arm around her soul. *Sammie Sternberg, I am your God. Trust in me. Not just for the flood. For your life.*

That moment, there was a knock at the door, and she recognized Mike's voice calling her name. His olive drab rain jacket was fastened tightly but his wet, dark blond hair was even darker and plastered to his head. "Have you checked the basement of the shop for water?" he asked in a voice crackling with anxiety.

She urged him in, and he stood dripping on the thick rug inside the doorway. "I was down there last night, and it was okay. Thanks for checking."

"This place didn't get it during the last flood. All the houses on this street were okay. But I feel responsible to make sure nothing happens here."

The phone rang and she heard Miss M.'s voice. "An emergency shelter has been set up at the church and we need volunteers. Can you come?"

Sammie's mind raced. She'd have to put a sign in the window of the shop that they'd be closed. "Absolutely. Be over in fifteen minutes."

Mike looked at her questioningly, and she filled him in. He frowned and looked down at the floor, then lifted his head. "I'll get Autumn and stop by for you. We can go in my van."

He was gone. Should she call Claudine and let her know? The idea prompted her to move to the phone. Claudine's answer was immediate and firm. "Have Mike stop by for me."

He drove cautiously through high water where drainage systems had failed. "Have you talked to Mrs. Nelson?" Sammie asked on a dry stretch. "I'm worried about her, since the nursing home is on the river."

"I've called or been by every day, and so far they're okay. But I don't like the idea of her being there. They are back on high ground, though. You know that she won't leave unless they call for an evacuation."

The main auditorium in the church where congregants worshipped on Sunday was now filled with rows of army cots and groupings of tables and chairs. Evacuees whose smiles had worn out milled around a long table of hot beverages and pancakes along one wall. At their sides and in their arms were children clutching teddy bears and sucking their thumbs.

Pastor Jack strode to them and extended his hand to each person in their group. His expression of gratitude was like a welcome mat.

"Am I glad to see you! They're bringing evacuees in fast. These folks spent last night here, but there'll be lots more tonight. There are boxes of donated food to organize in the kitchen and cooking to be done. Someone can help put up cots." He paused and adjusted his glasses. "These people need more than food and bed, though. They need comforting, reassurance."

He looked around the room, helplessly. "And the kids. They need someone to play with them. The moms need bottles warmed and babies held."

Sammie exchanged quick glances with Mike, Autumn, and Claudine. The minister added that people from emergency relief organizations were on their way. "This isn't something we trained for in seminary."

Waving at them, he hurried off to an elderly lady in a wheelchair who was sobbing quietly. "Right now, the kitchen crew is getting ready to make more pancakes," he called over his shoulder.

Claudine spoke. "I've found my calling. Point me to the kitchen."

She strode off as though flipping pancakes in a church evacuation center was something she did every day. Without a word, Mike headed for the group of men, some members of the Merchants Association, setting up cots. Autumn looked uncertainly after him.

Sammie waited, sensing that it was important to give

Autumn time to decide how to help. The girl looked as though she wanted to fold into herself, then spotted a table piled with children's books. "I could gather the kids and read them stories." She looked to Sammie questioningly.

"Go!" She shooed her off.

As Sammie headed toward the kitchen, she spotted a man and woman about her own age seated on the floor. Two children lay beside them, heads in their parents' laps.

Periodically, the young mother, who looked like she could have been last year's prom queen, wiped her eyes with the back of her hand. The young man, who probably had a Pineville Beach letter sweater in his closet, reached over and stroked her hair.

Kneeling next to them, Sammie asked, "Can I help? Get you some coffee? Juice for the kids? Blankets?"

The man answered. "Yeah. Thanks." Sammie extended her hand and introduced herself. She looked at the woman. "Haven't I seen you in my shop, the Treasure House?"

"Yeah. Just looking. Now I'm not sure we'll have a house, much less treasures to put in it." She inhaled tiny sobs and smoothed the butter-colored hair of the boy in her lap who'd fallen asleep.

Her husband spoke their names, "Deidre and Walt Wagner. The kids are Becky and Bill." So they wouldn't be a nameless family on the floor of a temporary shelter.

Sammie headed off for coffee and juice. On her way back from the refreshment table, Sammie spotted a stack of Bibles on the platform and managed to tuck one under her arm. After she sat on the floor beside them, she spoke, and her words flowed as naturally as breathing. "I've never lost my possessions in a flood. But I have lost an inheritance and a home and a…marriage. May I read you a psalm in the Bible that has comforted me?" The couple nodded as though from a far place.

"He who dwells in the shelter of the Most High will rest in the shadow of the Almighty," Sammie began. When she finished, she asked, "May I pray with you?"

Again they nodded, and Sammie suspected that prayer was a foreign language they hadn't learned. Without fear or self-consciousness, she spoke simply to God, the way she'd been doing these past months, expressing the Wagner's pain and asking for help.

When she lifted her head, she felt a hand on her shoulder and turned to see the pastor. "The Rivercrest Retirement Center is being evacuated. I thought you'd want to know."

Mrs. Nelson! An image of the ninety-year-old woman in a sweatshirt and eyeshade flashed through Sammie's mind. Smiling to the Wagners, she rose quickly to tell Mike.

Color drained from his face. "I've got to get over there. *Now!*"

Quickly, he told one of the men he'd been working with. "I'll let Autumn know," he called over his shoulder to Sammie, and, dodging evacuees and workers on the way, ran to the table where she was surrounded by children.

Sammie used those moments to dash to the kitchen and let Claudine know she was going with Mike to the retirement center and that she'd come back later to pick her up.

In the van, Sammie glanced at her watch. Nearly noontime. When they came to a road-closed sign and a detour, Mike muttered under his breath. The veins in his neck stood out. "I should have been there with her. If anything happens…"

They found a parking place behind the emergency vehicles that were lined up at the curb in front of the center and jumped out of the van. Mike knifed his words at the gray-haired female staff member in white slacks and waterproof jacket, carrying an outsized umbrella she used to escort residents down the sidewalk. "Mrs. Nelson! Where is she?"

In a grandmotherly voice, she assured Mike. "She's on the

second floor. There's no immediate danger, but we're not going to take any chances."

Mike tore inside the building, down the corridor, and up the stairs past volunteer firemen who had slowed their pace to that of the elderly on their arms. Sammie's short legs were no match for Mike's long ones, and she felt like a kid trying to keep up with a big brother.

He stopped at Mrs. Nelson's open door and called her name several times. When Sammie grinned at the poster on the door, she hoped Mike wouldn't notice. His sense of humor had probably gone south. "Love is hugging a porcupine." The picture was of a red-haired, freckle faced boy doing just that.

"Down here, kids." Mrs. Nelson, stuck her head out of the apartment two doors down. She was wearing a yellow eyeshade and matching sweatshirt with a bunny in a carrot patch, and it read: "Hop to it!" Mike groaned in obvious relief and hurried to her side.

"I'm trying to convince Harriet here that it's okay to leave all these family photographs." A heavy set woman wearing a hip-length, purple jacket and paisley head scarf held a grocery sack and was about to remove the gallery on one wall.

Mrs. Nelson patted Harriet's shoulder. "The river will never get up to the second floor." She laughed. "It's because we're old that they're being extra safe."

Grudgingly, Harriet allowed Mrs. Nelson to take the bag from her. With a last look over her shoulder, the woman turned and walked out the door beside Mrs. Nelson. A staff worker came by and led Harriet down the hallway.

Mike took Mrs. Nelson's arm. "Let's get you out of here."

She squinted up at him. "I'm ready. Harriet was the last holdout on this floor." She patted Mike's hand. "I'll be with you and Sammie in a minute." Disappearing into her apartment, she came out carrying a jacket and her Bible under her arm and pulled her door shut.

Mrs. Nelson addressed Sammie who'd stepped beside her. "What have you two been up to?"

"Working at the emergency shelter. Then we heard they were evacuating this building."

"I knew it! I knew you'd be helping!" She turned to Mike. "They need you on the third floor to help get the men out. Sammie can go downstairs with me."

The idea of working among more strangers on the third floor obviously didn't appeal to Mike.

Mrs. Nelson said quietly, "They need you, Mike."

Obediently, he nodded and turned to Sammie. "Take care of her."

The two women stood inside the entrance to the retirement home so Mrs. Nelson could encourage and cajole residents as they left. Once the older woman threw open her jacket to expose her message sweatshirt to a shuffling stick of a man buried in an overcoat who walked out reluctantly, leaning heavily on Mike's arm.

Only when the last resident had been transported to relatives, friends, or to the church was Mrs. Nelson ready to leave.

Mike joined them and spoke sharply to his mentor. "You're coming home with me." His words had no question mark after them.

"How about if we fight over you?" Sammie tossed at Mrs. Nelson as they got in his panel truck. "Mechiah would love someone else to talk to."

But Mike made clear that it was settled. He'd drop Sammie at her house and go home with Mrs. Nelson. Sammie would go to the church and pick up Autumn and Claudine.

He told Mrs. Nelson, "I thought I'd make donuts to take to the church. Ten dozen or so." He glanced at both of them. "If you think that's okay."

Mrs. Nelson grinned over at him. "I knew I raised you right.

Besides, who else in this town could do that but you?"

Without going inside her house, Sammie jumped in her own car and drove straight to the church. New volunteers had arrived, so Autumn, who was walking a crying baby, and Claudine, who was distributing kits of toiletries to evacuees, could be relieved.

Back home, she hung her wet coat in the bathroom to dry and put on the kettle for tea. Mechiah reminded her sternly that he hadn't had his daily treat. "Polly wants a cracker!"

Just as she was looking for something to satisfy him, the kettle whistled, and she remembered that she hadn't listened to the messages on her answering machine.

The first call was from Pop. "I hear the flood is bad, and people are being evacuated. If you don't call me tonight, I'm going to get the next plane out."

She groaned and turned off the phone machine. This time he had a right to be worried! There was no question in her mind that he'd do what he said.

He answered the first ring. "Pop? I'm sorry you've been worried, but I'm fine. As a matter of fact, I'm good. Better than in a long time."

"My daughter's in a flood and she's real good. How am I supposed to believe that? Are you safe? Do you have to evacuate?"

"No. The river isn't anywhere near my place. My neighbors and I have been helping those who have to get out."

"That's nice. Mom would be proud. Dave called. He said he'd been trying to get you and refused to talk to your machine. He wanted to find out about you and the flood and tell you that the case will come to trial next month."

"Good. That means it'll be over soon."

Mechiah interrupted with his newly learned phrase, "All wet."

259

Pop suggested she send him out the window like Noah sent the dove to look for dry land. "Maybe he'll never return."

"Hey! He heard that and he's hurt!" She wanted to tell her father about her confession to Brad. Instead she said, "God has been working in my life here. For a long time, I couldn't see it. Now I do." He may not want to hear that kind of talk, but she had to tell him.

There was silence the space of a slowed heartbeat. "Good, Sammie. I'm glad." His voice sounded wistful. "When you come home for the trial, let's go to the cemetery."

"I'd love to do that." Pop's voice was sounding different these days, but she'd have to wait until she saw him to find out why.

"So, Mrs. Noah, take care of yourself. Call me every day. It's the price you pay for moving to a place with a river called 'Iseeyousee.'"

"Every day, Pop. I love you."

"Me, too, Sammela."

She remembered there was another message on her phone machine. "Sammie? It's Brad. I have to make a quick trip to the city. The children's hospital is auctioning off one of my paintings, and I promised to be present. I hate to leave right now, but they're counting on me. I plan to drive back right afterward, so I'll get in late tonight. I wanted you to know. Sammie, when I get back, let's talk."

Her mind raced almost as fast as the tape she rewound on the phone machine. Brad wanted to talk. About what?

The river was scheduled to crest about twenty-four hours after Brad returned. She worried that he was cutting it pretty close.

The phone rang. It was Jennifer. "Sammie, I don't know what to do. They just came by telling us that we need to evacuate, and my father won't leave. He says all we own is here, and he's got to stay and try to save it. He won't listen to Autumn or Mom, either, of course. He says Mom and I can go, but I hate to ask Mike to come get us because he and Dad don't get along at all, and they might get into a big argument."

"Okay, Jen. Let me think." She shot up a silent prayer for help. "Maybe we should get help moving things off your place and to safety. Do you think your father would go along with that?"

Jen hesitated. "Maybe. He wanted to do that himself at first, but didn't see how he could."

"I'll call Mike and find someone with a truck to meet us out there."

After Jen hung up, Sammie called Art Humble and told him what she wanted. He agreed. "I'll meet you out there in say, half an hour with a truck."

As she was going out the door to talk to Mike and Autumn, the phone rang again. This time it was Miss M. "Sammie? I have good news, and I have bad news. The good news is that I've gotten all kinds of great responses to your photos.

"The bad news is that a Los Angeles paper picked up the photos and a tabloid is running a story about the well-known restaurateur's daughter and ex-news reporter at radio station KTWI who married a bigamist and is drowning in the flood in the Pacific Northwest. Digging up all the old dirt, of course." She took a deep breath. "I'm sorry about the notoriety. I know that's the last thing you want."

"Thanks for telling me. It's okay."

After she hung up, she gathered the pieces of celery she'd cut for her bird, who was drooping from lack of attention, and put them in his cage. He eyed her suspiciously as she rubbed his head. "Sorry. No time to take you out now."

He had no intention of forgiving her. "Poor Mechiah. It's not your fault we're being flooded."

She stopped in the center of the kitchen and laughed out loud. "Lord, if this isn't proof positive that I've changed. Everyone will know about my past, and all I can think about is being a good mother to my parrot!"

SIXTEEN

The blood drained from Autumn's face when Sammie told her the news about her family. "Mama kept telling me they were all right! I've got to get out there!"

Mindless that the pot of spaghetti she was cooking for dinner was boiling over, Autumn ran for her jacket, which was hanging by the door.

Mrs. Nelson, who'd been preparing a salad, pulled the spaghetti off the burner, then trotted across the room and put her arms around the girl. "They probably were all right when you talked with them." Autumn froze with her arm in one sleeve of the jacket and began to cry.

At the commotion, Mike came into the kitchen wearing baker's whites, his hands covered with flour. Sammie filled him in. "I'm going out there. Will you come help move some of their belongings if he'll let us? Since it's a single level home, that's their only alternative."

Mike's eyes swept over Autumn in Mrs. Nelson's arms, sobbing softly.

"Yeah." He untied his apron, washed his hands, and started for a jacket.

His wife broke away. "I want to go with you!"

Mike put his hands on her shoulders and looked into her face. "No. I'll take care of this."

Mike drove carefully along the dark roads. Riding beside him, Sammie remembered what Mrs. Nelson had told her about him and realized that the flood made him feel needed.

Some side streets were closed, and members of the National Guard stopped anyone trying to get through. They passed homes that had been evacuated. Places built with years of sweat. Now the people had to stand by helplessly and watch them being destroyed.

As they drove through water up to the hubcaps, she remembered Jesus' words, "In this world you will have trouble." A promise, she thought.

But hadn't Jesus also said that we shouldn't be dismayed because he'd overcome the world? The first part of the promise was the thorns, the second part was the blossom.

Mike pulled in the Hoffman driveway, and Sammie yanked her hood over her head as she jumped out of the van. The three Hoffmans were standing in about a foot of water in the old building that served as a barn, garage, and shop, loading tools into their pickup.

They looked up, not one of them saying a word, as Mike and Sammie trudged toward them through the water and mud. Like photographs of families in the dust bowl, she thought. Different disaster, same expressions.

Art Humble pulled in the driveway behind the wheel of Miller's furniture truck. Resolutely, he turned to Mr. Hoffman. "Hey, Frank. What do you want us to load first? I have room to store things at my place." Everyone in this town must know everyone else, Sammie decided. The logger was too beaten to do anything except agree. He pointed to cables, chain saws, a donkey engine, and other equipment.

"Okay. Let's go." Art grabbed a chain saw and headed for the truck.

Dossie Mae had already crated up as many of her chickens as she could find, and the women loaded them onto the furniture truck. In the house, the men hefted stove and refrigerator onto a dolly and the women followed with boxes of personal items Dossie Mae and Jen had hastily filled.

When they were finished, Dossie Mae timidly addressed Art. "Is there room on the truck for my rug-making supplies?"

Hoffman didn't object. Before Art could answer, Sammie stepped in quickly, "Sure there is." Mike went off with his mother-in-law while the rest of them pulled a tarp over the pickup bed. When Mike and Dossie Mae returned, they loaded her boxes onto the furniture truck.

The steady rain suddenly turned into a downpour, and they ducked inside the barn. Art turned to Frank. "You and the family can stay the night at my place. There's no one there but my animals and me." Quickly, he explained to Mike, "I probably have more room than you."

The logger narrowed his eyes, and Sammie was reminded that "Bull" stood for more than his size. His voice was a pounding fist. "I'm staying here!"

Taking a deep breath, he turned to Jen and lowered his voice so he sounded almost like a father. "You and Mama stay with him." He jerked his head toward Art Humble.

Mike looked as though he was going to argue, then thought better of it. Art nodded. "Okay, Frank. I understand."

Sammie remembered the sorrowful dog she'd seen her first trip here and asked Frank about him. "He's in the shed. I'll take care of him." In a voice that didn't seem at home in his mouth, he told Dossie Mae and Jen, "You go."

Sammie climbed into the van beside Mike. *How did you do that, Lord?* Frank "Bull" Hoffman hadn't said "I appreciate it" or even grunted his gratitude. But everything had gone smoothly. Pioneer spirit that he was, Hoffman would stay. He would let his family go to safety, but he'd stay and do his job.

Back home, Sammie was too tired to accept Autumn's invitation to stay for a spaghetti dinner. "I just need to crash."

The message light was blinking on her phone machine. "Sammie, it's Brad. The auction is over, but I just learned that the road to Pineville Beach has been closed. I should have paid more attention to the warnings. I don't know when I can get home. I'm worried about my paintings. Would you call the emergency rescue number and ask for help in taking them to a safe place? No one there has a key, so you'll have to break in. I keep blankets in the studio closet to wrap around paintings when I transport them. Oh, and don't worry about the furniture in the studio or anything in the house—except the photographs you'll see around. Thanks, Sammie. I'm sorry to have to ask you to do this. I'll get there as soon as I can."

She sprang from the couch, wired as though she'd just consumed a half-dozen cups of coffee. The emergency dispatcher took down all the pertinent information. "We'll send someone to that address as soon as we can, but it'll be at least an hour."

When Sammie arrived at Brad's, she retrieved a flashlight from the backseat and used it to light her way to the river side of the studio. The river had washed over the bank some, and she could see that the studio floor was wet. But Brad's paintings were either on easels or walls and, so far, were safe.

Please God, please God, send help soon. Right now, those paintings were her responsibility. She felt sick to her stomach. How long would it take someone to get here?

When she flashed her light into the kitchen, she could see that water covered the floor there too. Futilely, she rattled the doorknob. *Walk to the car,* she told herself. *Lock the doors and wait.* She laid her head back on the car seat and tried not to dwell on the fact that she was alone on a deserted, wooded road in a flood, late at night.

Brad was right. He should have stayed.

Desperate for something to keep her centered, she flipped through the pages of the Bible in her mind and stopped at a verse she'd read many times in the recent past.

"When you pass through the waters, I will be with you; and when you pass through the rivers, they will not sweep over you."

While she was waiting the half hour or so, she repeated those words over and over, and when sheriff's deputy Al Gonzalez drove up, she was considerably calmer.

Sammie had spoken briefly with the dark-haired, mustached deputy when he was in the village green with his grandchildren. Now as the two of them walked around to the patio, she filled him in.

Deputy Gonzalez had the patio door open quickly. He flicked the light switches on and off, but there was no response. "Power is out in most homes along here," he explained, shining his flashlight around the room.

With professional deliberation, the deputy instructed her to hold the flashlight, and he began removing paintings from the white walls. When he finished, she retrieved the blankets from a closet.

"Where does he want us to take them?"

She hesitated. "The Treasure House," she decided. There they'd be safe from the flood.

As they wrapped paintings, she was able to chuckle. "Only in Pineville Beach. Where else would a policeman take time to do a job like this?"

He grinned at her and looked closely at the painting they were about to wrap of wildflowers at the base of a tree in the woods. "My wife would go crazy over this." He glanced around the room. "This is one emergency call she's going to want to hear about."

After the paintings were loaded in Al Gonzalez's four-wheel drive, Sammie followed him to the Treasure House where they unloaded their valuable cargo. "I'm going back to Brad's house to salvage a few things with sentimental value," she told him.

"Be careful, young lady."

It was after midnight when she arrived back at Brad's place. The only items in the studio that might be in danger were art books on lower bookshelves, which she stacked up high.

The log walls gleamed with deceptive warmth as she entered the kitchen through the connecting door.

Her flashlight beam fell on a child's table, set with miniature dishes; glassy-eyed teddy bears sat in the chairs. A wave of sorrow splashed over her soul.

Get it together, Sammie. You're here to help. She grabbed table, chairs, bears, and dishes and carried them upstairs where they'd be safe.

What else? In the living room where the floor was also wet, her flashlight illuminated another bookcase across from the rock fireplace. After lighting fat, pine-scented candles she found on the mantle with matches she'd stuffed in her pocket before leaving home, she loaded her arms with stack after stack of books, hefted them up the stairs and lined them on the floor along the hallway.

Photographs of Bitsy were everywhere, but only one included Vonnie. Tenderly, she collected these prized items and moved them to safety.

Breathing hard now, she lifted a small, hand-painted chest, a hand-hooked rug, baskets, a child-sized fuzzy bunny, the framed photograph of the driftwood cross she'd given him, and set them in a second-floor bedroom where she found more candles to light. On her last trip upstairs, she stopped long enough to look around the room.

A shadow box framed in shades of pink hung over the bed and she stepped closer to examine the items inside. *My God, my God.* It held Bitsy's certificate of dedication, a snippet of her hair, a tiny gold locket, and a photograph of her as an infant in a white-ruffled dress. Sammie huddled in a heap on the bed hugging herself to contain the misery.

When she sat up, she realized how exhausted she was. And frightened at being alone in a dark house that shuddered with terrible memories during a flood in the middle of the night.

She'd make one more trip through the rooms to see if she'd missed something. Turning on her flashlight and blowing out the candles, she stood frozen, listening to the wind which had gathered force and was howling around the house. She listened to the Iseeyousee, pounding like a rampaging earth giant, and tree limbs scraping the house. The place felt as mournful as a grave site.

She imagined Brad in the living room, unable to sleep late at night, listening to memories, washed with anger and guilt and pain. She knew, because she'd done the same thing.

But somehow, some way, healing had also taken place for him. The question was: how deep and painful were his scars?

"Lord, I leave it all to you." As she ran to the car, sleet pelted against her face. She'd have to drive home with particular caution.

She made her way around slippery, hairpin curves and kept her soul facing God in wordless prayer. These past months, that had helped her the most.

Prayer. Isn't that what this town needs now? And Elk Creek, too? Slowly, she steered the car around a twist in the road.

Why not invite a few people to the cottage to pray together?

Whoa. Her critical side pressed with tenacity. *Who are you to be leading a prayer meeting?*

She slowed and made her way around a fallen tree. *I'm just me. Sammie Sternberg.*

It was settled.

Who should she invite?

Autumn and Mrs. Nelson. Dossie Mae and Jen.

And Claudine.

She started to toss the last name away as ridiculous.

No. Not ridiculous. Invite Claudine.

The next morning, she called Jen and Dossie Mae, Autumn,

Mrs. Nelson, and Claudine. "The river is supposed to crest tonight, and I'm inviting a few women over this morning to pray."

Jen and Dossie Mae, Autumn and Mrs. Nelson agreed immediately to come. Claudine sounded incredulous. "Pray? Me? Sammie, I'm hardly on speaking terms with God."

"I know."

"Are you sure you want the consummate hedonist at your prayer service?"

"I'm sure."

"I tell you what. I'll think about it."

Claudine was the first to knock at her door. "I thought about it. Of all the rotten things I've done, refusing to pray for flood victims would rate right up there at the head of the list."

As the five women sat quietly in Sammie's living room waiting, it suddenly occurred to her that she had no idea what to do first, and she said so. "To tell the truth, I'm scared."

Dossie Mae pulled her navy cardigan tightly around her. "I'm glad you said that because I'm scared to be here. I guess I feel ashamed because I haven't been in church since I was married, but I've loved Jesus since I was a little girl. And I taught Jen and Autumn about him, even though I never took them to church." She looked at the floor.

"It's okay, Dossie Mae," Mrs. Nelson said soothingly. She looked at the group. "Let's not worry about using the right words. Let's just say what's in our hearts."

So they did. Dossie Mae told God she was ashamed, Autumn and Jen thanked him for their mother, Sammie told God she was in awe of all he'd done for her, Mrs. Nelson said words from a psalm of praise, and Claudine simply stated, "I'm back."

"Let's ask God to stop the flood and help the people who've been forced to leave their homes," Sammie suggested next. The

270

little circle of women did that, like a family having a conversation with their father.

Sammie sensed that the meeting had been taken out of her hands and that no more suggestions were necessary.

Dossie Mae's prayers were as fragile as china in the Treasure House and just as lovely. Mrs. Nelson's had the feel of oak. Jen and Autumn spoke like children kneeling beside their beds. Claudine prayed little but said much.

A reverential hush, like a soft, warm blanket, fell over the room, and for long moments, they sat wrapped in it. As the women left, Jen and Dossie Mae said life had been so crazy that they hadn't said thank you for their Christmas gifts. Autumn chimed in. "It's the prettiest thing I own," Dossie Mae said softly.

After the women were gone, Sammie uncovered Mechiah's cage. "I wish Mom and Mina could have been here," she told him wistfully.

The phone line was dead, so she turned on the radio for news and learned that telephone service all over the area was out. The road into Pineville Beach on the other side of the Iseeyousee Bridge was still out. Just after midnight tonight, the river would crest.

Poor Pop! He'd be worried sick. *Reassure him, Lord.* She wasn't sure where his faith was. But hadn't he shown signs of change recently? She had to trust God to take care of him.

These past months she'd tried to make it through sheer determination, she realized now. The flood was teaching her that there was so much she couldn't do. She had to depend on God.

The house seemed strangely silent, and suddenly she realized that the sound of rain on the roof had finally stopped, and she ran to the window to be sure. At the sight of blue sky, she felt like sending out a dove to search for dry land. Instead, she decided to hurry over to the church and see if she could help.

The Treasure House would remain closed.

On her way, she stopped at the Le Ducs' and found Autumn and Mrs. Nelson folding bakery towels from the clothes drier. "Mike delivered the donuts to the church early this morning. He's gone back with bread he baked. They're still sandbagging places in town, and I wouldn't be surprised if he went on to help." She blew a wisp of hair from her face and stared wide-eyed at Sammie. "I can't believe the change in him."

Mrs. Nelson stopped folding towels. "Why is it that when we get what we pray for, we're surprised?"

When Sammie told them she was going to the church to see how she could help, Mrs. Nelson adjusted her visor and straightened her sweatshirt. "Want a hitchhiker?"

A ninety-year-old volunteer? Sure, she decided, because this one was a firecracker. Autumn went along as well.

As they entered the sanctuary, Sammie stood and looked at children sitting on the floor rolling balls to one another, at mothers feeding toddlers. Up front, where the cross hung, she imagined Jesus, his arms reaching out to the frightened people.

Mrs. Nelson and Autumn scurried off like ants, the older woman to a group of nursing home residents and the younger to the kitchen. Harvey Ellifson, who always carried a line of pens and a notebook in his pocket, gave her information.

"Claudine's in charge of the kitchen right now. If she has plenty of help, call the emergency number to see where they're sandbagging."

Sammie stood in the doorway of the kitchen and stared at Claudine, paring knife and potato in hand. Her neighbor grinned at Sammie's obvious shock and gestured with the knife at the four women and two men. "Somebody else will need you more."

Still dazed, Sammie made her way to the phone and called the emergency number. "We need help sandbagging the downtown stores." She let Autumn, Mrs. Nelson, and Harvey know where she was going and thanked Harvey for his promise to take the two women home later.

It wasn't hard to find the sandbagging crew, and she exchanged her raincoat for a rubberized slicker from her trunk, eyeing the bridge. Brad was still stuck on the other side!

Sammie filled and hefted sandbags throughout the afternoon with Mike, Abby, Miss M., Art Humble, and other Pineville Beachers. "Thank God, it's not raining," one would say as they passed sandbags down the line, and, "Is that yellow light in the sky what they call the sun?"

A grin sliced the face of a teenage boy named Sam, with spiked yellow hair and a dangling silver earring, when she responded that her name was Sammie. Sounding as though he'd just been offered a free trip to Disneyland he said, "Have you heard that Pearl has invited all the volunteers to the Farmer's Wife for a free dinner?"

Midafternoon, just as they broke for coffee, Harry drove up and surveyed the scene through his open window. "Come to help?" one of the men called.

Harry ignored the question. "Sammie Sternberg! How does it feel to marry a bigamist and lose your wad? Maybe there is justice in the world after all!"

Before she could decide what to do or say, Art Humble handed his Styrofoam cup of coffee to the woman next to him and walked swiftly to the car. "Stop blaming every Jew you meet for the one who hurt you." His voice rose with passion. *"Sammie didn't do it."*

Harry stared at the steering wheel. As a body, the volunteers eyed him unrelentingly. The Iseeyousee roared in the background.

After several moments, Harry turned the key in the ignition and drove off. Miss M. came to her side. "I'm sorry, Sammie."

Abby came next and put her arm around Sammie's shoulders. Art, along with several others in the group who'd been strangers until this afternoon joined in a circle of protection.

Art spoke up. "We're sorry, Sammie. About Harry, and about what the tabloid printed in the latest edition."

Sammie looked into their faces. "You knew when I got here to sandbag? And no one said anything?"

Miss M. looked around at the group. "Those who saw it probably didn't know if it was the truth, and it was right next to a story about a two-headed baby." She took the cup of coffee Sammie was holding in shaking hands. "You want to find some-place to sit down?"

"Sit down? No." She looked into each face, then over at Mike who obviously didn't know what was going on. "I don't know what they printed, but it is true that the man I married turned out to be a bigamist who fleeced me royally."

They shook their heads sympathetically. Abby gave her a hug.

"Okay, gang." Sammie shook rain from her slicker and stomped her feet. "Let's get back to work."

They worked steadily until twilight when someone led a parade to their cars singing, "Hi-ho, hi-ho, it's off to Pearl's we go." Sammie declined to join them.

The first thing she did when she got home was to transfer Mechiah to the perch she'd set up outside the cage, where he spread his wings and laughed, "Heh, heh, heh." After she soaked in a hot tub and ate a toasted-cheese sandwich, she gathered her journal, Mom's Bible and her own, and sank into pillows on the sofa.

The TV news reporter she watched while she ate confirmed that the Iseeyousee would crest about midnight. Mechiah flew over and perched on her shoulder. "Good Mechiah. Sammie's friend," she told him.

"Mechiah Sammie's friend," he assured her while she stroked him.

Then, opening her journal to a clean page, she began writing.

They know. Everyone in Pineville Beach will know soon.

If someone asked how that made her feel, what would she tell them? Scraped around the edges, but not stabbed in the gut, she decided.

It's okay, she wrote. *I even feel relieved. Because so many people were supportive. Because of what God has been doing these past months. Helping people during the flood has made me feel part of this town. Like Mike, it's made me feel contributive. I'll have to return to Los Angeles and testify against V.J. That'll be hard. But if V.J.'s accountable for what he did, so am I.*

Pop had urged her to wait, to find out more about V.J. before they married. Mina and Pastor Jim had pressed her to pray and wait until she was sure that V.J. was God's choice for her.

Instead, she told God she wanted V.J., and he gave her what she asked for. When she had to pay the price, she was angry.

Now she had to settle things.

Putting Mechiah in his cage with a profound apology, she tucked Mom's Bible, her own Bible, and her journal under her arm and headed for the turret room.

In front of the window where Mrs. Nelson had watched for Captain, held the wounded, and rocked their babies, Sammie knelt. "I'm guilty, too, God. Not just V.J. He was the thief, but I opened the front door wide. Forgive me."

She straightened up and looked out at the night sky, finally bright with stars. "Heal me from my anger and guilt over the loss of my virginity and the money Mom left me. I choose to forgive V.J. I leave him in your hands."

Peace so real she thought it must be tangible filled her soul.

She wept, but no longer because of pain. They were tears of healing. Time passed unnoticed as she filled pages in her journal, stopping to hold her mother's Bible close to her chest. *Thanks, Mom. Thanks for being there for me.* Opening the book to John 15, her mother's favorite passage, her eyes fell on words highlighted in yellow. "I chose you and appointed you to go and bear fruit."

She breathed the words into the depth of her soul. Bear fruit? In Pineville Beach? Was that a promise?

A glance at her watch revealed that it was a few minutes after midnight, and the river had crested. Back in the cottage, she heard the TV news reporter announce: "In downtown Pineville Beach, the river remains two feet under flood stage. Other areas have suffered no further damage."

She could sleep in peace.

Before she opened the shop the next morning, she drove to Brad's and found that the water level in his house hadn't risen much farther. Relieved, she headed for Hoffmans and found Dossie Mae and Jen there already, sweeping and bailing water in the house.

"Art Humble came by and picked up Frank to work on the cleanup crew," Dossie Mae said with wonder in her voice. "There's a job for him rebuilding roads if he wants it." She looked like she was going to cry. "Art Humble says he'll stay close to Frank."

I have overcome the world.

Standing inside the front door of the Treasure House, she reviewed recent events. Pop, waiting and worrying and Brad, not knowing what had happened to his place in the flood. According to the news, the road wouldn't be open for three or four days.

She remembered Brad at Fort Barker the day he told her about Vonnie and Bitsy, and the day she told him about V.J. As though to contain the memory, she folded her arms around herself.

She began to beg God: *Please don't say no to this relationship,* then dropped her hands to her side.

No. I refuse to do that again. Your will be done.

To celebrate clear sky and the waters receding, she dressed in a yellow-flowered skirt with a drawstring at the waist and a thick yellow sweater. She pinned a Noah's ark pin on one shoulder. The trickle of customers wore post-flood grins.

At noon as she ate a veggie sandwich and wished she could help Hoffmans with the cleanup, she found herself thinking, "Why not take meals to them after work for a few days?"

None of the Hoffmans knew what to say when she unloaded a steaming casserole of macaroni and cheese, buttered green beans, a fruit salad, and a lemon meringue pie from the bakery. Dossie Mae shook her head as though she were unable to comprehend what was happening. "Art was here helping us shovel mud today. Mike came when he finished at the bakery, and a crew from the church showed up, too."

A smile, shy and uncertain for lack of use, played at the corners of Frank's mouth. Sammie inspected the rooms. "You've made remarkable progress. I'll bring dinner tomorrow, so don't plan anything."

Jen sloshed through water and mud with her to the car. "Thanks doesn't say what I feel."

Mrs. Nelson and the other residents had returned to the nursing home. While Sammie bought the pie for the Hoffmans, Autumn had brought her up to date. "Mrs. Nelson is the unofficial chaplain, going from apartment to apartment listening to people tell how scared they were and telling them they're okay now. Can't you just hear her?"

The first thing Sammie did the next morning after peering out the bedroom window and welcoming another clear day was to pick up the phone. The dial tone was a sweet sound, but Pop's voice when he answered was the sweetest.

"God, Sammie! Are you all right?"

She wanted to ask if his words were a prayer. "Yes, Pop, I'm okay."

"It was hell waiting and wondering. I've become a news junkie. Sammie, I was afraid you were fish food by now!"

"I'm fine, but lots of others aren't." She recounted the story of the crisis at Elk Creek, at Brad's place, and the Hoffmans. "Thank God, no lives were lost. The church was the town evacuation center. We all pitched in and helped."

"That's the way it should be. Religion shouldn't just talk. It should do something. Sammie, as soon as I hang up, I'm calling Dave and Mina Bloom."

"Tell them thanks, and I'll call them soon."

"So, are you ready to come home now? Isn't one flood enough?"

"This is the first flood in years. Anyway, you have earthquakes."

"Well, your mountains blow up."

She shifted the conversation. "People here know now, Pop. About V.J. About everything."

"Sammie! My heart hurts for you. But I figured. I saw it here in one of those papers that wouldn't leave you alone. That's another reason I've been crazy."

"You know what? It didn't make me jump up and down and shout hooray. But I didn't fall apart either. People here are my friends. They accept me for who I am."

"So if you're not coming home, maybe when I retire I should open a restaurant up there. Maybe the first Jewish delicatessen in the north woods."

"And call it Sam's Place?"

"Restaurants are like boats—you name them after females. I'd call it 'Sammie's.' By the way. What's going on between you and Brad?"

She ran her hands through her hair in frustration. "What could be going on? He's stuck on the other side of the bridge."

"When he comes home, what then?"

I don't know what then.

"Mechiah sends his love."

"You know how to tell me to mind my business in a nice way, I'll say that."

"How about coming up for a visit in early spring? We could go fishing."

"I have this recipe for stuffed trout you wouldn't believe."

"I love you."

"I love you too, kid."

The following day, Sammie began an inventory of the Treasure House and made mental plans for another season. Mollie Holly phoned to discuss expansion of "Originally Yours." After dinner, Sammie returned to the shop to work on an oak rocker she was refinishing.

The bare wood took on a pleasant sheen, and she was admiring it when Autumn's face appeared in the window of the front door.

"Look! Thank-you messages in the *Pineville Beach Herald* for people who helped during the flood." After Sammie let her in, she opened the paper.

"'Thanks to volunteer Mike Le Duc for helping to evacuate the men's floor of the nursing home,'" Autumn read aloud. "And this one is from a little girl: 'What I liked was the donuts the baker brought for us to eat. He's a nice man.'"

"Mike pretends that it doesn't mean anything. But he did ask me to make sure and save the paper."

Early the next morning Sammie sipped her coffee and puttered leisurely when she heard a knock at the door. With dismay, she looked at her flannel pajamas, bathrobe, and bare feet, then ran her hands through her uncombed hair.

"Who is it?" she called through the closed door.

"An itinerant painter looking for a handout."

Brad! In seconds, she had the door open.

The broad smile on his face warmed his eyes with affection. He stepped inside the living room, extended his arms, and she walked into them. With her face nestled on his shoulder, she felt more content than she had in a long time. Then she remembered that she was still in her nightclothes. "You've seen me at my absolute worst. First Fort Barker and now this."

She left momentarily and returned wearing a long, button-front denim skirt, black turtleneck, and her star and cross necklace. Brad had poured himself coffee. "How about if we drink it in the porch swing?" she asked.

He settled beside her, and she closed her eyes and raised her face to the morning sun. After a few minutes, Brad asked how townspeople had fared during the flood, and she filled him in. He told her about being marooned without even a toothbrush on the other side of the Iseeyousee Bridge.

"A retired fisherman and his wife took me in. We played Scrabble each evening, and I even made a pot of clam chowder one night and baked biscuits to go with it." Their house was on a bluff overlooking the ocean, and Brad said he was going back to paint the scene as a gift to them.

He had been worried about her and had done a lot of pacing and praying. "I shouldn't have gone in the first place. After it was too late, I realized I should have called the emergency rescue number directly. But you were the only one I could think of then."

They rocked gently in the swing as she filled him in on the

rescue of the paintings and her trip back later that night. "I put some books, all the photographs, and things that belonged to Bitsy where they'd be safe."

Touched, he put his cup down on the ground, then slowly reached out and stroked her hair, letting a curl wind around his finger. "I wanted to take you to the house myself and show it to you, talk to you. But you probably figured most of it out." He picked up his cup again and they rocked quietly, watching sparrows on the feeder.

Interrupting the interlude, she told him that the town knew about her past. "It's okay. It really is okay," she told him.

He put his arm around her shoulders, and they rocked in silence.

"Spring's coming," Sammie remarked, thinking of the pair of birds that had nested under the eaves last year and wondering if they'd return. "It's been nearly a year since I drove into Pineville Beach for the first time." She paused, thinking back. "It's been one of the most amazing years of my life."

A faint breeze played with their faces. "I've been thinking," she went on. "This spring I'd really like to plant a rose garden here in the backyard. Mrs. Nelson wouldn't mind, I don't think. It won't be a big one like Mom's was, of course."

"How about the Peace Rose? Will you include that?"

She could see that he understood. "Especially the Peace Rose."

"I'll help you if you let me paint you among the roses this summer. Deal?"

"Deal!" Solemnly, they shook hands.

Suddenly, she sat up straight. "I'll need a compost bin. Mom had one."

"I could build you one behind the cottage."

She smiled with appreciation. "Mom used to say composting was one of her favorite everyday miracles." Sammie could see her mother now, beaming because God had mysteriously turned garbage into nutrients.

"You mother was a wise woman."

"She used to say that people need to compost, too. To give their garbage to God. I guess that's what I've been doing since I came to Pineville Beach." She gazed at the Treasure House. "And Mrs. Nelson before me."

"I let mine pile up far too long." He kissed one of his fingers, then traced it across her lips. His touch was gentle, and she sank into the feeling of it.

Sighing his reluctance, he rose. "I've got to get home. Later today, I'll be back to get the paintings you've been keeping safe for me." He set their cups on the front step, then turned, and took her in his arms. "How can I thank you?"

She was going to say she didn't want thanks. He interrupted with a whisper in her ear. "How about going with me soon some Sunday after church to the ski lodge for dinner? We could sit in front of the fireplace and drink our coffee afterward." His eyes spoke what her heart wanted to hear.

"Only if we sing Christmas carols on the way."

He grinned. "You're on."

Dear Readers,

Every few months during childhood, I snuggled into *Little House in the Big Woods* by Laura Ingalls Wilder. In my imagination, I was safe and protected by Pa Ingalls and not alone with my ill mother in a Coney Island, New York, flat.

The year I was twelve, I read *Gone with the Wind* for a book report. "Excellent," the teacher told me in front of the class. "That's what a book report should be like." I made a silent vow that when I grew up I would be a writer.

I grew up, married, raised three sons, and served with my husband, John, in ministry. Then I began to write for publication. While my sons were completing high school, attending college, and beginning careers, I became a freelance writer and saw a plethora of my articles and nonfiction books in print.

But my original dream had been to write stories that offered warmth and security and that modeled character. Like Wilder and Margaret Mitchell, I wanted to tell the truth in my stories. Life—even for Christians—can be terribly painful. But God is there. "When you pass through the waters, I will be with you....When you walk through the fire, you will not be burned.... For I am the LORD your God" (Isaiah 43:2–3).

Remembering the Roses is the fulfillment of that dream, the keeping of that vow. And because I've experienced God's miraculous healing of my soul, the message of his transforming power is the passion behind my words.

Warmly,

Marion Duckworth

PALISADES...PURE ROMANCE

Father by Faith, Annie Jones
Irish Rogue, Annie Jones
Glory, Marilyn Kok
Sierra, Shari MacDonald
Forget-Me-Not, Shari MacDonald
Diamonds, Shari MacDonald
Stardust, Shari MacDonald
Westward, Amanda MacLean
Stonehaven, Amanda MacLean
Everlasting, Amanda MacLean
Kingdom Come, Amanda MacLean
Betrayed, Lorena McCourtney
Escape, Lorena McCourtney
Dear Silver, Lorena McCourtney
Forgotten, Lorena McCourtney
Enough! Gayle Roper
The Key, Gayle Roper
Voyage, Elaine Schulte

⟶ ANTHOLOGIES ⟵

A Christmas Joy, Darty, Gillenwater, MacLean
Mistletoe, Ball, Hicks, McCourtney
A Mother's Love, Bergren, Colson, MacLean
Silver Bells, Bergren, Krause, MacDonald
Heart's Delight, Ball, Hicks, Noble
Fools for Love, Ball, Brooks, Jones

THE PALISADES LINE

Look for these new releases at your local bookstore. If the title you seek is not in stock, the store may order you a copy using the ISBN listed.

Heartland Skies, Melody Carlson
ISBN 1-57673-264-9
Jayne Morgan moves to the small town of Paradise with the prospect of marriage, a new job, and plenty of horses to ride. But when her fiancé dumps her, she's left with loose ends. Then she wins a horse in a raffle, and the handsome rancher who boards her horse makes things look decidedly better.

Memories, Peggy Darty
ISBN 1-57673-171-5
In this sequel to *Promises,* Elizabeth Calloway is left with amnesia after witnessing a hit-and-run accident. Her husband, Michael, takes her on a vacation to Cancún so that she can relax and recover her memory. What they don't realize is that a killer is following them, hoping to wipe out Elizabeth's memory permanently....

Remembering the Roses, Marion Duckworth
ISBN 1-57673-236-3
Sammie Sternberg is trying to escape her memories of the man who betrayed her, and she ends up in a small town on the Olympic Peninsula in Washington. There she opens her dream business—an antique shop in an old Victorian—and meets a reclusive watercolor artist who helps to heal her broken heart.

Waterfalls, Robin Jones Gunn
ISBN 1-57673-221-5
In a visit to Glenbrooke, Oregon, Meredith Graham meets movie star Jacob Wilde and is sure he's the one. But when Meri puts her

foot in her mouth, things fall apart. Is isn't until the two of them get thrown together working on a book-and-movie project that Jacob realizes his true feelings, and this time he's the one who's starstruck.

China Doll, Barbara Jean Hicks
ISBN 1-57673-262-2
Bronson Bailey is having a mid-life crisis: after years of globetrotting in his journalism career, he's feeling restless. Georgine Nichols has also reached a turning point: after years of longing for a child, she's decided to adopt. The problem is, now she's fallen in love with Bronson, and he doesn't want a child.

Angel in the Senate, Kristen Johnson Ingram
ISBN 1-57673-263-0
Newly elected senator Megan Likely heads to Washington with high hopes for making a difference in government. But accusations of election fraud, two shocking murders, and threats on her life make the Senate take a backseat. She needs to find answers, but she's not sure who she can trust anymore.

Irish Rogue, Annie Jones
ISBN 1-57673-189-8
Michael Shaughnessy has paid the price for stealing a pot of gold, and now he's ready to make amends to the people he's hurt. Fiona O'Dea is number one on his list. The problem is, Fiona doesn't want to let Michael near enough to hurt her again. But before she knows it, he's taken his Irish charm and worked his way back into her life…and her heart.

Forgotten, Lorena McCourtney
ISBN 1-57673-222-3
A woman wakes up in an Oregon hospital with no memory of who she is. When she's identified as Kat Cavanaugh, she returns to her home in California. As Kat struggles to recover her memory,

she meets a fiancé she doesn't trust and an attractive neighbor who can't believe how she's changed. She begins to wonder if she's really Kat Cavanaugh, but if she isn't, what happened to the real Kat?

The Key, Gayle Roper
ISBN 1-57673-223-1
On Kristie Matthews's first day living on an Amish farm, she gets bitten by a dog and is rushed to the emergency room by a handsome stranger. In the ER, an elderly man in the throes of a heart attack hands her a key and tells her to keep it safe. Suddenly odd accidents begin to happen to her, but no one's giving her any answers.

⌒ ANTHOLOGIES ⌒

Fools for Love, Ball, Brooks, Jones
ISBN 1-57673-235-5
By Karen Ball: Kitty starts pet-sitting, but when her clients turn out to be more than she can handle, she enlists help from a handsome handyman.
By Jennifer Brooks: Caleb Murphy tries to acquire a book collection from a widow, but she has one condition: he must marry her granddaughter first.
By Annie Jones: A college professor who has been burned by love vows not to be fooled twice, until her ex-fiancé shows up and ruins her plans!

Heart's Delight, Ball, Hicks, Noble
ISBN 1-57673-220-7
By Karen Ball: Corie receives a Valentine's Day date from her sisters and thinks she's finally found the one...until she learns she went out with the wrong man.
By Barbara Jean Hicks: Carina and Reid are determined to break up their parents' romance, but when it looks like things are

working, they have a change of heart.

By Diane Noble: Two elderly bird-watchers set aside their differences to try to save a park from disaster but learn they've bitten off more than they can chew.

BE SURE TO LOOK FOR ANY OF THE 1997 TITLES
YOU MAY HAVE MISSED:

Surrender, **Lynn Bulock** (ISBN 1-57673-104-9)
Single mom Cassie Neel accepts a blind date from her children for her birthday.

Wise Man's House, **Melody Carlson** (ISBN 1-57673-070-0)
A young widow buys her childhood dream house, and a mysterious stranger moves into her caretaker's cottage.

Moonglow, **Peggy Darty** (ISBN 1-57673-112-X)
Tracy Kosell comes back to Moonglow, Georgia, and investigates a case with a former schoolmate, who's now a detective.

Promises, **Peggy Darty** (ISBN 1-57673-149-9)
A Christian psychologist asks her detective husband to help her find a dangerous woman.

Texas Tender, **Sharon Gillenwater** (ISBN 1-57673-111-1)
Shelby Nolan inherits a watermelon farm and asks the sheriff for help when two elderly men begin digging holes in her fields.

Clouds, **Robin Jones Gunn** (ISBN 1-57673-113-8)
Flight attendant Shelly Graham runs into her old boyfriend, Jonathan Renfield, and learns he's engaged.

Sunsets, **Robin Jones Gunn** (ISBN 1-57673-103-0)
Alissa Benson has a run-in at work with Brad Phillips, and is more than a little upset when she finds out he's her neighbor!

Snow Swan, **Barbara Jean Hicks** (ISBN 1-57673-107-3)
Toni, an unwed mother and a recovering alcoholic, falls in love for the first time. But if Clark finds out the truth about her past, will he still love her?

Irish Eyes, **Annie Jones** (ISBN 1-57673-108-1)
Julia Reed gets drawn into a crime involving a pot of gold and has her life turned upside down by Interpol agent Cameron O'Dea.

Father by Faith, **Annie Jones** (ISBN 1-57673-117-0)
Nina Jackson buys a dude ranch and hires cowboy Clint Cooper as her foreman, but her son, Alex, thinks Clint is his new daddy!

Stardust, **Shari MacDonald** (ISBN 1-57673-109-X)
Gillian Spencer gets her dream assignment but is shocked to learn she must work with Maxwell Bishop, who once broke her heart.

Kingdom Come, **Amanda MacLean** (ISBN 1-57673-120-0)
Ivy Rose Clayborne, M.D., pairs up with the grandson of the coal baron to fight the mining company that is ravaging her town.

Dear Silver, **Lorena McCourtney** (ISBN 1-57673-110-3)
When Silver Sinclair receives a letter from Chris Bentley ending their relationship, she's shocked, since she's never met the man!

Enough! **Gayle Roper** (ISBN 1-57673-185-5)
When Molly Gregory gets fed up with her three teenaged children, she announces that she's going on strike.

A *Mother's Love,* **Bergren, Colson, MacLean**
(ISBN 1-57673-106-5)
Three heartwarming stories share the joy of a mother's love.

Silver Bells, **Bergren, Krause, MacDonald**
(ISBN 1-57673-119-7)
Three novellas focus on romance during Christmastime.